The Ones Who Remember

SECOND-GENERATION VOICES

OF THE HOLOCAUST

Edited by
Rita Benn, Julie Goldstein Ellis,
Joy Wolfe Ensor, and Ruth Wade

City Point Press

2022

Myra Fox

August 12, 1955–April 26, 2018

Myra joined our Ann Arbor Temple Beth Emeth Generations After community in its first year. She had the unrivaled ability to plumb the emotional depths of our group's difficult legacy, bringing us her enormous heart and creative gifts.

Myra was central to our endeavors as a writer, an editor, and a beloved friend. Her perspectives on her family, Jewish identity, and second-generation Holocaust experience had a profound effect on us, and are reflected throughout this anthology.

Myra died after a valiant battle with cancer, in the midst of our writing this book. It is with great love that we dedicate our book to her.

Myra Fox, Ann Arbor, Michigan, 2018

CONTENTS

FOREWORD

Irene Hasenberg Butter

In 2004, I attended the first Temple Beth Emeth Holocaust Remembrance Day service, written and led by Generations After. The stories that these children of survivors shared about their parents' experiences greatly moved me. As a Holocaust survivor who has spent years educating others and working toward peace and tolerance, I recognized the importance of their work.

When I came to the United States in 1945, the American relatives who took me in urged me to forget everything that had happened to my family—and to me—in the Holocaust. I was fifteen years old and they were adults, so I listened to them. For forty years I was quiet. I was not truly free until I started to tell what happened to me as a child.

The need to address how the Holocaust impacted me and the world drove me to work toward the establishment of the Raoul Wallenberg Award at the University of Michigan, where I was a professor in the School of Public Health. Raoul Wallenberg, while serving as a Swedish diplomat in Hungary between July and December 1944, saved tens of thousands of Jews from the gas chamber by issuing them protective passports and sheltering them in buildings designated as Swedish territory. With the mission to increase awareness of Wallenberg's heroic life-saving efforts in the Holocaust, each year the Raoul Wallenberg Award continues to recognize and bring to our community humanitarians and scholars working to combat the marginalization of peoples, to promote peace and reconciliation. Some of the past honorees include the Dalai Lama, Elie Wiesel, and Desmond Tutu.

Once retired, I focused on visiting local schools to talk about how

I survived during the war. The students were fascinated with my story. I saw their worlds open up in the way my experience resonated for them. Students confided to me that, after hearing my story and seeing how I was able to lead a successful life, they now felt they could overcome trauma in their own lives.

In 2011, I joined the Generations After group in participating in services for our temple community. I described how my idyllic early childhood was quickly followed by the terror and hell of concentration camps, the tragic death of my father, and my separation from my mother and brother when I was sent to a displaced persons camp in North Africa. I contributed perspectives and stories about returning to Germany many years later, where I spoke to high school students, surprisingly in my native German tongue. I also spoke of visiting the Stumbling Stones in front of the home of my grandparents in Berlin. These plaques are installed on the sidewalks in front of Holocaust victims' last known place of residence. Since most Holocaust victims do not have a grave, Stumbling Stones return names and places to victims who might otherwise have been forgotten. They serve as concrete individual memorials. I am very grateful to Gunter Demnig, the artist who created the *Stolpersteine* project, for the work he is undertaking to preserve the history of the Jewish people who were murdered. These have special importance to me, as now my children and grandchildren have an actual place in Germany where they can connect with their ancestors.

As some of the Generations After members began discussing the creation of an anthology based on our services, I encouraged them to focus on their own voices and their own second-generation experiences. I was fascinated by how well they had brought their parents' stories to life, but was even more engaged when they shared how these experiences impacted them. Each of them had a unique perspective on the personal effects of this singular tragedy. Each had a vital story to tell. All of them were committed to preserving their stories and insights for future generations. I asked my two children, Noah and Ella, to share a little bit about their own experiences growing up with a mother who had survived the Holocaust. As a small preview of what you will find in this book, here is what they wrote.

Noah's reflection:

I always knew that my mom was a Holocaust survivor. I do not remember not knowing this fact. It was not as if one day my mom sat down with me and explained what had happened to her family when she was an early teen, when they were arrested, taken away from their Amsterdam home, and sent to Westerbork concentration camp, later to be deported to Bergen-Belsen concentration camp.

One of my earliest memories of thinking about the Holocaust was walking with my mom in downtown Ann Arbor. I can still remember a flash of what was happening: we were walking down the street, with pedestrians and cars flowing by us, and I believe we had just come out of a shop. I remember thinking that there was something not quite right about me, some defect that I had, and that perhaps it was because my mom got roughed up in the war. In other words, I was attributing something that I imagined happened to Mom, physically in the concentration camp, to my own, tainted condition.

Ella's reflection:

From a very young age I knew that there was a story that needed to be told. One weekday night when I was about seven years old, in the second grade, I sat down with my mother on my bed and insisted that she tell me the whole story. Intuitively I had the sense that it was my duty and that I was given this responsibility. I think that hearing my mother's story transformed my life. Although I couldn't possibly understand, as such a young child, what it meant to be prisoners of Bergen-Belsen, to starve, and to be covered with lice, I listened attentively and made my mother's experience part of my personal journey. There were always more questions to be asked, and when I was in junior high school and had to choose a topic for my speech, I knew it would be the persecution of the Jews during World War II. As part of my presentation, I asked my mother to describe life in the concentration camps. I believe this was the first time she told her story in front of a group of teenagers.

When I was in my first year of law school at Tel Aviv University, I came upon an announcement about the first Holocaust survivors' gathering, to be held in Israel. It was obvious that my mother and I should be there together. We were on the bus to Kibbutz Netzer Sereni, and I fell asleep. When I woke up, there were children on the bus handing out flowers. This brought tears to my mother's eyes. Who would have imagined, in the midst of the Holocaust, that there would one day be children greeting survivors laden with flowers?

The Holocaust has always been for me a sign of the evil we are capable of. When I say "we," I mean that it's not merely the Germans who were capable of such atrocities. We the human race are all responsible and must find ways to fight our dark side. I felt the urge to study law and to fight for human rights and justice. My whole life I have felt that it is our responsibility and duty to stand up against injustice, to see the pain our neighbors are feeling and to bear that with them. Having endured my own share of crises and difficulties, I know what suffering is like. Whenever we bear a family history of the Holocaust or any other form of persecution, it shapes us into the humans we are. I look at my mother and see how such suffering can be transformed into love and care for others. Becoming a compassionate human being is what I would say growing up with the Holocaust is all about.

Remembrance is what shapes our lives and teaches us. And legacy has to be passed on to our children. This important book is compelling evidence that the legacy is being passed on. My children and the children in the Generations After community are our future, carrying our stories forward. It is both natural and essential that they lend their own inheritances to the tragedy of the Holocaust.

Every individual can make a difference, and it is our human duty to speak out against oppression and persecution wherever it exists. As you listen to the voices of the Generations After community, you will see how each one approaches their parents' history, seeking connection and a path toward restoring faith in humanity. In reading their stories, you will have the opportunity to deeply experience the notion that all people are our kin. And isn't that what we all are aiming for?

INTRODUCTION

Rita Benn, Julie Goldstein Ellis, Joy Wolfe Ensor, and Ruth Wade

It was a falling into. With a combination of sweetness and pluck, Martha Solent, the founding member of our Generations After group, suggested to our rabbi that we could enrich the liturgy for Holocaust Remembrance Day by inviting our own congregants to share their lived experiences of the Shoah and its aftermath. With his support, she approached friends and new acquaintances and invited them to join in this new group undertaking. Those who were hesitant were invited for coffee. A pair of cousins decided to join the group together. We all wanted to honor our parents, to give voice to the history many of them never could tell, and to find our own voices.

When we began meeting in 2004, we experienced a shock of familiarity with each other beyond the coincidence of having settled in the same Michigan college town and the same Reform Jewish congregation. We had in common an implicit understanding of what it was like growing up with Holocaust survivor parents: to be the namesakes of the "lost souls" who'd perished; to confront our parents' muteness, and sometimes anger, when we asked questions about their past; to bear the challenge of remembering when there was so much we didn't know. With one another, we didn't have to engage in emotional translation. Our stories became each other's stories.

Some of us had never learned more than fragments about our parents' past, while for others, there was more open and intentional sharing. Either way, our parents' suffering seeped into our souls. We absorbed their sorrow and shame, spoken or unspoken; their anxieties and their courage; and, most importantly, their lessons of endurance and resilience.

To plan our services, we gathered in each other's homes around abundant food, hugs, laughter, and sometimes tears. Our conversations moved organically from sharing what was happening in our own lives to telling our parents' stories to identifying a connecting theme that gave the annual memorial observances their own unique emphases, such as suffering, resistance, forgiveness, and grace. We then wove together our individual recollections with prayer and music. These services helped many members of our congregation move from trying to grasp the incomprehensible number of six million Jews murdered in the Holocaust, to hearing the clear singular voice of the person standing in front of them bearing witness to its meaning for an individual family. Our stories became all of our stories.

After ten years of confiding in each other within this community space, we decided to create an anthology that would preserve our parents' experiences for future generations of our families and beyond. In the process, we began to talk more about our *own* experiences of living in the shadow of the Holocaust while trying to lead "normal" lives. In one Generations After gathering, someone asked, "Who among us had parents who suffered from bouts of major depression?" Every hand went up. We realized that while we had been unflinching in describing the particulars of our parents' losses, we had kept private the impact of their trauma on themselves and on us. As we began to share this with each other, we asked ourselves, could we delve more deeply? Yes, we all could. And we did.

What did we learn? Our parents rebuilt their lives and raised a generation of successful children. Even so, there were ripple effects from growing up with this tragic family history. It was difficult to permit ourselves to disclose this impact—it felt self-indulgent and disloyal. After all that our parents had endured, how dare we portray them as in any way flawed? How could we even remotely think that we had problems worthy of mentioning? Our parents had stood in the freezing cold in their striped pajamas for hours on end, watching their friends and families die. How could our concerns and laments compare?

Still, we felt compelled to openly acknowledge that the suffering of our parents had significant effects on our lives as children and adults. For many of us it was a struggle to write more about ourselves, to say out loud what we had kept buried inside for so many years. We often had to dig through multiple layers of repression to find and express our true feelings. Over time, through this intense reflection, we deepened our understanding of ourselves and further recognized the impact of intergenerational trauma on how we moved through the world and raised our own children. In the end, writing these very personal narratives brought about unexpected healing.

The result is this book, a very different book than the one we first set out to write. Our parents, through grace, cleverness, and stubborn determination, managed to survive unimaginable horrors. These essays offer accounts of our families' courage and post-traumatic growth, as well as of our own second-generation struggles and reckonings. We hope that it will inspire healing for others facing adversity in their own lives.

Elie Wiesel, Holocaust survivor and Nobel laureate, said, "Whoever listens to a witness, becomes a witness."[1] Listening to each other's family histories has felt like a sacred act. We feel blessed to have a community interested in truly hearing each other, and grateful for the opportunity to carry on our parents' legacy while creating our own.

In encountering these recollections, you too are bearing witness. We hope that our stories will become your stories, and that the lessons of the Holocaust—and its continuing and expanding impact—will never be forgotten.

The
Ones Who
Remember

Screams in the Night

Ruth Taubman, daughter of Lola Goldstein/Mueller Taubman

Lola arriving in America, Port of New York, 1949

For as long as I can remember, my mother's screams of terror in the night were an ordinary occurrence. My siblings and I didn't ask questions. Being awakened several times a week or more was our family reality. We simply went back to sleep and didn't discuss it the next day. We certainly didn't mention my mother's night terrors to anyone outside of our family.

That's probably why I forgot to forewarn my friend Jesse when he came to our house for a visit one summer when I was sixteen. I'd been away at Interlochen, a fine arts camp, where Jesse and I had met the year before. He came to visit me at the end of camp, and then we made the trip together back to my family's home in Birmingham, Michigan. Jesse was going to stay with us for a few days.

In the middle of our first night at the house, my mother's shrieks pierced the dark. As I swam to consciousness, it clicked that Jesse would not know what was happening. I ran to his room. There, I found him standing up out of bed, shaking in utter fear of what horrible unknown event might be occurring.

I tried to tell him it was "nothing" and he should go back to sleep. That phrase, "it's nothing," sums up the disconnect between him, who could not imagine the origins of my mother's terror, and me—the child of a Holocaust survivor, familiar with its source.

• • •

Only recently have I discovered that my fellow members of the "club" known as Generations After have had uncannily similar experiences. My second-generation contemporaries and I have a shared sensibility. It took a long time for me to recognize the unbridgeable chasm between those who are aware of the Holocaust from some impersonal context—whether as scholars of history, or middle school readers of Anne Frank—and those who have been the direct witnesses to, and participants in, the aftermath of the Holocaust. No amount of reading and research, or seeing *Schindler's List* at the local multiplex, will parallel our experiences. We have an intrinsic knowing that cannot be shared or passed along; we are the link to our parents' ongoing, lifelong trauma. Even for our own descendants, the trauma eventually converts into what feels like little more than anecdotal stories. No teeth. No claws. No gut-wrenching screams out of nowhere, in the dead of night.

• • •

In the same way I tried (albeit unsuccessfully) to reassure my friend on that night long ago that everything was fine, I'm often assured by an owner with a dog lunging from a leash—or jumping on me as I come through the door to their home—that the animal is "friendly." Whether it's true or not, I'm always predisposed to be fearful, even if just walking near an approaching dog on a stroll. It's a vestige of my mother being terrorized by the Nazis' savage dogs, a direct physical transfer of her disturbance. I can still feel her grip tightening on my hand when she would see any dog—even from a block away—whether the dog was loudly barking in warning or quietly wagging its tail. That inadvertent communication of behavior has been impossible for me to unlearn. Whether I feign indifference or just slightly recoil, my innate, primal sense of danger is activated by any animal I encounter. However benign the situation, this deeply ingrained perpetuation of fear is a reflex; a reaction I never question or address.

• • •

By my mother's last decade, she had already publicly shared her Holocaust experiences, speaking dozens of times in schools and in many interviews. Beyond this, though, she was driven by a desire not to be defined solely by that wretched chapter of her life. She wanted to write a memoir, in her own voice, and she wanted it to be about her entire life.

And so, in her late eighties, in matter-of-fact sessions with a historian, my mother described her idyllic childhood in Svalava, a small town in the Carpathian Mountains that was originally part of the Austro-Hungarian Empire but was then part of Czechoslovakia. She diagrammed the floor plan of her house. She told of her jealousy of her three younger brothers' freedom to play, while she, as the oldest child—and only girl—of the family had a litany of seemingly unending domestic responsibilities.

> My mother made sure I learned to do things. I was the only girl, so besides going to school, my mother taught me how to sew, how to knit, how to crochet, and how to mend. I had to prepare a dowry, embroidered sheets and pillowcases and tablecloths. My mother also taught me how to garden . . . how to can fruits and vegetables. We couldn't go to the river to swim until we had done our jobs with the canning. We lived off that in the winter.[1]

During a frank discussion when I was a young teen, my mother surprised me by sharing that at my age, she dreaded becoming a woman in her community because she pictured her destiny as one of toil and drudgery. Her own mother worked constantly from dawn to night. I remember thinking how contemporary it seemed that she had such a nascent feminist attitude about her future.

In writing her memoir, she recalled her modern orthodox parents' deep emphasis on education. They sent her to the preeminent private Jewish high school in Europe, a co-ed Hebrew gymnasium in the larger nearby city of Munkács, highly unusual for girls at that time. She went on to describe the gradual curbing of her family's freedoms as Hitler rose to power. Eventually her entire town's Jewish population was rounded up and deported to two ghettos housed in former brick factories in Munkács.

After four weeks in the ghetto, they were abruptly gathered in groups and transported on a harrowing three-day rail journey by cattle car. They were crushed together, the conditions horrible; one woman gave birth to a child, one woman went berserk, people screamed. My mother was wedged between her mother and her father. The poignant moment that stood out from that horrendous boxcar was her father turning to her and saying, "No matter what they do to you—they can take everything away from you—but the little education you've got, they can't take away."

Their destination was Auschwitz. Upon their arrival, she recounted waiting in line as her family was selected by the infamous Josef Mengele for the gas chambers, while she was chosen to work—and to endure the unspeakable horrors that lay beyond the roaring chimneys that lit up the night, filling her nostrils with the stench of death.

With the historian as her interlocutor, my mother related the extremes of grit that were required to survive. Laying bare her fierce determination to live, she detailed many razor's-edge escapes from death. She also recounted her eventual liberation at the end of World War II, followed by years in displaced persons (DP) camps.

Two generations of uncles, aunts, and cousins were American citizens, willing to sponsor her immigration to the United States. But the postwar intricacies of redrawn European borders, combined with constantly changing U.S. policy for the priority quota of refugees, left my mother unable to get a visa to come to America. She had unwittingly lost her eligibility for priority status for papers because she had briefly left Germany for Czechoslovakia; merely having crossed the border to her country of origin meant she was considered as having a "home." She desperately wanted to reunite with her closest surviving relatives who had all successfully emigrated. Her uncanny talent for speaking many languages led to her working as a translator for a sympathetic American Army officer in the DP camp, helping register applicants for visas. The nature of the work allowed the officer access to make false papers on my mother's behalf, using the name of another survivor close to her own height and age who had never applied for a visa. Because this fellow survivor was illegally smuggled into what was then Palestine (now Israel), she effectively "disappeared." My mother assumed her identity, acquired a visa, and finally arrived in New York as Leah Mueller on March 1, 1949.

Two years later, my mother moved to Detroit, where she met and fell in love with my father, Samuel Taubman. Together they built a home life that eventually included my sister, my brother, and me.

When I was about ten, I began to understand how family names were passed along, and asked my mother why her last name was Mueller while her entire immediate and extended family name was Goldstein. In simple terms, she began to reveal how she had acquired Leah's identity. As an adult, I came to learn the full story, realizing the risks she took to finally be safely in the United States. Forty years after that first conversation, we discovered her actual age through a distant relative's genealogy search. My mother had so fully incorporated the facts of her naturalization papers into her own life that she never even revealed her true birth date to my father.

The complexities of living under a false identity had its own reach of quiet terror beyond the safe harbor of my mother's home and young family. I got the first inkling of this as a small child during a pleasure

Lola with her children (Richard, Ruth, and Alyssa) at Ruth's first birthday, Southfield, Michigan, March, 1960

day trip to Windsor, Canada, just a forty-five-minute drive from our house. For the border crossing, my mother placed her naturalization papers in their red leatherette tri-fold case on the front seat of the car, nervously gripping the steering wheel as we approached the entrance of the tunnel to Canada manned by the Border Patrol officers. She delivered choked replies in her lilting, Hungarian-accented English to the officers' standard questions about where each of us were born. She was virtually undone by this brief and seemingly mundane excursion and was visibly drained every subsequent time she had to cross a border. Throughout her life, though fully a U.S. citizen by her marriage to my father, there was never a time when she did not fear her initial illegal status being found out by "the authorities." The cloud of her own imagining of being "sent back" cast a pall from which she never fully escaped.

After a fifty-plus-year marriage, my mother survived the loss of her dear Sam. Soon after, she moved to Ann Arbor, where another whole chapter of her life began. She made dozens of friends in her retirement community. A few years after the move, an amalgamation of her interviews with the historian, together with photos, was self-published as her memoir, *My Story*, by Lola Taubman.

· · ·

As my mother's book project came to fruition, my job was to edit the galley proofs. One day during this period, I was boarding a small plane in a tiny town in the mountains of Montana. The time had come to work on the chapters of her memoir where she described some of her most horrific experiences in the death camps.

My flight departed during a winter storm, with the pilot warning us before takeoff that it was going to be a rough trip. This was a great understatement, considering the white-knuckle ride that followed. As the plane pitched, the wings torqued and rattled. People's personal belongings began to fall from the overhead bins, which popped open in the tumult. I forged onward with my edits, gripping my red Sharpie as I persisted in correcting small grammatical errors and minor misspellings—a prosaic function, so clinical in comparison to the dreadful content on the page.

My presence on that turbulent plane was a story in itself. I was returning from the onerous task of being interviewed for my child's admission to a therapeutic boarding school, far from the comforts of our own home. Yet even this, one of the most challenging moments in my life, paled in contrast to what my mother had survived. How could I indulge in self-pity, no matter how dire the circumstances felt to me? As I once said during a meeting of our Generations After group, my worst day was a pimple compared to what my mother had experienced. To be stoic in the face of adversity—and avoid wallowing—were my instinctive responses, thanks to my bittersweet inheritance.

A wise counselor once asked about an unrelated difficult situation, "Where are you in all of this?" In my own way, I have harnessed my mother's ability to prevail, beyond all odds, to know on a deep level that I can't be overwhelmed—and won't be defeated. I have an unshakeable sense that I can prevail in any situation. After all, as my mother's story proves, it is possible to overcome anything—and no amount of trouble can equal the monolith that is the Holocaust.

The inescapable shadow of the Holocaust is one from which I won't emerge. Yet that very same shadow has provided a resilience that I am always aware of, and for which I am perversely grateful.

This attitude is not self-invented. It is another piece of the complex puzzle that made up my mother's life view, which I was fortunate to inherit. As anyone who knew her will tell you, Lola was an upbeat optimist. She made a conscious decision to be positive. Her trademark response to difficulties, "It's better to be happy than to be sad," was a simple summation of what allowed her to go forward in her life. Its very simplicity belies an infinite darkness lingering just below the surface of the fierce determination that propelled her.

I don't recall exactly which kind of sound pierced that long-ago night when Jesse came to stay. Was it just my mother's cries? Or was she yelling about something specific? Often, she would shout about a man with a gun. This man was so vividly present and real to her in her terror that once, in her sleep, she managed—with the superhuman strength that is only possible in the face of enormous fear—to push my father out of the bed they shared, despite his much larger frame. This episode reminded me that her torment was related, in part, to being the sole member of her immediate family to survive the Holocaust.

My mother died in December 2015, as did her screams in the night. I'm thankful that she is not here to witness our current atmosphere of hatred, a common refrain among my second-generation cohort. Not a day goes by without my seeing a headline in the news, a comment on a social media feed, or the first line of an email that I scan before even getting out of bed with the word HOLOCAUST. When I read that word, or hear the latest contemporary dark story of antisemitism, I quake at the horrifying reverberation of events so similar to those that led to all my mother survived. The shot of adrenaline that jolted me awake—several nights a week, for years on end—surges again. It takes me back to those nights as a small girl. And I'm still shaking.

2

The Attic Full of Photographs

Julie Goldstein Ellis, daughter of Magda Blaufeld Goldstein
and Louis Goldstein, cousin of Lola Goldstein/Mueller Taubman

*Blaufeld family and friends. Front row left to right: Magda, brother Béla,
mother Gisella, Béla's wife Juliska, Svalava, Czechoslovakia, 1937*

My mother had a blue number on her arm. A string of digits, six or seven of them, was tattooed on her left forearm. In front of the numbers was the letter A.

It's strange, but although I grew up seeing that number every day, I can't tell you what the number was. I never memorized it, never said it out loud. I don't remember ever reading it silently to myself. But I know the A was for Auschwitz.

When I was young, I must have asked about it, but I don't remember doing so. I don't remember my mother saying anything about it at all, until much later in life. Only as a teenager did I start to learn about the dehumanizing horrors associated with that number.

At some point as a child, I must have realized that my parents had a very troubled background that my older sister and I should not ask about. We wanted to protect them from any further sadness and pain, so we never made trouble ourselves. We were always good. I remember at about age eight cutting myself on a piece of broken glass and my sister admonishing me, "Don't tell Mom." She secretly gave me a Band-Aid to take care of it. I felt frustrated and sad that I couldn't tell my mommy I got a cut. Only now do I recognize how this small episode in my life was emblematic of the thought processes and dilemmas of the second generation.

When my son was very young, and we were visiting my parents in New York, he noticed the number on my mother's arm. "Bobie Magda has a number," he said. "Yes," I said, "she does." Here he was, an innocent, observant little boy and he had noticed. The secret. The thing we didn't talk about. I didn't even attempt to explain why she had a number tattooed on her arm, and he didn't ask why. He just accepted it as a fact, as I must have when I was little, too. My parents had always tried to shelter me and my sister from knowing about the horrors they lived through. In the same way, I did not want to burden my son with the knowledge of how awful human beings could be to one another.

When I was growing up, there had always been a reticence in our home about World War II. No one wanted to talk about the subject to anyone else, let alone tune into their own feelings. Silence became a refuge, a safe place. When I was very young, I wasn't always so silent. I was a gregarious girl in elementary school. I had lots of friends and was an outgoing student, eagerly raising my hand in class.

That changed in the summer of 1967, after I finished the eighth grade. My family took a trip to Israel, where my parents were reunited with friends and family they hadn't seen since just after World War II. These were people from their hometown in Hungary, people with whom they had survived the war. They were thrilled to see each other, singing songs and sharing stories of the good times when they were young.

Just after the Six-Day War, this was an exhilarating time to visit Israel and to see Israeli Jews as victorious. But our tour included visits to Holocaust memorials and museums, where I saw my parents break down crying. There I learned more details about the Holocaust than I had ever wanted to know. In one museum our guide made a dramatic presentation of artifacts from concentration camps, including soap made from human fat and a lampshade made from human skin. Seeing these actual objects in addition to all the photographic displays of what took place in the camps was staggering. Then there was no turning back. There was no way to shake the memory of my father sobbing as he showed other people on the tour the name of his hometown engraved on the wall of remembrance. The wall listed hundreds and hundreds of towns whose Jews had been murdered.

After that trip I became quieter, more introspective. I began to feel different from my classmates. I trained myself not to think very often about the image of my parents getting so upset at the Holocaust memorials, but it is something I will never forget. I can count on one hand the number of times I ever saw my father cry. That was one of them.

• • •

In the years following our trip to Israel, my parents still didn't reveal much about their wartime experiences. Their nieces and nephews, who were also survivors, did not say much either. These were my cousins and their children, whom we saw regularly while we were all growing up in the New York area, not just on holidays, but on most weekends. All of us kids knew our parents had been in the war, but we didn't know the details. In 1978, after the airing of the TV miniseries *Holocaust*, starring a young Meryl Streep, the ice seemed to break. Although the series was criticized for trivializing certain aspects of the Holocaust, it raised awareness and educated the hundreds of millions of people who watched it worldwide. For me, it was mesmerizing as well as shocking. However inaccurately they were portrayed, the scenes in the concentration camps became all too real. One part showed family members led into a gas chamber, holding each other close. That image and the sound of the gas pellets dropping into the room has been stuck in my mind ever since. I didn't watch the TV series with my parents when it aired, as I was married and no longer living with them, but everyone in our family watched it and talked about it. Our extended family started to tell their stories. And they bravely made recordings for Steven Spielberg's Shoah Foundation.

Anyone can go to the United States Holocaust Memorial Museum in Washington or to Yad Vashem in Israel, look up Magda and Louis Goldstein in the database, and watch the videos in which they bear witness to the atrocities of the Holocaust. I have found it too upsetting to watch their recordings at home. But in the years since my parents died, when I visited those museums, I sat and watched parts of their tapes. It was an eerie feeling to see my parents' faces appear on the screen and hear their Hungarian accents, there in the museums. Odd that I never registered their accents in person when they were alive. I only notice them on video recordings. It is comforting to know that my parents live on in the museum archives, always ready to tell their story to me, to my family, to the world.

• • •

I am named for my aunt, Julia Sternbach Blaufeld. The family called her Juliska (YOOL-eesh-kah). She was married to my mother's oldest brother Béla, who was an attorney. They had a son, Jóska, and a daughter, Zsuzsi. Even though I don't know very much about her, I am certain Juliska would have been a wonderful aunt, always ready with a warm hug and a smile. I am lucky enough to have a couple photographs of Juliska and, indeed, she had a beautiful smile. She is outfitted in smartly tailored suits and dresses, her smooth dark hair neatly pulled back. One picture is from the day of her wedding to Uncle Béla. A radiant Juliska is wearing a long, flowing white dress. In the photos, she looks so happy and comfortable with her life, not knowing what would befall her and her family in Auschwitz.

I have always considered it an honor and a privilege to carry on Juliska's name. However, when I was about thirty, I told an acquaintance that I am named for my aunt who perished in the Holocaust. She remarked, "Oh what a terrible burden that is." At the time I thought, how could she say that? How could she be so insensitive? But now when I think more deeply about it, I realize that in addition to being an honor, it is a heavy burden as well. By carrying Juliska's name, am I obligated to make up for a lost life in whatever I do in my own life?

During high school I was quiet, often feeling like an outsider, yet I was an excellent student. When I went away to the University of Michigan, I was finally able to get free from a very cliquey high school, to relax, to have fun. This was also the time in my life when I met my wonderful husband, Charlie. Still, I tried to please my parents by deciding to go to medical school, even though I knew deep down that I didn't really want to. Perhaps I felt an obligation to pursue the highest professional degree that they never could. My father had wanted to be an attorney and had started to study law at Charles University in Prague in the late 1930s. After the Germans occupied Czechoslovakia, their antisemitic laws prevented Jews from studying in universities. I hated every minute of medical school and was desperately unhappy. I took a leave of absence a couple of times before finally deciding to drop out. It was one of the hardest decisions I've ever made, imagining how disappointed my parents would be.

After leaving medical school, I made an about-face from choosing goals that caused me stress and unhappiness. I became the manager of a gourmet kitchen shop and eventually was fortunate to be able to be a stay-at-home mom, both of which I loved doing. As it turned out, my parents were very forgiving and understanding. However, I frequently faced questions from others about how I could possibly give up the chance to be a doctor. Those questions aroused guilt feelings that plagued me for a long time. I eventually realized that it is much more important to be happy than to follow someone else's version of success. I am proud to carry on my Aunt Juliska's name, but I know I have to live my own life. Even as I approach the age of seventy, at times I feel like I am still learning how to do that.

• • •

My parents, Magda and Louis Goldstein, must have had a deep-rooted sense of hope when they decided to get married in 1942 in Svalava, a small town in the Carpathian Mountains. This had been part of Czechoslovakia, but was annexed by Hungary, an ally of Germany. Soon after my parents were married, my father, along with other young Jewish men, was forced to serve in a slave labor battalion attached to the Hungarian army and was sent to the Russian front. His unit was captured by the Russians and taken to a POW camp deep in Russia. My mother did not hear from him again until after the war ended. My mother's brother Martzi was also taken away in a labor battalion, but he never returned after the war. He is thought to have perished on a frozen field somewhere in Russia.

Although some of the Jews remaining in Hungary lived in relative safety for a while, life there got progressively worse. In 1944, German troops invaded Hungary. That spring my mother and the remaining Jews of Svalava were forced out of their homes and were eventually taken to Auschwitz. There, my mother's entire immediate family was murdered.

These are my mother's words, taken from a short memoir of her life before and during the war, which she typed up in 1975 and gave to my sister Susan and me several years later. We aren't sure why she decided to write it then, but we hope it gave her relief from what she had kept inside herself for so long. For us, it put together pieces of a puzzling past and gave us a more complete picture of her life: one that was achingly tragic but also full of courage and inspiration.

My Aunt Zali always told us that all would be well as long as we could sleep in our own beds. This became a wishful prayer and proved to be prophetic words. The fateful knock on the door came the day after Passover in 1944. I was hurried out of the house along with Aunt Zali, my brother Béla, his wife

Juliska, and their children, four-year-old Jóska and two-year-old Zsuzsi. The few measly belongings that we were permitted to take along seemed to weigh a ton after a few minutes' walk. Since it was right after Passover, we didn't even have any bread to take along. The Hungarian police and army made sure we left all our valuables behind. The streets seemed to be deserted. Some soldiers were visible here and there. Only our dog ran after us, howling in bewilderment. He was captured by some soldiers.

Where were we going? What was next? We were led into the local temple, where quite a few other families were congregated already. All the Goldsteins were there, among others. Fear was taking hold of us and the dreadful odyssey to the final tragedy had just begun. More Jewish families joined us during the night. Everybody was hoping for a miracle, that in the morning we would be set free.

In the morning, we were herded into cattle cars and taken to the nearby city of Munkács. An abandoned brick factory was converted into a temporary ghetto. We stayed there four long weeks. Our nerves were shattered, our physical strength diminished, we were humiliated. One night, before trying to fall asleep in our corner of the shack, I heard my little nephew Jóska say, "Am I not going to sleep in my little bed ever again?" I tried very hard to stifle my sobs.

After four weeks, the cattle cars appeared again. The cattle cars, the symbol of annihilation. After being shoved, pushed, and packed into the wagons, our journey continued for four days.

In the evening of the fourth day, the train finally stopped and the doors opened. This was Auschwitz. Spotlights, noise, screaming, dogs barking . . . above all, German commands.

Who were these creatures in striped pajamas, trying to orga-
nize people into groups? I tried to carry one of my brother's
children but was shoved away and forced to march in another
direction. I soon found out that I would never see my immediate family again. I was part of the group chosen to work. With
our clothes discarded and our heads shaven, we became mere
numbers. Lost numbers at that. Did anybody in the world
know where Auschwitz was, or that it even existed?

For a few days, I was in absolute limbo. I had no sister
or cousin or anybody to belong to. To be alone in a place like
this could be disastrous. I could not find a safe place to sleep.
One day, I mentioned this predicament to my husband Louis's
niece, Irene Goldstein, who promptly invited me to join her
and her sisters. They did not have much room on their bunk
bed, but we managed. In retrospect, to belong to a group and
have mutual concerns became the major factor in survival.
Irene's good-hearted offer saved my life.

My mother was twenty-four years old, Irene was twenty-two. If
you have ever seen the photos of concentration camp barracks that
show the horrifically crowded bunk beds, then you can imagine what
it would mean to be embraced by and share comfort with someone
under those conditions. A simple act of loving-kindness made the difference between life and death.

After a few days, fifty or sixty women from our group were
formed into a work unit. Each day, we walked about two miles
into another part of the camp, called Birkenau. Our work there
consisted of separating and baling all the clothing discarded
by the arriving throngs.

After a while, we were moved closer to our work, to a

bunkhouse in Birkenau. Most of our friends and Louis's nieces were included in this group. It was comforting to know that we had a nucleus of people from our hometown around. In Birkenau, the matter of survival was eased somewhat for us. But one of the crematoria was practically next door.

In the meantime, thousands and thousands of people went through the gates. Left or right, who shall live or who shall die . . . all according to the infamous Dr. Mengele.

Weeks went by, and summer turned into fall. We managed to figure out the dates of the High Holidays. We had a little prayer service with my friend Leah singing some of the prayers. We even managed to fast on Yom Kippur.

My mother somehow survived the horrors of Auschwitz. I once asked her if they had tried to rebel in any way. She told me that in Birkenau one of the girls, who had been working there for quite a while, showed them how to sabotage the clothing they were baling together to be sent to Germany. They reached into the bundles with scissors and cut up as much of the clothing as they could, without it being noticeable on the outside. I was proud of her for these moments of quiet subversiveness.

In January 1945, the camp was evacuated ahead of the advancing Russian army. On foot and by train, the prisoners made their way to another concentration camp, Ravensbrück.

If there was a worse hellhole than Auschwitz, this was it. Unbelievably crowded conditions, sanitary facilities were almost nil. The constant harassment was unbearable. We were lucky if we got our bread ration and managed to eat it before it was stolen. The stench was suffocating. Luckily, we did not stay long here. The cattle cars, symbols of our journey, appeared again.

Our next stop was Malchow, but not before a harrowing night in the railroad station at Magdeburg. That night this important railroad crossing was bombed for about four hours. And we were sitting there in the open cattle cars, literally exposed. The bombs lit up the night sky like a Christmas tree. I gazed into the sky, almost jubilant, that there were some people up there who were willing to put things right.

Over the next several weeks, my mother, along with my father's nieces and other women from Svalava, spent time in the Malchow camp and then endured forced marches, with little food. They slept in open fields. One morning, they realized the Nazi guards had disappeared during the night. The women eventually made their way to a refugee center in Grimma.

My father, after surviving horrendous conditions in Russia, managed to join up with the Czech Legion and fought his way back to Prague in 1945. He maintained a vigil on the streets there, hoping to find my mother. Meanwhile, my mother was able to get on a Czech Red Cross bus headed from the refugee center to Prague, as she wrote:

As we came nearer and nearer to Prague, with everybody in a jubilant mood, I kept having a sinking feeling about our return. We knew that there might be nobody waiting for us at the other end. But we were finally liberated and I could not help but be elated in leaving so much tragedy behind.

The first week in May we finally drove into Prague. The bus stopped at a crossroad. Louis's nieces Clara and Irene got out of the bus and almost immediately met a soldier from our hometown. He said, "You know your uncle Louis Goldstein is here in Prague." I could not believe this information and could not move or talk for quite some time. The ultimate miracle had happened. My husband was alive. We spent the night at the Catholic center, Charitas. I met Louis the following day, after almost a three-year separation. What a day that was.

After all the horrific losses of the war, my parents somehow started life over. My father had become an officer in the Czech army and they provided him with an apartment. But life in Prague was still very rough. Meat was hard to come by. My mother learned to cook rabbit. That winter in Prague, every apartment facing the courtyard had rabbits hanging out the window to keep them chilled. My parents opened their new home to my father's surviving family, friends, former teachers—anyone who was passing through Prague and needed a bed or a spot on the floor to sleep. My parents and the survivors they embraced became each other's family. But in Eastern Europe after the war, there was no guarantee of freedom. The Communist party was coming to power in Prague and signs of repression were everywhere. My parents began looking for a way out.

My father was the youngest of fourteen children, thirteen boys and one girl. Three brothers had died in infancy. Four brothers and their only sister were killed in the Holocaust, along with their spouses and most of their children. My father's three oldest brothers, Jacob, Isidor, and Harry Goldstein, had moved to America at the turn of the twentieth century before my father was even born. Jacob was twenty-eight years older than my father. When the war ended, these brothers reached out to their surviving family and helped bring them to the United States, beginning with my parents, in 1946. When my parents arrived in New York, my father met these three brothers for the first time.

• • •

My father's niece Lola had been with my mother at Auschwitz, where Lola's entire immediate family had been murdered. Her father Max was one of my father's much older brothers. After the war, Lola was with my parents in Prague for a while. They became her surrogate parents, even though she was only five years younger than my mother. Years later, at Lola's wedding, they walked her down the aisle.

We all adored Lola. When I came to Ann Arbor to attend the University of Michigan, Lola and her family lived about forty-five minutes away. I often went to her house for holidays or just to get some love and support. My first cousin Lola was thirty years older than I, and she often felt more like a surrogate mom or a sister. She and her husband Sam later retired to Florida, but after Sam died, Lola moved to Ann Arbor, near her daughter Ruth, for the last ten years of her life. Lola ended up living around the corner from my home, allowing us to spend a great deal of time together, which I cherished.

Later in life as Lola sorted through her many boxes of letters, cards, and photographs, she often presented me with envelopes filled with cards and copies of photos. The most special letter she gave me is slightly yellowed, written on a plain piece of writing paper. It is dated exactly three months after my parents arrived in America and contains messages from both of them. It was sent to Lola in a displaced persons (DP) camp in Zeilsheim, Germany. While my parents had succeeded in immigrating to the United States, Lola had to stay in a series of DP camps due to complex and antisemitic immigration laws. When I first held this letter, I immediately recognized my parents' European-style handwriting.

Brooklyn, Nov. 6th, 1946

Dear Lola,

We received your letter of Oct. 25th and you can imagine how happy we were to read some news. Unfortunately, you are still not writing us about those things that we would wish mostly to know. Why are you not writing exactly if we have to make out a new affidavit or have you some possibility with the one sent by my uncle?

We really are shocked that you couldn't get over here till now, but please you must hope still and you will see everything will be all right. I know it is hard for you there, but unfortunately nothing goes so smoothly as we would wish.

We will try to send you a package this week. I hope it won't pass a long time and we will be able to see each other again.

Much love and many kisses,
Magda

My dear Loli,

We received your letter. Write to us more often and exactly what is to do in your interest. If the affidavit from Uncle Maurice isn't good, write at once and we make out a new one. Learn English, it is very important. If you have occasion to learn some trade, so do it, it is very important, too. Enclosed 1 Dollar.

Many regards from,
Louis

My parents were, of course, trying to help Lola immigrate to the United States. The words in these notes are emblematic of their lifetime of caring for others, their very special relationship with Lola, and their generosity. Scraping together an extra dollar was a big deal at that time.

My parents sent several packages to Lola in the DP camp. One included camel hair fabric along with material for a lining, thread, and buttons to make a coat. Lola was not able to come to the United States until 1949. After a long journey, she arrived by ship in New York harbor. A photo taken of Lola on the deck of the ship shows her beautiful, radiant smile, and she is wearing the camel hair coat.

• • •

My parents worked hard to start their new lives in the United States. They had many setbacks and challenges, but eventually began to build a new family. My sister Susan was born in New York in 1948. Later the family moved to Detroit, where I was born in 1952. My parents established a new life for themselves there, enjoying a circle of friends in their neighborhood and among fellow survivors. My father worked at Winkelman's, a women's specialty department store chain. In 1960, when I was seven, my father's work took our family back to New York, where he worked for Franklin Simon stores. My parents had to start all over again, make new friends, and find a new home. That proved to be overwhelming for my mother, and she succumbed to periods of depression and "nervous breakdowns."

While I was growing up, my mother was hospitalized a couple times to treat her depression, which was very hard on my sister and me, and on our father. I remember a day when I was in second grade and walked home from school to our apartment building. Waiting outside for me was a teenage cousin who had been sent over by his parents to bring me to their home. They explained that my mother had been

*Magda and Louis Goldstein with baby Julie and Susan, Detroit,
Michigan, 1953*

taken to the hospital and that my sister and I would stay with them for
a few days. Although I loved the cousins who took care of us, this was
an upsetting time for me. I felt like my world just stopped for a while.
I needed my mom.

I can barely stand to think about what it must have been like for
her to be separated from us. My sister remembers that this episode of
our mother's depression was the first time she ever saw our father cry.
Susan was twelve or thirteen at the time, a terribly tender age to have to
deal with parents so vulnerable to distress, and only a sister five years
younger with whom to share this experience. It's no wonder we grew

up feeling like we never wanted to cause our parents any further harm.

Despite these difficult times, my parents were always helping others, which I think gave them a mission in life and kept them going. They continued to do whatever they could to support my father's surviving brothers, nieces, and nephews. They helped bring them to America, gave them food and a place to stay, and assisted them in finding work. They continued the tradition of welcome they had begun after the war, opening their home to all newcomers and sharing my mother's delicious Hungarian food. In addition, my parents saved up so they could send packages to my father's brother Martin, who had stayed behind and was trapped behind the Iron Curtain in their hometown of Svalava, which had become part of the Soviet Union.

In the 1960s, my father went to Europe once a year on a business trip. It was exciting for us to go to JFK Airport to pick him up after these trips. In those days, we could look from a bank of windows down below to the international area and see arriving passengers line up for customs inspection. Until we spotted my father in line, we didn't know if he and his brother Martin had both succeeded in getting permission to rendezvous with each other in Prague. If my father wasn't wearing his hat and coat, then we knew he had seen Uncle Martin and given them to him, among many other gifts.

• • •

Next to my desk, I keep two black-and-white photos of my mother and father, taken when they were in their seventies. In my mother's photo, she is standing at the kitchen sink. Though she's looking at the camera, her hands are under the faucet, preparations underway for a holiday. In his photo, my dad is looking at the camera as well, but he's working on setting up the drink buffet for the holiday gathering. You couldn't be a good host without offering a good schnapps.

I treasure these photographs more than any professional portrait. I feel like my parents are still there, in their house, and I could come stand next to them to help out. My parents were totally absorbed, especially at holiday time, with taking care of and providing for their extended family.

I wish I could ask my parents how they did it all. I would ask my mom, "How much fish should I buy to make enough gefilte fish for twenty people?" My dad would say, "You can never have too much." Clearly, it was a lot of work to prepare for the holidays. But somehow, my parents made it look so easy. Perhaps because love of family was so important to them, everything else came naturally. Perhaps because they lost so much in the war—and struggled for so many years to rebuild their lives—working hard to bring pleasure to the family was not really work at all. It was a source of pure joy.

Today, my sister and I proudly continue the tradition of hosting our extended family on Rosh Hashanah at Susan's home in New York. There are usually forty to fifty cousins in attendance, all descendants of my father's nieces and nephews. Most live in the New York area, but several join us from other states as well. We put out an amazing spread of food, including Hungarian delicacies. We always display photos of our parents, our survivor cousins who have passed away, and our father's oldest brothers, who helped bring the family to America.

• • •

In the summer of 1993, my sister and I traveled to the Carpathian Mountains of Eastern Europe with our parents and our cousin Lola. We went to their hometown, where they had never returned after the Nazis took them away almost fifty years earlier. The breakup of the Soviet Union made this trip possible, and a couple of our cousins had paved the way by visiting there a year earlier. Given my mother's history of depression, I was apprehensive as to how she would deal with this journey. But in the end my parents' stamina and upbeat spirit amazed me.

In the town of Svalava, we found my mother Magda's house, which had been built by her family, the Blaufelds. We were able to go inside, and my mother recognized the layout of the rooms, the original parquet floor, and the decorative designs stenciled on the walls. It was now being used as an appliance repair shop, filled with broken refrigerators and stoves. We asked her if she had hidden any valuables in the house. But no, there had been no time for that when the Nazis deported them. I think my mother's heart must have been breaking when she saw her former home under these conditions.

Lola remembered who had lived in all the nearby houses. Further down the street was where Lola's family's house should have been. It had been torn down and replaced with an apartment building.

At the former synagogue, my parents said that the façade of the building had the same shape it had fifty years before, but it had been painted over. It was here that the Jewish families had been taken the first night they were forced to leave their homes. The interior had been gutted and converted into a bread bakery, which had been moved there from across the street. The director of the bakery showed us around and gave us a sample of some bread. I couldn't bring myself to taste it.

After the war, survivors who returned to Svalava discovered the synagogue attic was strewn with the personal photographs of Jewish families who had been deported. It is unclear how or why the photographs were put there. A network of survivors sorted through them and returned as many as possible to family members. For us, these family photos had become an incredible visual record of our parents' lives before the war, a validation of another world.

In the walled Jewish cemetery in Svalava, we found the gravestone of Uncle Martin, the only one of my father's brothers who had lived out his life in their hometown. We looked for the gravestones of my mother's parents, who had both died of cancer before the war, but couldn't find them. The older gravestones were illegible, decaying and falling over in a jumble of weeds. Together we said Kaddish among the graves of our family. My parents and Lola wept. My sister and I wept, too, grieving the loss of grandparents we never had a chance to know.

Driving out into the countryside, we stopped at a small two-room hut by the side of the main road. An old man with a shock of white hair and an animated personality tended beehives behind the hut. About a hundred yards further, up a beautiful green hillside, there was a small cemetery, which he also tended. He led us up that hill and we found the tombstones of my father's parents, Esther and Zev Goldstein. I have always been amazed that my grandparents were born in the 1860s. They died of natural causes before World War II. To me, they'd always seemed part of a dream from a far-off world. But here they were. Touching their gravestones was the closest I would ever get to having grandparents. I will never forget the view from that hillside. Lush green fields were dotted with small farms and cone-shaped haystacks. In the distance, beyond clusters of small square houses rose the slopes of the Carpathian Mountains.

We continued down the road to Izvor, the tiny village where my father Louis was born. Before the war, the Goldsteins were the only Jewish family in the village, and in their home, they ran the only general store and a café of sorts. A lumber train used to run along the other side of the road. The engineers would stop across from the Goldsteins' house just so they could eat some of my grandmother's food. When my sister and I were young, we heard lots of stories about the house and the village of Izvor. My mother compared it to the TV show *Petticoat Junction*.

We found my father's house still standing, uninhabited and boarded up. It had a steep roof and outer walls made of flaking plaster. We broke off pieces of the plaster to bring home. The backyard was overgrown and the river behind the house had dried up to a small stream. While we took photos, children from the village came up to us and we handed out candy.

In the 1930s, my father had been the teacher of local peasant children in a one-room schoolhouse in Izvor. As we looked around, a man on a bicycle happened to stop and started talking to my father. After a few minutes, he realized that he had been one of my father's students. He said in Ukrainian, "Mr. Teacher, you came back! You came back! You're a hero!" People gathered around us. A few more turned out to be my father's former students. They were so excited to see him and we were thrilled to meet these people. They told us that the whole village would be talking that night about their teacher's return.

Our "Return to Izvor," as we named our trip, put together parts of the fairy tale that I'd heard about while growing up. A fairy tale with an impossibly monstrous ending. If you read between the lines of the story, you find out that the original owner of the bread bakery was my father's brother Joseph, who was gassed in Auschwitz. And what of my father's former students? While they happily welcomed him back, one man assured my father that he had taken over and run the Goldstein family store after the Hungarians took the family away. But had they tried to save the Goldsteins when they desperately needed help?

These are some of the conflicting thoughts that run through my head to this day. But most importantly, I remember how honored and privileged my sister and I felt to make this journey with our parents and Lola. I hope that it gave them some closure on a very dark period of their lives, and also an opportunity to reclaim the good memories. For me, it made my family history more tangible. I felt like I had found pieces of my past. To this day, tucked away in my dresser drawer, I keep the bits of plaster taken from the walls of my father's house.

• • •

When my parents were older, they traveled frequently. On a trip to Austria, they made a journey to the Eagle's Nest, which had been Hitler's retreat in the mountains between Austria and Germany. My sister and I were surprised they decided to visit this place. When we asked them what it was like to be there, they said it made them feel victorious. They were alive and Hitler was dead.

I can picture them there, holding their heads high with dignity as they looked out over the hills and looked back on their lives. Before the war, my parents, Uncle Béla and Aunt Juliska, my mother's brother Martzi, and other family and friends would go on picnics together. I have photographs that show them on these outings in the country-side. Often the women are posing with bouquets of wildflowers. In one photo the young men and women are lolling on the grass, in each other's arms, laughing. My Uncle Martzi, always said to be the witty life of the party, is playing the guitar. My mother's friend Leah and her sisters would have been singing. That is how I imagine them all now: reunited in heaven, having an eternal picnic on the slopes of the mountain outside their town, with a small river running nearby.

• • •

After a few months of suffering mini-strokes and the onset of dementia, my father died on July 6, 1999, at age eighty-five. Almost exactly a year later, my mother died of a stroke on the Fourth of July 2000, at age eighty. She was buried next to my father in a cemetery in New York, on eastern Long Island. A few yards away are the graves of my father's oldest brother Jacob, and his wife Pauline.

After my parents died and my sister and I were cleaning out their house, we found a file cabinet with records of my mother's treatment for depression. Flipping through the papers, we noticed that she'd had electroshock therapy, which we had never known about. This was so utterly disturbing to us that we immediately threw away the papers and have rarely mentioned them again. I regret not doing more to help my mother with her depression, perhaps to have helped her find a therapist, but I am thankful that she did much better later in her life.

While dealing with our parents' possessions, we gave some of their things to family and friends who had been important to them. One day, my sister and I decided to take one of our mother's necklaces to her longtime hairdresser, Ursula. We had never actually met Ursula, but when we walked into the hair salon, she looked up and said, "I know who you are." She recognized us from all the photographs our mother had shared with her. "I miss your mom," she said. "Oh, we would talk. She would tell me about her bad dreams." Then we realized Ursula had been her therapist all along.

· · ·

I myself sought out therapy from a social worker several times in my life. I think that I've always just wanted to be normal. I didn't really know what normal was, but I definitely felt different.

I tend to worry. Is it any surprise that I worry, with a family history full of horrible suffering? I am drawn to news about natural disasters and I imagine disasters befalling me and my family—crazy unlikely accidents and mishaps. My social worker advised me that, when I get into these thought cycles, I should tell myself that's enough and move on. I have, for the most part, learned to shake off these thoughts when they rise up. It's not easy, but I like to think I have absorbed some of my parents' ability to adapt and carry on in difficult situations.

Personal disaster did strike when I was diagnosed with breast cancer at age forty-three. Facing a double mastectomy, chemotherapy, and radiation in the months ahead, the most difficult hurdle for me was telling my parents about my diagnosis. As always, I wanted to protect them; I was worried about upsetting them. The burden of trying not to inflict more pain in their lives is something I think only children of Holocaust survivors and other survivors of genocide can fully understand. After I told them, though, they showed me the love and support they had given me my entire life. Any visible upset they kept hidden. I had failed to realize that my parents had an inherent strength born out of the challenges they faced during and after the war. My dad had often told me throughout my life, "Everything will be okay."

A further burden for me was the dilemma of calling myself a cancer survivor. Did I have the right to be called a survivor, albeit a different type of survivor? In my experience, any reference to a survivor had always meant a Holocaust survivor. They were survivors of a different magnitude. They were Survivors with a capital S. My situation paled in comparison.

After my cancer diagnosis, my wonderful social worker guided me during my recovery. She helped me to recognize that there really is no such thing as normal. That was an amazing and wonderful gift. While I had been seeking a "normal" life, I realized how lucky I was to have parents who were extraordinary in so many ways. Despite, and perhaps partly because of, their wartime experiences, they were always loving, kind, generous, and courageous.

• • •

My son Jonathan adored his grandparents, as well as our dear cousin Lola. After Lola died in December 2015, Jonathan, then thirty-two, wrote about her passing.

THE LAST HOLOCAUST SURVIVORS[1]

"It is better to be happy than sad." That was the message that my cousin Lola Taubman carried with her for her entire life, even after witnessing the horrors of the Holocaust firsthand.

Lola died last December at age ninety. She had been in declining health for several years, but there's still a missing part of my family now. For my entire life, it's been a given that there have been [living] Holocaust survivors among my relatives. Now, we've lost one more of them, one more eyewitness to a grievous part of history that must never be forgotten—or denied.

Of course, Lola herself was more than a Holocaust survivor. She was a loving mother and grandmother—and was like an extra grandmother to me. If you were her guest, she insisted that you never leave hungry, even after your repeated protests that you had had your fill. She loved to give sweet "birdie" kisses on your neck. She was the furthest thing from a statistic.

Recently I found myself wondering about the dwindling number of remaining survivors. How many more years do we have left when we can still talk to them? Their memories live on in books and movies, and filmed testimonials. But no matter what, there's nothing like talking to a Holocaust survivor in person.

No one keeps an official count of survivors. But the U.S. Senate estimated [in 2014] that one hundred nine thousand to one hundred forty thousand remain in the United States. You can still meet them. The United States Holocaust Memorial Museum in Washington, D.C., is a good place to start if you have a chance to visit. And there are many other resources available at local Holocaust museums and community groups.

For Lola, sharing her story was important. She wanted young people to "understand what happens when hate and intolerance prevail." She worked with a Holocaust center in Florida and often spoke to students. She even self-published an autobiography so her memories would live on.

"I have found that telling my story in school is so important," she wrote, "because there is still so much ignorance in the world."

. . .

At my parents' house in New York they had a sun porch, where they loved to spend much of their days. After they died, we sold their house, and movers came to take away their furniture. While one of the men was rolling up the sun porch rug, he found a photograph underneath it and gave it to me. A photo from the treasure trove found in the attic of the synagogue. There she was: my mom at age seventeen, with her family in their backyard. I had seen that photo many years before. It is dated 1937. In it my mother looks totally relaxed and happy. She is seated with her ankle crossed over her knee, her head tilted to one side as she smiles and leans into her brother Béla. He has one arm around her, the other around their mother. Aunt Juliska is there, too, along with her sister and brother. And everything is okay.

We are compelled to speak about our family of Holocaust survivors to ensure that their stories will never be forgotten. In sharing our experiences growing up in the second generation, we find strength in our common bonds and feelings. What is the purpose of diving deeply into such personal events and feelings? Is it to validate our own suffering? I have included stories, such as my mother's treatment for depression, that my parents would not have revealed to the public. Is that fair to them?

Here I am trying to protect my parents again. Now I understand why.

Drinking from a Half-Full Broken Glass

Avishay Hayut, son of Aliza and Aharon Chajut

Blended Hayut family (Hayim, Lea, Aliza, and Aharon) after the war, Warsaw, Poland, 1948

It recently dawned on me that we might think of Kristallnacht as a metaphor for the lives of the second-generation children of survivors. Kristallnacht, the Night of Shattered (Broken) Glass, took place on November 9 and 10 in the year 1938, and spread its virulence across Nazi Germany. During that horrific event, Jewish establishments including stores, schools, hospitals, and synagogues were attacked by German paramilitary and members of the Nazi Party. Glass was shattered everywhere and fires were set to destroy heaps of books and sacred Jewish scrolls along with buildings. This was the thunder and lightning before the storm of what we call the Holocaust. When we try to uncover the hidden stories of our families' experiences during and after this calamity, it's like trying to excavate the archeological artifacts of our parents' silence. Just as the shards of glass cannot be put back together and the burnt pages of books can't make whole books again, we can never recover the whole truth of what happened to our family members lost during the Holocaust. In some cases, even those who survived took their secrets with them to their graves, trying to protect themselves from the pain of reliving their experiences, as well as others from the horror of hearing about what happened. Yet, those of us who came after often feel compelled to seek to unearth their stories from the broken glass and charred embers—even though we may become scarred with emotional cuts and burns too.

This past Holocaust Memorial Day, my sister asked if any of us—my mother, my brother or myself—remembered the name of our father's brother, whom we'd never met. He had been killed at the age of ten, shot with his mother by the Nazis, as they were rounding up women and children as one of the final cleansing actions in the Vilnius Ghetto.

To whom do we refer when we have no name? I remember seeing a picture of my father's mother and brother in my parents' bedroom in the house where my mother still lives. A black-and-white photo of mother and child almost expressionless. I think it had been under the mirror, but it wasn't there when I last visited.

I don't recall if my father ever said his brother's name, if we ever even asked. In the Jewish tradition you name someone after a relative who has died. My poor uncle has no one named after him. His name is lost in the ether of a dark history.

· · ·

I was born in Israel twelve years after the end of World War II, shortly after the Sinai War of 1956, and eight years after Israel's War of Independence. I believe my birth as the firstborn child to Holocaust survivors signaled to my parents the promise of a new beginning: a new generation that could vindicate the annihilation of their families, a celebration of planting ground in a newfound country, and a confirmation of their love and commitment.

Israel, a country made up mostly of Jewish refugees who gathered from all over the world, was formed as a place where Jews could feel safe from persecution, a refuge where they would not have to feel afraid that people would scapegoat them for the maladies and weaknesses of mankind. It was a glorious and noble ideal. Unfortunately, the plan neglected to take into account that other people were already living on this same piece of land. Nowadays I am keenly aware of how the tensions in the region are connected to the understandable fact that the Palestinians did not want to give up their homes to the new Israeli state. As a child growing up in Israel, I hadn't thought of that. The way I viewed it, we were just in survival mode because we wanted to prevent the Arab nations from throwing us into the sea. We wanted to prove to ourselves (and the world) that we would not let another Holocaust happen to us, that we were capable of surviving by using military force, rather than going to the gallows like sheep to the slaughter. Today I understand that the politics were far more complex, and that there was a nation caught in the middle between its aspirations and its own survival. Just as school curricula on American history have omitted much of the plight and the perspectives of the Native Americans and the African American slaves, so too did history in Israeli schools often neglect the plight and perspectives of the Palestinians.

Until the age of thirty I lived in Israel, enjoying and suffering the everyday life of a young country trying to establish itself as a modern, successful democracy in the Middle East. When I left Israel to come to the United States to pursue graduate studies, I didn't think I would be leaving permanently. Whether or not I ever do go back to live there, I will always remain a product of this challenging history. I think my family struggled with the Israeli view of Holocaust survivors as weak, while in America, it seemed that their survivor counterparts were treated with more compassion, especially by the Jewish community. I see my own personal history and impact of the Holocaust through this lens.

I know every person has their *pekale*, Yiddish for proverbial baggage that they carry with them. My complicated family history may have caused me to carry more than most. It has been a rough journey, trying to look at and untangle the effects of the Holocaust from the country in which I was raised, and the interpersonal and family dynamics that have contributed to who I am.

• • •

As a boy of ten or eleven, I used to poke fun at the Holocaust with one of my friends. I remember acting out the "Heil Hitler" salute, sarcastically saying things like "it's springtime for Hitler," and pretending to shoot people. I cringe now when thinking about what we did. Perhaps playing the part of the aggressor as children was our way of dealing with trying to understand what happened or overcome our fears that this could happen to us.

No one event stands out in which I remember being told about the Holocaust. Every year Holocaust Remembrance Day is strongly acknowledged in Israel. We hear what is said on the radio, typically through stories shared by survivors we do not know. In my house, that day was always a very somber one, though no one, especially not my parents, discussed what made them sad. I think they didn't want to burden us with their personal horror stories and hoped to shield us from their terrifying past. Nonetheless, I always felt that there was some kind of dark cloud from the Holocaust hanging over our house. As a child, I experienced continuous tension in the air, accompanied by my father's shouting, my mother's crying, and one instance where my mother was close to mental breakdown.

Bits and pieces of my parents' story came out over the years. When I was about twenty years old, my mother shared a memoir she had written of her Holocaust days. While I found what she wrote to be very interesting and disturbing, the depth of the horror of that phase in her life didn't fully sink in. Other information came after my father died in 1995, from his cousin who had lived with him in Poland after the war. As I grew older and asked more questions, a greater sense of the enormity of my parents' wartime experiences seeped into my consciousness. Today, I still find it hard to fathom that my parents were part of that catastrophe and that so many of our family members were exterminated.

• • •

September 1, 1939 marked my mother Aliza's third birthday at her family home in Radomsko, Poland. That was the day that bombs fell all around her town and her world changed forever. The Jews were put in the ghetto. When a rumor spread that Jewish children were going to be separated from their parents, my grandmother gave my mother to her colleague, a non-Jewish unmarried teacher friend in a village outside the city. That was the last time my mother saw her father. Sometime after, he was deported to his last destination, Buchenwald.

Aliza's life in the village was fairly pleasant and she was well cared for until people started to suspect that she was Jewish. Leah, my grandmother, then paid a king's ransom for the two of them to flee to Warsaw. There they moved from one apartment to another, until finally obtaining false documents stating that my grandmother was a Polish teacher and my mother an orphaned Polish girl. A few months later, my mother was given to a head nun who knowingly hid her at a convent under her new identity. My grandmother survived the rest of the war as a nanny to a Polish family. After the war, when my mother was around eight, she reunited with her mother.

During my last visit to my mother's home in Israel, I was looking for vinyl records for my older son, which I remembered I had stored there. When my brother pulled a very dusty box from the attic, it contained a magazine with an interview of my grandfather Hayim, which told the horrific story of their Holocaust survival. I learned that mothers and children up to age sixteen were rounded up and taken from the ghetto in Vilnius, Lithuania, to their deaths, including my father's mother and ten-year-old brother who were shot and killed preceding this round up. My father Aharon, who was sixteen years old, and three other teens were able to escape and run back to their fathers. From that moment on, my grandfather had to protect and guard his only last possession—my father—more than ever.

To survive in the ghetto, my father sold cigarettes. My grandfather

Hayim drew a mustache on him to make him look older so he wouldn't be rounded up and killed. In Vilnius they worked as tailors in one of the work camps and survived by the grace of a guard who helped them obtain more food and safer living conditions. My father and grandfather were later deported to the Stutthof concentration camp in Germany. By the end of the war, in Stutthof, my grandfather got typhoid fever and almost died. My father fed him breadcrumbs until he recuperated and somehow they both survived.

Immediately after the war ended, in 1946, the paths of my widowed grandfather Hayim and my widowed grandmother Leah crossed at a train station in Poland. They fell in love and got married, probably in part because they shared this common suffering. At first they made a home in Poland, where my grandfather sold bolts of fabrics given by a Jewish charity organization in the United States to help Jewish refugees rehabilitate their lives. Leah and Hayim left communist Poland for Israel a few years later with their new blended family—my mother Aliza, who was fourteen at the time, and my father Aharon, who was twenty-two. The government gave them a very small room in which to live, and they had to share it with another refugee family from Romania. At that time, there was considerable fear about threats to Israel from their Arab neighbors both within and outside of the country. I think it must have felt to my parents as if they were in survival mode all over again, only now in a new environment.

The resourceful Leah adapted quickly, learning Hebrew and beginning to study to resume her teaching career. She sent Aliza to boarding school in the countryside, as she needed time to get herself ahead. My mother did not yet speak Hebrew and had to learn farming and gardening on top of the other regular high school subjects. The teachers, many of whom came from Poland, loved my mother, with her warm personality and her ability to speak Polish. Aliza, however, did not get along with some of the other students. Most of them came from the Middle East, and she could not communicate well with them. They were jealous of my mother's good standing with the teachers and treated her poorly. My mother described her stay at this boarding school as worse than living in the convent in Poland where she was hiding during the war. Being a sensitive teenage girl, she often fainted from stress and despair.

As the older stepbrother, Aharon felt a responsibility to come and visit Aliza every once in a while. He was studying mathematics and physics at the Jerusalem university. Noticing her distress, he decided to bring her back to the city where the family lived and get her enrolled in a regular high school. My mother did very well in the humanities, but when it came to math, she performed so poorly that the career placement director said she would only be able to find work in menial jobs like housekeeping or tailoring.

My grandmother did not agree with this assessment. She knew her daughter could do better. She found someone at a nursing school who was able to get Aliza registered. My mother passed the admission exam and four years later graduated from nursing school with honors. She became a very skilled and compassionate nurse, deeply loved by her patients.

During Aliza's time in nursing school, my grandmother and grandfather had a lot of marital disputes and finally formally separated. My mother loved her stepfather who was more warm and nurturing than her mother. Shortly after the divorce, Hayim moved to South Africa.

While they were still officially step-siblings, my parents were secretly seeing each other. It wasn't until after they found out that their parents were divorcing that they announced their intention to marry. My father married my mother when she was twenty and still in nursing school—in part out of love, in part to get her out of her mother's home, and in part to be able to care for her.

My mother always felt indebted to my grandmother for saving

her life. I think she respected her mother for being so adaptable and resourceful, for not caving in to the many horrible circumstances she experienced as a young woman. There was much to admire. In later life, in Israel, Leah became the chair of the surviving community from her hometown in Poland. Unfortunately, my grandmother was not capable of giving my mother the emotional support and love she needed. Despite her resentment towards my grandmother, my mother never shirked from her responsibility to help or take care of her. As Leah aged and started to decline mentally and physically, my mother brought her to live with her and my father. Her presence in their home was a source of continuing tension between my parents.

• • •

My grandmother had wanted me to be named Honi, after her first husband, Henrik, my mother's father. It is common in Eastern European Jewish tradition to name children after the dead. But my mother felt that Honi sounded like what you called a boy from the old shtetl in Europe. For both my parents, this name brought back the feeling of living in persecution and exile. They were not willing to use a name from the diaspora, since families that chose such names for their young Israeli children were looked down upon for not leaving the shameful past behind. This new Israeli society was creating the culture of bravery needed to build a Jewish country that would never let another Holocaust happen again. Israelis wanted to establish a homeland that would serve as the antithesis of the life of Jews since the destruction of the Temple, always in fear of persecution and at the mercy of the rulers and the locals wherever they lived. My parents preferred a Hebrew name that they thought sounded both Biblical and modern and was well suited for a young Israeli child.

Avishay, literally translated from Hebrew, means "father's gift." My mother called me a gift from her father, a father she recalled always with great love and yearning. This name, this legacy, has often felt like a double-edged sword. How could I fill the impossible void of a lost beloved father?

I learned recently from my mother that on every Holocaust Remembrance Day she writes letters to her father. She is now eighty-four years old, and I know to this day she feels that her father is watching over her. She told me that he is like a mythical guardian angel of sorts from whom she can ask for help and protection for her and her family. I too would like to believe that he is looking out for her. It's funny how we each comprehend the survival of the spirit.

Would I like to see these letters? I don't know. Perhaps, after she dies. A part of me is interested in getting a better understanding of her, to know what has been going on in her mind over the years. But another part of me isn't sure that I'll be okay with what she is writing. Surely while she is alive, I don't want to pry.

Growing up, I always wanted to be on good terms with my mother. She was the generally more even-tempered one of my parents, less prone to anger, screaming, and outbursts when dealing with life's stresses. I was not afraid to share my thoughts or my troubles with her. I felt she gave me levelheaded responses that didn't conjure up her own inadequacies or anxieties. My mother was very warm and caring, but at times she seemed to be overwhelmed by life as a young mom. She did not get much moral support from my father or from her own mother. When overwhelmed, my mother became distraught over small stuff, like cleaning the house. She would cry and behave like a small child. This emotional volatility made me anxious. I remember very vividly an argument between my parents when I was about ten or eleven. My mother was talking incomprehensibly, with saliva coming out of her mouth. As a child, you don't quite know anything is wrong in your family, as this is the environment in which you are raised. Yet somewhere deep inside, I knew something was not altogether right with my mother.

In her mid-fifties, my mother was hospitalized with a nervous breakdown. Later, after my father died, she was diagnosed as bipolar. She subsequently had a couple more severe episodes of depression and mania. The two major times that it happened, within a period of just over a year, I immediately took time off from work to go to Israel, even though I was leaving my wife alone with two babies in the United States. With the help of my brother, my sister, my mother's close friends, and the rest of our family in Israel, my mother was able to stabilize and get back to her normal self. I also felt that my presence was material in her recovery, since I was the one who stayed with her in her house the whole time and gave her the constant attention and support she needed to return to reality.

I think the Holocaust was a key precipitant in the development of her disorder. The unstable times of that period were breeding grounds for the development of an unstable personality. I also imagine that her leaving Poland, the continuing survival threats of life in Israel, marital tensions in her new blended family, and later, conflict in her own marriage, all contributed to unmanageable stress.

• • •

From an early age, I had the sense that I could not meet the expectations of my father or my mother. I was "not a typical boy," my mother voiced frequently. Though this was said lovingly, I also heard undertones of disappointment and sarcasm. I was not a rough and tumble type of boy. I was neat and polite, and while I was quite a good student, I was not very focused. There was a popular song in Israel called "*Heimke Sheli*" ("My Heimke," a diasporic nickname for Hayim), about her soldier son who was not marching in line with all the other soldiers. My mother often referred to me as her "Heimke." She spoke this nickname in an endearing way, but there was also a mean twist to it, implying that because I was a daydreamer, I wouldn't be fit to be a good soldier. In the song the mother is proud of her son who does not follow in line with the rest of the marching regiment, but we are meant to laugh at the stupidity of the mother thinking her son is a special soldier. I always resented this association but never told my mother how awful it made me feel, how it validated my inadequacies.

I believe my mother wanted me to be a macho kind of guy, one who stands up to others and doesn't take a beating from anyone: a prototype for the new Israeli warrior ready to fight for and protect the

Aharon, Eran, Avishay and Aliza Hayut near the beach, Tel Aviv, Israel, c. 1965

country's future. As a boy, I did not fight back readily when someone posed a threat to me. I would get beaten up because I was not quick enough to sufficiently respond physically or verbally. My younger brother, five years my junior, would not let anyone get the better of him. In fact, my brother was everything I wasn't. I envied that he didn't take any crap from anyone. To this day, I and everyone else consider him the head of the family. He manages the finances and other matters for my mother. While we have a good relationship, I have always felt inferior to him.

My father contributed to my feeling of being "less than." I don't recall him ever really complimenting me, except for the occasions when he said that I was talented in music. I loved to listen to the records my father used to buy. I tried to connect with him through the joy in music that ran deep in my family. On my father's side, my grandfather was often singing and used to play the balalaika (a Russian mandolin). My father also liked to sing as well as play both the accordion and piano by ear, though not so well. On my mother's side, my great-grandfather was a cantor and my grandmother also loved to sing and had a lovely voice.

When I was around eight, my father bought me an accordion and arranged lessons for me. But my real musical passion was the guitar, and I eventually got one for my bar mitzvah. In those days, campfires and sing-alongs were a common social activity. Playing guitar was a way for me to be more popular. While I had a hard time reading music, I was able to teach myself how to play by ear. Three years later, during the Yom Kippur War, I started writing some songs, and my parents got me a teacher who I loved, a famous composer of Israeli music. Music brought me and my father closer together. I would play the guitar and he would bring out the accordion, and both of us would play some new and old songs together. They were mostly popular Israeli songs or world music that we both knew and loved.

• • •

My father was a real Litvak. This is a term used pejoratively to describe someone from Lithuania who likes to argue just for the sake of an argument. My father and my grandfather were both hot-tempered. At age two and a half, I remember my grandpa cursing me in Russian when I accidentally broke something in his apartment. My grandfather and father also constantly fought whenever they were together. In fact, my father was always getting into arguments with everybody because he felt he was always being wronged. I remember periods of time when he wouldn't talk to neighbors, friends, or even the grocer for long stretches. Eventually he would let it go because he forgot what he was angry about. Our friends and members of our community were understanding, and willing to forgive his anger. I assume that was because at the end of the day, they saw something good in him and appreciated him. I saw it too, the caring and the help he jumped to give me, even though it was hard to internalize that because I felt bombarded by his negativity. I was often the one who bore the brunt of his wrath.

Looking back on that time with the benefit of years of therapy, I think the shadow of my father's brother's death, the survivor's guilt, and the reversal in caretaking he took on with his father as the war progressed probably played into the intensity of my father and grandfather's dynamic. While they each may have had some innate tendency to react more angrily than most, I think their anger became exacerbated and more ingrained as a result of the inhumane conditions and fears of imminent death they experienced during the Holocaust, as well as the subsequent difficulties of everyday life in Israel.

I felt I could never live up to my father's expectations and was almost always letting him down. I knew that my parents wanted me to be in an esteemed profession as a doctor or an engineer, which is why I started my undergraduate education in civil engineering. After one semester, though, I realized this was not the profession I wanted to be doing for the rest of my life. I could not imagine sitting in an office and working on computations and building plans. That was boring, dry work in my opinion. I wanted a profession where I would be engaged on a daily basis with other people in a more intimate way. When I was sixteen, I'd suffered a serious leg injury that required surgery followed by intense physical therapy in the hospital. I was very impressed with the results of my rehabilitation and thought I could see myself doing this kind of work. So I decided to become a physical therapist even though my parents tried to discourage me. When I had floated the possibility even before attending engineering school, my mother said that I would never make enough money as a physical therapist.

I enjoyed my studies in physical therapy, excelled at them, and was appreciated by my colleagues and professors so much that I planned to become a professor. At that point in time there was no further education in Israel available in this field past the undergraduate degree. When I shared with my father that I wanted to get my masters in physical therapy in New York, he responded, "You'll never make it in New York." The message I heard was that I couldn't manage my own life, which made me feel awful. How do you tell that to your son? I left for New York feeling both worried that I wouldn't succeed and also determined to show him that I was able to make it on my own. Now I wonder if my father's reaction was related to his experience in the Holocaust: to the belief that you can't survive without your parents, or you shouldn't abandon your parents. Perhaps he was afraid to lose me to the United States. Living in Israel, I had been a dedicated son. Maybe he didn't believe that once I moved, I would come to help out anytime that I was needed.

The feeling of not achieving our full professional potential is a running theme on my father's side of my family. Neither my father nor I fulfilled our professional aspirations. My father had wanted to be an engineer, but his schooling was interrupted by the war and then later interrupted again in Israel. After he began to study at the university, he needed to stop for a two-year stint of service in the army. When he finished his mandatory army obligation, he did not go back to the university. He needed to support his family and ended up taking a job at an electric power company that was neither physically nor intellectually challenging. He stayed there until his early retirement when the plant was closed.

At age fifty-one, I suffered from clinical depression. I was the same age as my mother when she had her first mental breakdown. Though it was not as severe as my mother's, and it was only one episode, it took approximately two years for me to recover. I had palpitations and dizziness and went to the emergency room on three occasions because I thought I was having a heart attack. No, depression with anxiety was what my primary care doctor later diagnosed. It was a surprising revelation. On one hand, I was relieved that I did not have a serious life-threatening illness. On the other hand, I struggled with feeling burnt out at work, and I worried that I would not be able to continue to provide for my family, including two elementary school-aged children. I felt my father's voice coming back to haunt me that maybe I wasn't able to make it after all.

This episode occurred at the height of the financial meltdown of 2008. I was doing home care physical therapy full time, which was not so intellectually challenging. But it was emotionally draining, because I was working primarily with the elderly, many of whom were very sick and did not have good social support. With medication, psychotherapy, vigorous exercise, and the great support I got from my lovely wife, I was able to regain and improve my emotional health. I was never hospitalized or out of work because of my condition, but it was a very dark and hard period that took a lot of mental and physical effort to overcome.

I have not told my mother about this time in my life. I didn't want to burden her with the worry of mental illness passed on in the family. I only recently discussed it with my sister and my brother, who is a psychologist. I thought they would be able to take in this information without having it affect them emotionally. My children are aware that I've experienced depression and that their grandmother has bipolar disorder. I told them because I want them to be assured that they can find the strength to fight sad or anxious feelings if they arise and that they can get help. I'm not worried about my sons having bipolar disorder like my mother, since they don't display any of the same tendencies, nor have they suffered from the same horrible past. However, I continue to worry about the thread of mental illness in our family.

• • •

Becoming a father was joyous but very challenging. I saw myself in my firstborn son Yoav, and found myself enacting the same pattern of anger that had played out between my father and me. Though I tried very hard, I found I could not escape beating him up psychologically and sometimes physically as well. In many ways, I repeated my father's mistakes, having expectations for my son to behave a certain way and to succeed according to my conceptions. I didn't accept how his brain might work differently or allow him to just be himself. I can't solely blame the Holocaust for the way my father parented me and I parented my son, though I know patterns of learned behaviors become a part of our DNA. My own insecurity probably led me to feel less confident about my child's ability to stay on the "right" path.

Yoav was diagnosed with ADHD and received treatment for that behavioral disorder starting at an early age. Even though the medication helped, I still feel I have to monitor him closely. What I didn't get from my father, and which I consequently do with my own son, is to share with him how much I believe in his potential to succeed. I often tell him that he is gifted artistically and very intelligent. I encourage him to not give in to the tendencies of our primal mind that can lead to behavior like wasting hours playing games and watching things on our multimedia devices. "You cannot use having ADHD as a reason to not function well in society; do not use your disability as an excuse! You have the advantage of great intelligence and creativity and talent. You can and have to fight the tendencies." This is my discourse to him, and my struggle with him. He hates to hear these words, but he also knows they're true.

Yoav happens to be a very talented violinist. He is in college now pursuing a career in music education. Alon, my youngest, plays the cello beautifully and is pursuing a cello performance career in college. Both my children have academic scholarships, for which I feel very fortunate and proud. At the same time, I worry about them (particularly Yoav) losing the scholarships. I have a hard time trusting that things will work out. The fear that something bad will happen plagues me. I believe this fear is magnified in the life of a second-generation survivor given our history: that at any moment something can go terribly wrong.

• • •

While I may not be as accomplished as I had hoped, at this point in my life, I can say that I am satisfied. I am doing what I like to do, working in a clinic seeing a variety of patients and using all my skills in a way that I feel is stimulating and gratifying. I am good at taking care of people, both physically and emotionally. Along with my wife Regina, who is a cantor, I am able to express my love for music, a love I'd left behind for a very long time. Now, I sing in the choir at the synagogue, play the guitar at a few services during the year, and sometimes, when I join our friends at gatherings, I sing and even play the accordion.

I feel very grateful for my father's love and recognition of my musical gift; for the transmission through the generations of musical talent; and for my ability, in turn, to nurture in my sons their unique musical strengths. If I were allowed to go back in time to change the trajectory of my life, I would probably make all the same choices because they brought me to where I am today. I enjoy a career that satisfies me, music that fills me, and wonderful people in my life that I love. This is my half-full broken glass.

At age seventeen, Yoav wrote of our family's legacy in this poem. He understands that when we pray on the High Holidays, we acknowledge our ability to survive even under the most dire circumstances. He knows that even though the Holocaust changed the course of our family's narrative, we were still given the grace to be here today.

AVINU MALKEINU

I will be able to endure,
    Because on my father's mother's third birthday the beautiful skies of Poland turned ashy gray as the jackboots took her people's heritage with guns,
    And she is still here.

I will be able to endure,
    Because my father's mother got on her knees to pray in a temple that was not hers in order to not die, and her mother risked her life to stay close by.

I will be able to endure,
    Because though my father's father saw his mother and baby brother get shot in the streets of Lithuania,

He survived past it,

Through Buchenwald,

Where the barbed wire was so thick, staring at it would pierce one's skin and hopes.

I will be able to endure,

Because my people still survived through the gas chambers and the cold winters without food,

Because they still saw the sunlight at the end of the muzzle of Hitler's gun,

Which gave them more reason to sing their songs of freedom . . .

I will endure,

Because my parents have endured me and much worse,

And my grandparents' circumstances were much worse than mine.

So whatever they can endure, so can I,

Because I am their family,

And their durable blood runs through my genes.

I will sing my song of praise at their graves one day,

Proclaiming to them,

"I will always endure, because it is why I am here today."

"Avinu Malkeinu"

4

I Don't Remember

Nancy Szabo, daughter of Daniel Szabo

Daniel Szabo with his mother Maria and sister Eve, Lake Balaton, Hungary c. 1939

Are our parents responsible for sharing with us the pain of their youth? The struggles of their young adulthood? The landmines in their marriage? How much of their legacy is what's told? How much is withheld? We sometimes judge them harshly because they've kept secrets from us. We've been angry at feeling left out of the "truth." We've had to accept that much of what our parents went through will remain a mystery to us.

I know I never got the full story from my father of what happened to him during the Holocaust, but I tell myself, he gave me morsels, tastes of his pain. "What was it like to be in hiding? What did you do there? How did you get through this time?" I asked. His usual response to such questions was "I don't remember." So much I ached to know, but most of it my father seemed to have blocked out. As young adults, my brother and I were able, with some prodding, to get a few disconnected memories out of him about his childhood. We learned that his father walked him to school every morning, that his parents forced him to eat everything on his plate for dinner or else he would have to eat it for breakfast, and that he spent summer vacations at his Aunt Margaret's home in the countryside. But about the dark periods when he was hiding, and later when his family escaped Hungary, we got very little. I had the distinct sense that he was consciously keeping some things private—whether to protect himself or us, I'll never know.

Mainly, my father spoke of his mother's bravery and grit. He'd shake his head in amazement at her strength, but never acknowledged his own. Though I was incredibly curious about my father's wartime experiences, I treaded lightly. I knew my father must have harbored terrible memories and probably wanted to shield me from them, to keep them as his burden alone. I went along with this because I could see his pain. I thought by talking about it he would be hurt more. I didn't want to make my father sad, sadder than he already was.

• • •

My father Daniel was a six-year-old boy in Budapest when the war broke out. Though both his parents were Jewish, he was not raised as a Jew. Their family name, Szabo, very common in Hungary, had replaced their Jewish last name, Gansel, by the time my father was born. Maria and Alexander, his parents, essentially hid his Judaism from him. Several of his aunts converted to Catholicism, though there is no evidence that Maria and Alexander converted. With Hitler's rise, my grandparents may have reassured themselves that raising their children as Catholics would help them survive. My father recalled celebrating Christmas, exchanging gifts and singing carols. His mother's family was from the countryside and apparently did identify as Jewish. They were likely ridiculed by the Budapest Jews in the family, who looked down on the "less sophisticated" country Jews. Assimilation was the norm among Budapest Jews. Identity submerged. Hidden.

In 1943, when Daniel was ten, his father died suddenly. My father and his sister were not allowed to go to his funeral. His death was barely spoken about. Feelings buried. Not long afterwards, my father was sent to a Jesuit boarding school in southern Hungary. He recalled registering with the police on his way there. When asked to identify his parents' religion, he wrote *Israelite*. "How I knew, I don't know. I never had this kind of conversation with my parents."

Imagine his reaction when, less than a year later, his uncle Pali retrieved him from school, explaining that he would have to wear a Jewish star and the family would now live in a Jews-only apartment building owned by his uncle. My father was shocked. "I wasn't Jewish,

I didn't feel Jewish. I knew nothing about Judaism." What a jolt it must have been to be introduced to Judaism, for which he had no feeling or experience, by being forced to wear the punishing Jewish star, to be singled out, banished from his home, and made to live in fear because of an identity that had no meaning to him. "Who am I?" he may have asked himself. "I don't feel like a Jew."

In the summer of 1944, spurred to action after terrifying raids of their apartment house by the Hungarian Nazis, my grandmother left the relative safety of the apartment, venturing out into the streets without her Jewish star, risking her life to obtain protective papers from the Swiss embassy. Our family lore contains another story in which my grandmother got false identity papers from "brave Christian friends." I don't know the source of either story and I don't know which one was true—the Swiss embassy or brave Christian friends. It's another frustrating gap I've learned to accept.

Clearly, these papers were a key first step in their survival and, for my father, they entailed another switch of identity. His papers said he was a refugee orphan from a southern Hungarian city. This new identity became an entry pass into a Nazi-oriented orphanage. My grandmother took him there, at eleven years old, when it became too dangerous to stay in the Jewish apartment building. He lived in the orphanage for months during the war and wore the armband of the Hungarian Nazis. "From that point on, I was acting, but I had no problem passing as a Christian," he told me. "If I had to pass as a Jew, I would have had a terrible problem because I knew nothing." His survival hinged on his ability to appear Christian. Indeed, his ignorance of Judaism may have saved him.

While the other boys in the orphanage were raising their hands in "Heil, Hitler" salutes, how did my father feel? He characterized this time as play-acting, as a game, but he was a boy all by himself, lonely and vulnerable. He had just lost his father, was forced to leave his mother and only sibling, and was living among Christian boys who might have killed him if they knew the truth. But he was smart enough to play along to survive.

After threats of Nazi raids, his mother had to move him out of the orphanage to the basement of another apartment house in Budapest. My father described it as dark and crowded, during a time filled with Russian artillery barrages and intense air raids. When he recounted this period to us, he would shake his head sorrowfully, and with some shame, admit that he had limits and needed his mother. Eventually, when his mother was able to visit, he begged her to take him with her. "I couldn't stand being alone anymore," he said. "She was fearless. I was scared to death."

The next day, they retrieved his sister, Eve, who was three years older than him. She had also been hidden alone and twice moved: first to a convent and then to a cellar wood closet in my grandmother's friend's home. My father, aunt, and grandmother stayed in hiding until Budapest was liberated in January of 1945.

After the war, they remained in Budapest for several years. During that time, my father found great solace in the Catholic Church, where he served as an altar boy at St. Stephen's Basilica, the largest church in Budapest. He said he was comforted by the Catholic rituals, the music, the incense, the rich vestments. I do wonder, though: did his experiences during the war make him averse to acknowledging his Judaism, so instead he sought comfort in the rituals of Catholicism? Was he trying to fit in after the torturous persecution of Jews? Did any part of him acknowledge that he was a Jew underneath it all? Was his Jewish soul in waiting, hiding until it was safe to come out?

• • •

Budapest Székesfővárosi Közlekedési Rt.

36671

Daniel Szabo's Budapest transit ID, c. 1947

My grandmother, Maria Berger, grew up in the Hungarian town of Herend, deep in the countryside, but she met her husband, my grandfather Alexander, in the city of Budapest, where she lived and survived during World War II. When asked how many people she knew who were lost in the camps, my grandmother would woefully reply, "About sixty friends and family. About thirty were family. They lived in the countryside." This was a far more dangerous place for Hungarian Jews than Budapest.

When we asked about these family members, we got only the barest response. Her cousins István and Simon, "two brothers, who looked like twins," were the only ones my grandmother described. These fun-loving cousins lived in a town called Nagykanizsa, off the southern end of Lake Balaton in Hungary, 170 kilometers from her home in Herend. She used to visit them as a child, and they would take her for wild rides on their motorcycle.

Recounting their playful antics, her face would light up, and then become grief-stricken when she recalled their fate in a heavy voice: "The Nazis came and they took István away. Him and his wife and their children, and his mother, too." We assumed that Simon met a similar fate. This made me think about my own cousins, the trio of boys—Billy, Dicky, and Jimmy—whom I adored and with whom I shared many family visits in New York when I was growing up. I thought of Jimmy's contagious laughter, Dicky's gentle soul, Billy's brilliant athleticism. And my "sister" cousins—Jana and Julie—with whom I shared music, Hungarian desserts, and so much laughter. I could only imagine the heartbreak if I were to lose them the way my grandmother lost hers.

Though I've tried to find out what happened to Simon and István, I still do not know where and how they died. It's a strange feeling, the "unknowingness" of it all. So many people I will never be able to mourn. Only a handful of stories told and written down as proof of the miracle of my family's survival.

• • •

By August of 1949, having survived the war in hiding, my grandmother felt it imperative that she and her children leave. Refusing to join the Communist Party, she had been blacklisted and craved a life of freedom. I can barely fathom how she managed it, but with much preparation and courage, my grandmother arranged for their escape from Budapest. When they got off the train at a town in northeastern Hungary, it was dark. They walked along a highway, a car came, and they got in. The driver (who was he?) left them near the Hungarian border with Czechoslovakia. They met another man there (and who was he?), joined some people who were hiding in the woods, and walked all night. Who were their companions on this trek? Strangers they'd never see again, taking a journey together that was both terrifying and miraculous.

Sometime during the walk, or perhaps in the barn where they were hidden after crossing into Czechoslovakia, my grandmother lost her wallet. She had to find someone who would drive them through the Tatra Mountains to Bratislava on credit, and she did: "a very nice driver, I will never forget him," my grandmother told me solemnly. In Pozsony, they took a trolley to the end of the line—a village near the Czech-Austrian border—and here, an interesting thing happened. After they got off the trolley, a man on a motorcycle approached them but then turned around and drove away. The people in the village, who could have turned the travelers in to the police, saw them but ignored them. Why did they look the other way when a group of ragtag Jews walked openly through their village? Maybe they were weary of the lost souls trudging through their town. Regardless of the reason, it was a huge stroke of luck that no one lifted a hand to prevent them from continuing on their journey.

Finally, they walked across the Czech-Austrian border. My father recalled throwing himself to the ground, wailing that he could walk no further. The guide told him to get up and keep on walking. They arrived in a wooded area near the highway that went to Vienna. The guide left to get a car and told them to lie down in the ditch near the highway and wait. Early the next morning, the guide arrived in a car and drove them safely through the Vienna checkpoint to the Rothschild Hospital. From there, they went to a refugee camp run by the Joint Distribution Committee.

The giver of false documents. The apartment owners. The drivers.

The guides. The people who escaped with them. The people who saw them, but said nothing. Without these individuals—all of whom were willing to risk their lives, whether for pay or with simple good will in their hearts—my father and his family would likely not have made it to America. Without them, I would not be here. How do I repay such a debt?

• • •

My father and his sister spent the next year in the refugee camp in Vienna. There, my father experienced a turning point. "I met a man," he explained, "who had these numbers burned on his arm, from the concentration camp. He showed me soap made of Jews and he told me of lampshades made of Jewish skin. I was shocked." My father was still attached to the Catholic religion, but he was starting to see the incongruity of it all. "That's when I began to realize that I was Christian in the chapel and Jewish in the camp." As he gained more knowledge of the fate of other Jews, it shook his consciousness.

My amazingly resourceful grandmother, determined to make a better life for her children, reconnected with a childhood friend, Emery, who had been in love with her. Emery had left Hungary for America in 1938, and she imagined he might be her family's ticket to freedom.

"You married Emery to get out," my brother concluded.

"I would have married the devil," my grandmother replied. "Anybody would have, to get out of Hungary. I could not live under Communism."

By July 1950, the four of them were living in New York together, but my father's new home life was not a happy one, as Emery was terribly abusive to my grandmother. Nonetheless, my grandmother stayed married to him until he died about twenty-five years later. I did not witness these abuses firsthand. During the few times I saw him when

I was a child, I remember feeling that Emery was a bit strange and reserved. I never saw good feelings pass between him and my grandmother or my father. Whenever my grandmother would visit us in Maryland, she always came alone, never with Emery.

I learned about his abusiveness much later, when I was an adult. My father compared living with him to surviving during the war: "More or less, the war was to me some kind of an adventure. The first time that I was afraid in my life was in that apartment because of Emery." That took my breath away.

I know my father felt tremendously guilty that he could not protect his mother. He felt he owed his survival to her, and yet he could not shield her from the pain of her cruel husband. My father also felt indebted to Emery for marrying his mother and bringing them all to America; without his help, they might never have been able to leave Europe. This mixture of guilt, powerlessness, rage, and gratitude proved a familiar and tormenting blend for my father.

• • •

I had a wonderful relationship with my grandmother. She lived in New York and we lived in Maryland, but we saw each other often when I was growing up. When Granny visited, she brought us boxes of Hungarian pastries, and she was always laughing and interested in my life. From an early age, I was struck by her positive attitude, by how much she was involved with us and with the world around her.

I have always admired my grandmother's independence. In Budapest, after her first husband died, she ran his store, paying off his debt. After the war, she opened and successfully ran a retail store called Nivo (which translates as "something fine"), selling beautiful fabrics and making dresses. In her elder years, after Emery's death, she took classes at Hunter College—in French, politics, art history—well into her eighties, and rode the bus into the city from Queens for the various season subscriptions she had to the Metropolitan Opera and New York Philharmonic. She exercised every morning and as long as I knew her, she would outpace all of us with her focus and stamina when we'd visit art museums. I identify with my grandmother's zest for life, her passion for the arts. But what I consider my greatest inheritance from her is the positive attitude she maintained in the face of terrible challenges.

My grandmother was fearless. She walked through wartime Budapest streets without wearing her Jewish star so that she could obtain papers to shield her children with false identities. She arranged for special hiding places for each of her children during the war and visited them at great peril. She took the bold step of planning for their escape from Budapest.

My Aunt Eve told us that permission had been given to the Russian soldiers to rape women for a forty-eight-hour period during the time their town was liberated. When Eve was hiding in their family friends' basement, my grandmother stood her ground in between my aunt and a Russian soldier with an Uzi, screaming at him, and eventually pushing him over. Eve was spared.

My grandmother showed me by her example that one can go through hell in life, survive it, and even thrive. When I was twenty-nine years old, I lost my first husband to cancer. My grandmother was very consoling to me. I remember her visiting us in Maryland not long after he died. We were standing in my parents' basement, just outside the small guest room where she would stay. "Deee-her Naaan-cee," she said in her strong Hungarian accent. She looked me soberly in the eye, with understanding. "You have to move on. You have to be strong. You will be okay."

She had lost her first husband, "the love of my life," she called him. And I knew, because of her example, that I would indeed be okay, that I would survive this awful loss. She gave me confidence that I would be able to create a new life for myself, even return to life with love. Even now, when I feel most daunted, I know she is part of the life force that keeps me going.

My grandmother has also given me the hope that as I age, I will be as engaged with the world as she was, taking a hearty interest in the people and things I love. She also pampered herself with beauty potions from Hungary, took great care to always dress nicely, and balanced her daily exercise regimen with occasional rich and indulgent meals. I know she'd approve of similar ways in which I take good care of myself.

• • •

It wasn't until my father met my mother, Corinne, one summer at Jones Beach, that he began to feel a meaningful connection to Judaism. Her Brooklyn Jewish family embraced him. Though a couple of generations removed from family who had come here as immigrants, my mother's parents were steadfastly Jewish. I imagine they must have been quite taken with my father's polite, respectful manner, and his love of their daughter. They were not deterred by a refugee's small status; they themselves lived modest lives. My parents' Jewish wedding in 1955 led to a family of two children: my brother Peter and me. We were raised as Jews, and though not very observant, we eventually became members of a Reform Jewish congregation in Washington, D.C. When I was young and we were heading out to temple, my father always joked, "We're off to church!" I took my cue from my father's nonchalant attitude and didn't think much of it.

Over the years, he and my mother joined a kallah, an adult study group at our temple. The rich intellectual discussions resonated with him; that was one of the things he loved best about being a Jew. He also joined the temple's adult choir. I remember banging out melodies on the piano to help him practice for High Holiday service songs. I can see him standing proudly with the choir, belting out those songs with gusto. One day, he heard a good friend describing her process of becoming an adult bat mitzvah. He and my mother decided to do it, too. When my father was preparing for his bar mitzvah in 2008, he said, "After this, I'm really becoming a member of the tribe. I wasn't when I was thirteen, but now I'm seventy-five by the time I'm going to do this. So it's very meaningful to me, for that reason: that I'm really an authentic Jew. All those cultures that co-existed with the Hebrews have disappeared and yet somehow the Jews have survived. And it's a constant mystery, why the Jewish race survived. There must be a purpose. There must be a reason. I'm just glad to belong to it."

• • •

I was forty-seven years old at the time of my parents' b'nai mitzvah. I hadn't had a bat mitzvah as a girl, since, when I was young, this event was primarily reserved for boys. Before my brother's approaching bar mitzvah and our joining a temple, we had belonged to an informal group run by several Jewish cantors. It was a wonderful collection of like-minded families, refreshingly non-doctrinal in its educational approach. There was a great focus on the Holocaust, which would have provided a perfect occasion for my father to share his experiences. But no, he stayed in the background. Instead, I learned from the cantors—a group of passionate educators—about the horrors of that time. I wonder if the cantors had asked my father to speak and he demurred. In any case, it was a lost opportunity for all of us.

As a sophomore in college, I was asked to be president of the student Hillel group. I felt stunned to be chosen for this position, as I had almost no knowledge of traditional Jewish prayers and observances. My family would light candles for Hanukkah and attend Passover Seders, and we always went to temple for the High Holidays, but that was it. Didn't they know this about me? I felt like an imposter, that echo of inauthenticity from my father's experience. So I taught myself the Sabbath prayers and led our small group in a short Friday night gathering, sharing fresh challah and sipping Manischewitz wine. When I'd return home during school breaks, I noticed for the first time that my parents didn't participate in these Friday night blessings. Through my encouragement, my parents began observing Shabbat, though it became a running joke in my family that my father repeatedly asked me to write down the blessings for the lights, wine, and bread. They probably weren't routinely doing the blessings, but it was okay; when I came home, they knew it was important to me, and would buy some challah and we'd say the prayers together.

I always knew I would raise my own children in the Jewish tradition. Though my first husband, Neil, was raised as a Catholic, he was open to Judaism, but he died a couple of months shy of our second anniversary, so we never got to fulfill our dream of having children together. When I met my husband Steve, our common Jewish heritage meant it would be easier for us to create a Jewish family. Indeed, after twenty-five years of marriage, we have infused our life together with many Jewish traditions, and our children, Benjamin and Isabel, seem secure in their Jewish identity.

When I was fifty-two years old, I finally decided that it was time for me to become an adult bat mitzvah. During that year of study, my father's health deteriorated, and then he had a terrible fall. I chanted my Torah portion to him as he lay unconscious in the hospital in June 2013. He died on July 1, 2013. I became a bat mitzvah that December.

• • •

As I think about how the Holocaust has influenced my life, I can't help but ask, what do my feelings about the Holocaust matter? What do *my* feelings matter? In all this catastrophe, the scale of it, the scope of it, I am but a speck. I am not a survivor. I am not a victim.

My father and I share a kindred sense of non-importance. For years, my father claimed he was *not* a survivor. He was never in a concentration camp, so he felt that his experiences were nothing compared to those who had endured that horror. He denied his own suffering. And he denied his own strength. My father claimed his survival was all due to the Herculean courage and resourcefulness of his mother. As if he had no independent source of strength and resilience.

I ask myself often, what was the cost to my father for keeping things hidden? I think it manifested in periodic bursts of all-consuming anger—a "Hungarian temper" is how my brother and I thought about it—directed toward many things: politics, sports, his sister. His anger at us was usually prompted by occasional challenges to his authority as a parent, when we'd say "no" or ask "why." He was a man of deep emotions and we as his children learned not to push too far or the darker emotions would be unleashed. My father always apologized soon after his outbursts, knocking quietly at the door, saying he was sorry. I was quick to forgive. There was something concrete and predictable about his emotions that I couldn't find in my mother's. I learned from my father that anger was scary, but it was not going to decimate me and that apology and forgiveness were always part of it. I am grateful for that. It has helped me in my marriage and in raising my children.

My father would often become incensed about societal injustice. Some of this came from his work for Senator Jacob Javits in the early 1960s. Javits valued my father and his Jewish refugee story. He had been active in helping to procure reparations from the Germans. Maybe this helped my father feel proud of his Jewish story. Maybe it helped him feel he didn't have to hide what had happened. That he could show his feelings. He could be angry. I remember my father saying that the senator was like a father to him.

My father was with Javits on the steps of the Lincoln Memorial on August 28, 1963, when Martin Luther King, Jr. gave his "I Have a Dream" speech. I was not yet three years old at the time, so it wasn't until much later that I realized the incredible opportunity my father had to witness history. On Martin Luther King Day in the mid-1990s, he shared this experience with the fourth grade class I was teaching in Austin, Texas. The children were mesmerized as he talked. I felt so very proud that he, a Hungarian refugee, was able to connect in such a meaningful way to my class of students and to transmit this piece of history to them. I realize now that I never asked him to speak to my students about his wartime experiences. Would he have done it if I'd asked? Why did I consider his one day at the Lincoln Memorial more important than sharing what it was like to be a Jewish child during the Holocaust? Was I protecting him?

My father never wanted to promote himself professionally. He was modest and humble, even as a Deputy Assistant Secretary of State. I was a bit surprised when he told me later in life that he felt like an imposter in his profession. I hadn't realized that he felt so unfulfilled in his career. He had wanted to be an engineer as a young man, but with so much schooling missed during the war, he lacked the math skills to pursue this direction in college. So he hid as an economist, feeling inauthentic. Another cruel legacy of the Holocaust. And another way that my father could not be his true self.

• • •

A sensitive, artistic soul, my mother was dedicated to our family. Her analytical mind and insights about people were among her strengths. But she suffered from mental illness, with her worst period taking place during my adolescence. Her inconsistent, unpredictable behavior terrified me as a young person and took a terrible toll.

I felt the need to escape and hide from her overwhelming emotions, so I would try to disappear, casting out—no, banishing—my feelings, needs, wants. I thought maybe if I made myself small enough, she wouldn't see me, find me, hurt me.

I wonder if that was in some way how my father felt when he was in hiding in Budapest during the war. In the Nazi-run orphanage, did he make himself small, trying to blend in, not to be seen? With false papers, he was supposedly an orphan from the Hungarian country-side. This alternate identity was a shield, but how did it feel to pretend to be someone he was not?

When my mother felt anxious or angry, her troubles overflowed, exposing my brother and me to her turmoil. My father did not share with us his dark inner feelings like my mother did. Despite his occasional outbursts, he maintained good, healthy boundaries. My father's restraint in this respect was a great relief for me. Perhaps I didn't try harder to get my father to talk about his past because I got too much intensity from my mom. When I was older and became more curious about his wartime experiences, I hesitated even then, wondering what it might be like for my father to uncork his demons. Perhaps, like him, I needed to keep the lid closed.

After my father died, my mother remained in our family home for a few years. One day during a visit, I opened a small closet that used to house my father's ties, shirts, shoes. There, standing in plain view, was a white banker's box marked in big handwritten letters: "Do Not Open, Destroy Contents." The lid rested lightly on the box, almost daring me to open it. This closet was situated near the carport door, where I'd pass it every day, walking up a few steps and either making a right into the study or going straight ahead into the kitchen.

One day, when my mother was out of the house on an errand, I lifted the top of the box and looked inside. I saw many small journals with my father's writing on the covers. The only notebooks I had ever seen my father keep were for accounts of our family travels; the sheer number of journals in this box had to contain more than our trips abroad. I noticed a white envelope tucked in the front of the box that said "To Danny" in my mother's handwriting.

I felt the push and pull of a magnetic force—of wanting to know, being hungry for the truth, but also not wanting to know, being afraid of what I might find out. I was so curious to see what was in there, but I wrestled with wanting to respect the boundaries my father had created. Opening the journals would entail the crossing of a boundary. I always took my cues from my father. I waited and hoped he'd tell me things. It wasn't until much later in life that he began to share a bit of his story. A brief memoir—"for the grandchildren"—conveyed some of the facts, if not the emotion, of what he went through. Conversations with my brother led to more unearthing of family history. I asked my father to do interviews with me for narratives I wanted to write for Yom HaShoah services, and what he said shed some more light. So, his earlier claims of "I don't remember" were not the whole story.

Why did my father want the contents of that box destroyed? Why hadn't he destroyed it earlier? What was my mother's role in keeping the box in the closet? Why did I never ask her about it? Why didn't I look through those journals? And why, when the house was sold and my mother was moving out, didn't I grab the box and keep it? I realize now that the practice of hiding—hiding important things and not disturbing them—was an unspoken value in our house. My father's wartime experiences in Hungary taught him that sometimes you choose to hide who you are, sometimes the truth about yourself can be hidden by others, and sometimes you must hide to survive.

Those unopened journals, like the closed off parts of his memories, I have to accept will remain a mystery. But accepting that there is so much I won't know about my father feels like a punch to the stomach. I wish I had gotten more from him. More about his past, his struggles, how he managed to live with his demons. I would have liked to have known him better. I wish he had protected me less. When hiding becomes a habit, so much is lost. For my father, hiding when it was no longer necessary meant denying himself full acceptance of what he had been through. He denied himself his own story. And thus he also denied us, his children and his grandchildren, part of our inheritance.

Still, the joy he found in life, his great gusto for travel, food, culture, politics, and justice are burnished in my memory as acts of resilience. That he went through so much and managed to be such a giving, warm, and generous human being is a miracle. The boundless love he had for me and our family I will carry with me for the rest of my life. That much he could give us. So I try and pull the threads together the best I can to weave his story, which has become my story, and bring it out of hiding.

5

Shades of Chanel No. 5

Rita Benn, daughter of Alice and Phillipe Benn

Alice Benn dressed for a charity ball, Montreal, Quebec, 1963

Growing up, I relished watching my mother get dressed. With her hair flattened, she reminded me of Marlene Dietrich, sultry and refugee-like. When she was ready to go out, Zsa Zsa Gabor and Barbara Walters seemed the more à propos mix. Fashion was my mother's love, and elegance her trademark. Accompanied by the lingering smell of Chanel No. 5, it didn't matter if my mother was going out to buy groceries or play bridge with friends. She was determined to leave the house as if she came out of a 1960s photo shoot for *Vogue*. It took forty years in Canada and chemotherapy appointments before she dared to buy herself a pair of sweats and sneakers.

As a young girl, I regularly accompanied her to Bubnick's, her Romanian dressmaker, where she was outfitted with Yves St. Laurent and Christian Dior lookalike designs. In the basement of Bubnick's home, the two of them chatted in their Eastern European version of English about Jackie Kennedy's latest hat or dress featured in *Women's Wear Daily*. When I asked my mother why Bubnick's speech sounded so heavily accented, she replied, "Is his accent more noticeable than mine?" I nodded.

Puffing her chest proudly she told me, "I have an ear for languages: French, German, Yiddish, Lithuanian, Russian. English is the hardest of languages to learn. The earlier you start to learn a language the better. You'll be happy later in life to be able to communicate with so many people." Unfortunately, she was greatly disappointed by my poor intonation and lack of motivation to master any languages other than English and French.

You could never tell by looking at my mother that she had suffered in any way. Her thin strands of blond hair were well coiffed into a bouffant elevated by her neatly tucked-in hairpiece. Nightly applications of Estée Lauder protected her face from showing the lines of wear and tear that marked each loss in her life. Though she was impeccable to the outside world, the pain of the Holocaust did not stop gnawing at my mother's insides. I saw her tears streaming on Yom Kippur when she permitted herself to mourn all the relatives taken from her. With her new life in Montreal and her insistent focus on a pristine appearance, my mother tried to wipe clean the history that included her wartime years. The nine months of concentration camp incarceration, the itching from lice, the standing for hours on end in the rain while other inmates, family members, and friends collapsed or were shot. Even the first day of spring after our freezing Montreal winters could never fully bring her joy, as March 21st marked the anniversary of her mother Rebekka's death.

It didn't matter how many times my mother spritzed her sweet French perfume over her clothes. She could not cover the stench of the Holocaust from seeping out. Despite her remarkable resilience, invisible ghosts of sadness hovered, casting shadows on the makeshift beauty of a life she tried to create for herself and our family.

• • •

In 1941, my parents and thirty-two family members were detained in Kaunas (Kovno) Ghetto in Lithuania, along with twenty-nine thousand other Jews in their community. By the end of the war, three thousand of these ghetto inhabitants remained alive. From my family, five people survived: my mother Alice, which was pronounced Alyse (née Zlata Ginas); my father, Philippe Benn (né Philippe Allen Benjaminovitsch); my mother's sister and husband; and their younger cousin Tanya, who was about four years old by the end of the war.

My parents, both twenty-two, had married earlier that winter of

1941. At first they lived in a small apartment with my mother's family: her parents, Josef Ginas and Rebekka Virovichiute Giniene, and her younger sister, Sara, who was almost seventeen at the time. A year earlier, Alice and Philippe had returned home for summer vacation from the college they attended in Belgium. With the war imminent, both families had urged them not to visit. My father and mother refused to listen. They never dreamed Lithuania would fall under communist occupation and that they would get stuck behind these borders. Nor could they imagine what else was to come. How could they? How could anyone?

Every survivor has stories of incredible luck regarding their escape from death. As amazed as I have been by the horrors my parents endured, I have been equally astounded by the miracles that enabled their survival, the extraordinary acts of courage, devotion, and resilience that my mother, in particular, showed at that time. Most of what I learned about my parents' wartime experiences came in fragments from my mother over the course of my childhood and in stories later shared in my adult years.

When asked any questions, my parents volunteered very little information. Their responses were typically general and clipped.

"Terrible things happened. There was a war."

"The Germans hated the Jewish people. You don't need to know about it."

If pressed, my mother resorted to, "I don't remember. It was a long time ago." I only learned a few bare facts here and there about her family.

"My father was a salesman for Dupont and used to travel to Europe. That's why I went to school in Belgium. He did a lot of work there."

"My mother was very chic. I was very close to my parents."

I don't remember my father ever saying a word about his family. It wasn't until college when I was taking a class about the Holocaust and then later, in my forties, with the widespread introduction of Stephen Spielberg's Shoah project, and my aunt Sara's permanent move from the USSR to Canada, that I heard more complete stories.

I assume my parents thought that by not talking about their experiences, they could contain their own sadness and pain, as well as protect me and my brother from the cruelty that exists in the world. Likely, they had no inkling about what we as children or adults might imagine or pick up from that which was left unsaid.

• • •

In June, exactly six months after my parents' marriage and two days after Germany invaded the Soviet Union, my father was kidnapped from his home. Two men who represented the interim provisional Lithuanian government broke into their apartment. The pretext for the arrest was alleged activities of treason. My father was brought to the outskirts of the city, to the Seventh Fort, a Czarist-like fortress surrounded by a large iron gate.

When my mother returned home from the airport laundry division where she'd been assigned to work, she immediately began to check with her connections about what to do. She found someone who personally knew the military commandant in charge of the city's operations. Within a day, he arranged for an appointment for her at the commandant's office. My mother, dressed in her best feminine attire, and using her beautiful blond Aryan looks to her fullest advantage, assured him in fluent German that my father was innocent of any wrongdoing. "There has to be some mistake. It was just an after-school club where the boys planned nice activities for people in the community. Nothing Zionist. It was not a political group!" She pleaded for my father's release and the commandant promised to help.

Three days passed without a word. On the fourth day, she received a phone message asking her to return to the commandant's headquarters. People who lived close to the Seventh Fort had reported hearing frequent gunshots and screams. What if she found out her newlywed husband was among those gunned down? During this second meeting, the commandant interrogated her with more questions about my father's well-to-do family. When the phone rang and interrupted them, he instructed my mother to wait down the hall in a room where military sentries were stationed outside the door. She didn't know whether the meeting was going to resume or whether she too might be arrested.

While captive, my father and the other Jewish inmates were ordered to lie face down on the cold concrete prison floor, their bodies jammed together like sardines. My father was careful not to make any movement that would single him out. The guards liked to play a game for target practice. Each took turns shouting out a prisoner's name to see if they could shoot that person when they saw a head lift. If a prisoner didn't make a move to stand up, they sometimes randomly shot into the pack. By the time my father heard his name called for a third time and no gunshots had been fired, he identified himself. The guards directed him to go outside where he was whisked away in a car. He had no idea what was going to happen next. It was only when my mother walked into the room at the military headquarters that he realized he was safe.

In the week my father was imprisoned at the Seventh Fort and the following week, approximately ten thousand Jewish men and two-thousand Jewish women and children had been rounded up. Almost all were murdered.

How was my mother able to set my father free when so many others perished? Was it just luck or kindness on the part of the commandant, or was there more to the story that she never told us? My brother and I both wondered if some exchange was provided: sexual relations for sparing his life. After all, my mother Alice was quite the beauty in her youth, with her thick long blond curls, green eyes, lanky legs, and slender shape. We never asked her and she would never have admitted this to us. But we raised the question to each other as adults. Did my father wonder about this too? Did he ask? Did he feel burdened by his imagination or his indebtedness to her for his survival? These answers remain unknown. We learned the story of my father's imprisonment from my mother's Shoah testimony in 1995, decades after my father's death.

• • •

As a second-generation, I keep trying to make sense of it all—not just of the impact of the Holocaust on my parents' or my life, but of so many inexplicable events that occurred during that period in history. How could people be so hateful to other human beings? Why did ordinary individuals turn a blind eye to what was happening? These big questions nagged at me early in life, beginning in second or third grade. The shadows of the Holocaust that loomed in my house must have made me more sensitive to issues of discrimination and injustice. Like Anne Frank, I wanted to "believe that people are basically good at heart."

I remember coming home one day from school feeling sad for Lisa, with her awkward bow-legged gait, walking alone ahead of me. She didn't look like the other kids on our block. Her clothes always seemed to be one or two sizes too big. Her eyes squinted behind the thick lenses of her eyeglasses. "Lisa was a blue baby," my mother explained. "She was born too early." Although Lisa lived across the street and was in my grade, she never came out to play with me or any of the other elementary school-age kids on the block. I used to stare at her house from our porch and wonder what it was like to be her, to have no friends, to always stay indoors. Was she lonely or sad the way I often felt on Sundays, the day all my friends had visits from their grandparents and cousins and I had none?

When the new girl Ava (my future best friend) was repeatedly ostracized by our fifth-grade peer group, this made me very uncomfortable, even more so when she later disclosed that she vomited in fear every day before coming to school. One day at recess, I announced that I was going to invite Ava to join me at lunch on some playground activity. I felt too bad seeing her all by herself on the playground. As one of the more popular girls, I hoped that others would accept her if I did.

I felt grateful and at the same time frightened that my peers followed my lead so readily. I had my first glimpse into how a leader can provoke beneficial or terrible outcomes. Did I connect this to what happened with Hitler and the German people? I don't think I consciously did at that time, but as I grew up, I became increasingly interested in psychology and ended up choosing it as a career. I remember hearing my mother tell her friends in a joking manner that she would be my first patient. I was determined to try to understand human behavior, certainly how she survived, and see if I could somehow contribute to relieving suffering of others less fortunate in the world.

• • •

I was seven or eight years old when I first became aware of the extent of mass murder that occurred during the Holocaust. Adolf Eichmann's trial was broadcast nationally on television, and every night after dinner, my father headed down into the den of our split-level home to situate himself in front of the screen. I wasn't allowed to join him for TV time as I usually did, nor did he come upstairs to tuck me into bed. "Eichmann was in charge of killing a lot of Jews during the war," explained my mother. "He was a horrible man. You don't need to watch anything about it." I knew my grandparents had died in the war. Had he personally killed them?

I remember experiencing antisemitic vitriol once, as a ten-year-old child, while I was standing in line at the movie theater with my older brother. A teenage boy spit on the ground when he saw us, muttering under his breath, *"maudit juif"* (bad Jew). Despite living in Canada, I am not sure my parents felt totally safe from antisemitic persecution. My mother was very vocal, expressing her disdain for the supposed ignorant Quebecois who wanted to separate from Canada, and who had eleven children and no education beyond high school, and who hated the Jews. Throughout my childhood and adolescence, recurrent threats of Quebec separating from Canada swelled in the media. The FLQ (Front de Libération du Québec) set off a number of explosions throughout the city, including mailbox bombs concentrated in the main suburb where many wealthy English Canadians lived. Newspaper headlines suggested and rumors soared that English Canadians, which meant we Jews, might be forced to leave.

During this period, the Cold War was also at its height. I heard my parents talk in Russian about building a bomb shelter. Whenever issues were serious or private, they always conversed in Russian, peppering the conversation with some English or Yiddish words. I usually could get the gist of what they were discussing, and I always understood the tone. "Why a bomb shelter?" I asked. They told me a war might break out between the Soviet Union and the United States, and this might affect us in Montreal.

I became increasingly anxious. The Soviet Union, I believed, was to be feared. It was a communist country that did not allow my mother's sister Sara and her family, who were living there, to visit us. I imagined that Russian spies might arrest us. Once every three to six months, my mother and Aunt Sara talked excitedly and loudly by telephone for just a few minutes. The collect calls were very expensive and frequently the connection garbled their words. My mother couldn't always decipher the intent of my aunt's coded communication. She explained, "Sara cannot talk freely. The government may be listening to our

calls and she may get in trouble if she says something they don't like."
(I later learned that my aunt was a Professor of Marxist Economics and
a card-carrying member of the Communist party.) My mother often
prepared trunks of medicines and clothes to send off to Sara and her
family and deliberately included multiple pairs and different sizes of
identical items, especially prized Levi jeans. When I asked why she
packed duplicates, she replied, "The agents look through everything.
Usually, they take out things they want for themselves and let the other
things that are not allowed into the country to pass through. Sara can
sell anything she doesn't need on the black market for extra money."

The Cold War threat and discussion of a bomb shelter made the
possibility of war very real to me. I began to worry that my parents or I
might die. After all, that had been the fate of my grandparents and the
other Rita, my father's sister. I started to have trouble sleeping. Scam-
pering into my parents' bed in the middle of the night, squeezing in
between them, I tried to steady my breath from the bouts of panic rising in my chest. I told them the dark made me afraid. After a week or
so, my parents requested that I stay out of their room. So heaving my
sheets, blankets, pillow, and special stuffed animal from my bedroom,
I camped out by the threshold of their bedroom door until the morning sunrise woke me. I don't know if they ever knew that had become
my routine. I usually was back in my room before my parents woke
up. This period of heightened anxiety may have gone on for months.
I doubt my parents would have really understood its intensity. I think
the Holocaust erased their experience of any felt sense of vulnerability
we had as children. Maybe this was when I began to learn that I had
to rely more on myself than my parents to help me feel inwardly safe.

At around this time I asked my mother why my Aunt Rita, who
died at twenty years old, was not protected by a bomb shelter. "She was
hiding in a house," my mother said. "We couldn't build bomb shelters
in the homes where we had to live."

"Did they bomb the house?" I asked.

"No. We think the Nazis burned it."

"Did they know she was in it?"

"We don't know."

This response did little to alleviate the fear of my parents' or my own mortality. I seriously entertained the irrational fear that because my Aunt Rita died at twenty years of age, that same fate would await me. In celebrating my twenty-first birthday, I distinctly recall breathing a huge sigh of relief that I'd made it alive until then.

As I contemplated having children in my twenties, I made a decision that when the time came, I did not want to pass any names from my ancestral lineage on to my children. I did not want them to feel weighted down in the way that I had about my name. With my husband's agreement, we didn't follow the Jewish custom of naming any of our three children, David, Jeremy, and Marissa, after relatives who'd passed away. Luckily, none of our family's parents or relatives gave us grief for taking this non-conformist stance.

• • •

The fear of death has been an ever present, quiet companion in life. Since I was around eight years old, I worried about my mother's dying. She seemed the weaker one of my two parents. Whenever arguments flared in the house, her migraines came on afterwards with a vengeance. In the darkened bedroom, with the window shades drawn down, I tried to ease her distress, bringing cups of hot tea or re-warming the washcloth compresses I carefully placed on her forehead. I feared the bulging, varicose-like veins popping out from her temples. The echoes of her rhythmic moans through our adjacent bedroom walls eventually gave way to sleep, for her and me.

Most of the time, I never really knew what precipitated the yelling matches between my parents. Usually, they occurred on the weekends in the living room. As the pitch of their voices raised, their English switched to Russian. I knew it was time to seek refuge in my older brother's room when I heard my mother scream the ultimate pejorative, *Chaleryeh*. After I heard my mother's muffled sobs leaking from her bedroom down the hall and the stomping of my father's feet on the stairway to the lower level of our home, I ventured out to check on her.

The pill bottles on my mother's nightstand scared me. I had learned about Marilyn Monroe's suicide while on a family vacation at my parents' friends' cottage in Hyannis Port. I remember the large black block letters in the tabloid headlines: "Marilyn Monroe . . . 40 pills . . . Sleeping Overdose . . . Suicide," and the photos of her beautiful face. She was not that much younger than my mother. I became concerned that perhaps this same fate would befall my mother. When I eyed an uncapped pill bottle or two on her nightstand, particularly after one of her migraine episodes or their marital arguments, I felt my anxiety grab hold. I would tiptoe furtively to the bedside where she was resting or sleeping to make sure I could see or hear her breath. My need to check on her in this way became routine. My mother relied on prescription tranquilizers to help her sleep and "calm her nerves" throughout her life. And my need to check in with her continued, even when we were living far apart.

• • •

My father Philippe was a passionate man—passionate about food, his family, his work, and his opinions. He loved a good party and his boisterous laughter was so contagious that even strangers who heard him at a restaurant joined in. He was extremely generous with gifts to my mother and me, and to organizations that supported Israel or Jewish education. He was equally lavish with the peace offerings he made following my parents' arguments. Bouquets of long-stemmed red roses frequently arrived via the florist delivery truck to our house.

I always looked forward to playing cards and board games with my father on the weekends, despite the fact that I often ended up in tears. He never let me win and we both hated to lose. When the game was close, I occasionally caught him cheating, changing his letters surreptitiously in Scrabble or peeking to see the next card in the deck before deciding on his move. My mother always came to comfort me, often chastising my father for his behavior. To this day, I still love a competitive game of Scrabble.

My mother and I often felt angry and disempowered by my father's paternalistic stance towards us. He did not like when we questioned his authority. At the dinner table, I was frequently admonished to not talk back, reminded that little girls should be seen and not heard. Talking back meant I voiced my opinion over parental decisions that I perceived as "unfair" and restrictive of my autonomy or that I supported my mother's position in family disputes. I remember on one occasion, at age fifteen and a half, I became so incensed that I refused to engage in any further conversation with my father for several days. My mother begged me to stop this silent treatment, so to appease her, I finally apologized to my father. I realized the extent of distress that I had caused him when I saw his teary eyes and felt his arms around me, hugging me tightly as if he would never let me go. I've forgotten now what made me so mad at him, but I'll never forget how I felt six months later, when it was my turn to not want to let him go.

On June 21, 1969, the phone rang at 6:00 a.m. to inform our family that my father, Philippe Allen Benn, had died at fifty-one years old. I was sixteen. Only three and a half weeks earlier, he had been admitted to the hospital to investigate unexplained abdominal pain he'd been experiencing for several months. Cause of death? The doctors said cancer, metastasized to the liver. What did my mother say? Dachau.

My father was extremely ill upon liberation from Dachau. At five feet eleven inches, he weighed only seventy-five pounds and had to spend three months in recovery at a hospital where he almost died. The beatings, lack of food, freezing winter without heat or clothing, chemicals emitted from the gassing, and disease from the corpses around him may well have taken a long-term toll on his body. Perhaps my mother thought his overindulgence with sweets, excess second helpings, and preference for filet mignon and other red meat and rich sauces was a reaction to his deprivation, and contributed to the rise of his cancer. More likely, I believe she saw his workaholic behavior— the sixty-hour work week he regularly put in to build his engineering company and the pressures that led to his quick temper and inability to compromise—as the main culprit. With no financial resources after the war, he felt driven to achieve and attain the level of wealth that he had growing up and which had been taken away from him. Dachau, with its attendant loss and victimization, set the course for his premature death.

It pains me to not have heard anything from my father about his experiences during the war, his relationships with his sister and parents, or his interests as a boy. All I know about my paternal grandparents are their names, Rosa Sonimsky and Leiba (Leon) Benjaminovitsch—not where they were born, how old they were when they married or died, not even if they had any biological siblings. I have just two photos of my father's parents and three of him as a teen. With the death of my father, I lost the chance to connect to this half of my lineage. To this day, I keep searching for clues, scouring for resemblances of their names in new digital records and databases that become publicly available in English.

With my father's death, I could sense the desolation of Dachau within my own house. My mother's loneliness and sadness were overwhelming, and I didn't know how to support her except to listen to

her worries and laments and not leave her by herself for very long. I
didn't give myself permission to feel my own grief. My mother was so
wrapped up in her own suffering that she never inquired as to how I
was faring. My older brother couldn't wait to get back to his girlfriend
and graduate school life at MIT in Boston. He had come home for
a week or so before my father died and stayed through the week of
shiva. "You'll be fine," he informed me before he left. "You'll be busy
with your friends. Dad was mostly at work anyway. There is plenty of
money. Everything will stay pretty much the same."

It is true that I had a large social network and several very close
friends. Yet, I was the only one in my peer group with a parent who'd
died. I didn't want to feel any different from my friends, and when they
tried to offer me sympathy it made me and them uncomfortable. It
became very natural to hide my grief—from my friends, my mother,
and even myself. Numbness quickly set in. It took me well into my
adulthood to feel the enormity of my father's death.

• • •

When I was twenty, I sat stunned in my mother's bedroom, listening to my friend Lois interview her for a course she was taking on
the Holocaust at McGill University. This was the first time I heard the
entire account of how my Aunt Sara had come to adopt her cousin
Tanya as her daughter.

On March 13, 1944, the Nazis began to perform *Kinder Aktion*,
rounding up all children under the age of thirteen living in the Kovno
Ghetto. Tanya, then two and a half years old, was hiding in a bunker
with her mother beneath the home in which my parents and several
other families had been forced to live. They knew they couldn't keep
this child hidden quietly for much longer before she was discovered and
then they all would be killed. My grandmother Rebekka and Tanya's

mother, my great-aunt Fanya, asked my mother for help. They thought that with her German-like beauty and language fluency, she could sneak out of the ghetto and blend in easily on the other side. They wanted her to locate their former Christian housekeeper and request that Tanya stay hidden with her until the war ended.

The next evening, my mother removed her coat that had the Jewish Star of David sewn on it and slipped out of the fenced-off compound. The housekeeper refused to harbor Tanya in her home but said she would try to find her safe cover elsewhere. "Come back in a few days," she told my mother.

When my mother returned to the ghetto, the families decided they could not take the chance to wait that long. They wanted my mother to smuggle Tanya out the following day and bring her to the housekeeper. My grandmother called a ghetto physician neighbor to medically sedate the toddler. Weeping, my great-aunt Fanya wrapped her daughter up with blankets and placed her gently into the bottom of a large black satchel that she slung onto my mother's shoulder.

This second night outside of the ghetto, two young German soldiers approached my mother. She realized fairly quickly that they did not intend to hurt her and were more interested in having some fun with a pretty German girl. My mother smiled, spoke a few flirtatious words, and waved them off. She picked up her pace to make sure she was not being followed. At the housekeeper's house, she left the satchel containing Tanya on the doorstep and ran away.

Tanya's mother became increasingly distraught during the next week. She begged my mother again to sneak out and find out if her daughter was indeed safe. So, a third time, my mother risked her life by leaving the confines of the ghetto. She returned with a photograph of Tanya standing alone outside a farmhouse that belonged to the housekeeper's sister in the countryside. There she remained hidden until the end of the war.

Exactly four months to the day after *Kinder Aktion*, my mother, father, maternal grandmother, and several other relatives were deported to concentration camps: the women to Stutthoff and my father to Dachau. My grandmother, feeling claustrophobic in the bunker where they were hiding, ran outside to get some air. Fearful that she might faint or fall into the wrong hands, my mother chased after her. My father, wanting to protect them both, immediately followed. All three were captured in the street. This evacuation formed the last concentration camp transport out of Kovno, just three weeks before the Russians arrived to liberate this town from the Nazis.

After these transports, the Germans set fire to the ghetto, killing the two thousand or so Jews that remained in hiding, including both Rosa and Leiba, my father's parents, and his twenty-year-old sister Rita, my namesake.

My Aunt Sara was nineteen when she left the ghetto to join the Jewish Partisans as a resistance fighter. Just before *Kinder Aktion*, she sneaked back into the ghetto to plead with my parents and my father's sister to join her. They refused, not wanting to abandon their parents. It was the last time Sara saw her mother or my parents before they were deported. After the war, Sara located Tanya, who was by then three and a half or four years old. While Tanya suspected she was not Sara's biological daughter, she never felt comfortable asking her directly. It was only in 1966, when my mother was given permission by the governments of Canada and the Soviet Union to visit my aunt and her family in the USSR that Tanya, at age twenty-six, learned about her real identity. As a result of my mother's courage and her financial generosity in sponsoring her two nieces, their spouses, and her sister's immigration in 1975 and 1980, Tanya lives today in Toronto, a grandmother to two grandchildren. She is close to eighty years old.

• • •

Alice with husband Phillipe and sister Sara on Sara's first visit to Canada. Montreal, 1967

"Murderers, all of them—the Lithuanians were far worse than the Nazis!" my mother said to me after a conversation with Sara. Historical reports indicate that close to two hundred thousand Lithuanian Jews were slaughtered during the war: 95 percent of the prewar Jewish community. Most of these deaths occurred in Lithuania, often initiated or aided by their own citizens. In 1941, my mother's three uncles, one of whom was Tanya's father, were apprehended in the middle of the night by a Lithuanian antisemitic gang and shot dead outside their home. That same evening, my great-grandmother Malka, the mother of these three uncles, died from shock—from a fatal heart attack.

Sara did not disagree that the murders of her uncles were motivated by antisemitism. However, she fervently believed the country had moved significantly forward since the war: that it was becoming a more tolerant modern society. Later in her life, when publicly and falsely accused by her Lithuanian (non-Jewish) colleagues of killing

Lithuanian civilians during her Partisan activities, Sara still refused to find fault with the Lithuanian government or to see any antisemitic bias to their claims. My mother said, "Your Aunt Sara, she wears rose-colored glasses when it comes to Lithuania."

Sara immigrated to Ontario at the age of sixty, only because her husband had died and her adult children chose to leave the Soviet Union when it opened up emigration laws for Jews. Sara did not want to live apart from them. However, her loyalty stayed strong to the country of her birth. I'm not sure my mother and she ever came to terms with their residual anger and guilt, stemming from Sara's decision to join the resistance and abandon the family during the war, the years of separation they endured from one another, and the different trajectories that resulted. The sisters were quite dissimilar in both their physique and personality. Though both were strong-willed, Sara was brasher and would never back down from a conflict. Like my father, she insisted on being right. Sensitivity to others and any penchant for *largesse* was not her strength. Often my mother left their phone and in-person visits exhausted and exasperated.

As Sara began to rebuild her life in Canada, she became a guest lecturer at York University in political and social science. With time on her hands, she researched and documented her experience during the Partisan resistance in Kovno, eventually publishing a book that was later translated into English, called *Resistance and Survival.* She promoted her book by giving many presentations at various Jewish congresses and museums on the topic of the Resistance and more generally about the Holocaust. An iconic photo of her holding a rifle across her chest hangs prominently in the United States Holocaust Memorial Museum in Washington, D.C.

My mother was very ambivalent about Sara's emergence as a Holocaust speaker. While extremely proud that her sister had been a World War II female resistance fighter, and was a professor and a published author, she perceived these speaking events to be opportunistically motivated, as a means to gain personal glory and take advantage of the growing public interest in the Shoah newly inspired by Stephen Spielberg's project. In my mother's mind, her sister was not a Holocaust survivor. That identity belonged to my mother alone.

I was flabbergasted when, several years after my mother's death, I learned that my aunt had arranged (through her ambassador friend in the Lithuanian government) to have the Lithuanian Life Saving Cross award bestowed posthumously on my mother. This award was established in 1994 to pay tribute to those Lithuanians who'd placed their families and themselves in danger by saving Jewish people from the Nazi-sponsored genocide. My mother had been granted the award for saving her niece: Sara's adopted daughter, Tanya. My aunt informed me of the award because she'd learned from the Office of the Lithuanian President that she needed my written permission to allow her to participate in the ceremony and receive it on my behalf. She had never discussed any of this with me beforehand.

What were her motivations exactly? Did she really think my mother would have been pleased? Did she feel this award would absolve her from her own survivor's guilt? Or did she want to still be in the limelight as a Lithuanian Partisan and expert? I believed my mother would have been furious with her sister and vehemently opposed to accepting this award from the Lithuanian government, who, in addition to the murders of my mother's relatives, had imprisoned and tortured my father for no reason at the Seventh Fort, and had taken away my paternal grandfather's business, home, and financial assets before the Nazis even came into power.

I was angry with my aunt and concerned that accepting this award meant betraying my mother. Could I live with myself for being complicit?

I let my aunt know exactly how I felt. She was surprised to hear me so upset with her and not at all contrite, refusing to consider the validity of my perspective. She could not see the irony of the situation. I experienced firsthand the insensitivity and brazenness that my mother found so challenging in their relationship. The tint in my rose-colored glasses for Aunt Sara dimmed significantly.

In the end, I emailed the government office to give permission for my aunt to accept the award. I informed them that this recognition of my mother in no way exonerated their country's culpability for killing so many Lithuanian Jews, including my mother's family, and I hoped they would publicly acknowledge this culpability during the event that included this award ceremony. I could not bring myself to say thank you.

I copied my aunt on the email.

• • •

Over my adult life, my mother and I lived six hundred miles away, a ten-hour drive. Although we visited each other several times a year when my children were young, as my family grew and we got busier with work and the children's commitments, the visits went down to once or twice a year at most. My mother and I spoke on the phone at least once a week, but I often got off our phone calls feeling depleted or triggered. I was my mother's confidante pretty much all her life—the one who heard the cries of disappointment in herself, her marriage, her children, her sister; her fears of recurrent illness and suffering and her harsh judgments of others; and her perceptions of insecurity and oppression. With my father's death and her subsequent struggle with cancer and other health issues, my mother's sense of victimization and her depressive moods increased. The mastectomy of one of her breasts at age fifty-five devastated her dream to remarry. For her, this bodily defilement closed off any opportunity for a future intimate relationship.

She couldn't imagine that Randy, the man she was seriously dating after my father's death, who aptly called her "La Contessa," would continue to see her in this light. She broke off the relationship.

Despite how much I, along with several of her good friends, listened, consoled, and tried to support my mother throughout her life, we could not fill her cup beyond the half-empty way she viewed it. "After all I have been through" was the common refrain. A psychiatrist friend my mother once saw for consultation said to me, "Your mother is remarkably normal, given her experiences. What she suffers from is chronic, a profound sense of isolation and aloneness. There is nothing I can do for her. Or you, for that matter. Go live your life."

As my mother and I grew older, I found it harder and harder to bear her relentless unburdening. I felt I could not fix the trajectory of her life or her victim mentality. I wished she could find happiness. Yet, I was not her solution. I knew what I needed for my own growth was to create distance—first physically and then emotionally. In deciding to reside permanently in Ann Arbor after my initial move for graduate school, I hoped to instill a boundary that would keep me from falling into her vortex of sadness, or trigger my frustration and helplessness in not being able to alleviate it. I struggled with guilt for trying to enforce this choice until she died.

My mother described her relationship with her own mother, Rebekka, as very close. It saddened her that ours was not as smooth sailing as what she remembered about hers. She spoke many times about how much she loved and missed her mother. "A mother's love can never be equaled by her child," was another favorite lament. "One day I won't be here. You will miss me when I'm gone; then you will understand." I often wondered, would I really miss her?

I was almost forty-five years old when I learned the details of how my grandmother Rebekka died. One weekend when I returned to Montreal to visit, my mother asked me to watch the videotapes of her Shoah testimony. She seemed to feel affirmed by Stephen Spielberg's project, believing that she was making a significant contribution to history. It was the first time that she'd described her experience in full to anyone. She told me that in the interview she'd wanted to be accurate and not break down. Indeed, throughout, she remained calm and collected, conveying horrific events in a matter-of-fact tone, with no tears.

Rebekka was forty-seven years old in Stutthof concentration camp. She had been feeling ill and asked my mother to spend the night with her. My mother did not want to stay in the same crowded bunk bed with her, so she left. "I was afraid . . . afraid of seeing her die," she reported. In the morning, my mother returned, only to drag her own mother's cold body out of the barracks, and place her on top of the heap of other corpses in the camp yard. Two weeks later, the camp of Stutthoff was liberated.

My heart sank into my stomach when I heard her describe her mother's death. I vowed to myself and immediately afterwards to her, "I will never let you die alone. When the time comes, I will stay with you. I want you to know that and never worry about it." For all my mother felt I couldn't give her, I knew at least I could do this for her. My mother quickly dismissed this avowal with a slight smirk and a quick "Okay." She had something else on her mind. "How did I look on the tape? Was my lipstick okay? Did I seem composed? Was it logical? How was my accent . . . could you understand me clearly?" She beamed as I praised her coherence, her demeanor, and, as important, her shade of red lipstick.

The day after my mother's eighty-eighth birthday, she entered the hospital battling a high fever. After a bout of severe respiratory distress, she lay still, with her eyes closed. For the next day and a half I remained by her side, intermittently getting up to wet her lips with a washcloth. I was reminded of the many times during my childhood when I brought warm compresses to her forehead to relieve her recurrent migraines. I began grieving in anticipation of her passing, sometimes quietly and sometimes very loudly, feeling the full regret of not having done enough to ease her suffering during her lifetime.

In the evening, my mother suddenly opened her eyes. My brother and I moved closer. She gazed directly at me and I felt the love streaming out of her eyes, even though she could not speak. Holding her hand, I said, "I love you," and assured her that she had done her best as a mother. I began softly chanting, "*Shema Yisrael, Adonai Eloheinu, Adonai Echad. Shema Yisrael, Adonai Eloheinu, Adonai Echad*" ("Hear, O Israel, the Lord is our God, the Lord is One"). I knew this to be one of the most religious prayers in our Jewish liturgy, but wasn't aware that it is invoked as a formal rite of passage during a person's final moments of life. Though my mother was not sure what to make of God's existence ("How could a God allow the Holocaust to occur?"), I knew that when it came time for my mother to leave her body, I wanted her to hear the Hebrew sound of God around her. For a full minute and a half, my mother eyes were locked with mine and I sang.

Just as unexpectedly as she opened her eyes for this last time, my mother turned her head away to face the wall in front of her. Her last breath was barely audible, her end, peaceful. I was grateful that my mother did not suffer in death as she did in life and that she did not die alone.

And yes, I do miss her. And yes, having raised three children, I do understand.

• • •

The day I closed up my mother's apartment, I arranged for most of her personal and treasured belongings to be given away. The larger items that my brother and I loved were shipped to our houses. As I closed the door to leave for this last time, all that I carried out of hers fit into one suitcase. How strange and how sad, I thought, that what remained of such a full life could be held just in one suitcase. What I have come to appreciate now, is how much my mother's life could not neatly be packed away or confined into one piece of baggage; that she continues to live within and outside of me. Our mother-daughter relationship has not stopped with her death.

Growing up, I never perceived my mother to be independent and resourceful. I didn't realize all the risks she took in her life. My mother always downplayed what she had done to save Tanya's life. In a matter-of-fact tone, she said, "It is what you do for family." But really, the bravery she demonstrated was extraordinary, and the humility with which she spoke about it was amazing, too.

In April 1945, Russian bombs began hitting Stutthoff, mistaking it for a military camp. The Nazis marched my mother and the other inmates to a shipping port, crowded them onto the lower deck of a ship, and set out from the shore. From the ship, the Germans began shooting at the British liberators stationed on land. The inmates on the boat started to scramble amidst the gunfire and my mother jumped off the boat, even though she did not know how to swim. Somehow, she made her way to shore, wading through waters red with blood.

She was interned in a Soviet transit camp in Germany, where she learned that my father had been seen alive in a German hospital a couple of weeks earlier. Having no choice but to board the train going to Lithuania, she decided to jump off when it slowed down through the next town. As she wandered through the countryside by herself, she was falsely arrested as a German spy. With no identification papers to prove otherwise, my mother spent the next few days in jail while the police verified her identity with the displacement authorities. When they released her, the police helped her find the train to Łódź, where she was given temporary housing. My father received news of her location and, miraculously, they were reunited.

In 1953, seven months pregnant with me, my mother traversed the Atlantic by boat with my brother, then four years old, to join my father who was already in Montreal working. Immigrating to a new country without close friends or relatives, and unfamiliar with the English language or culture, she found her way, creating a close-knit group of Eastern European survivor friends with a few select Canadians in the mix. At age fifty-one, after sixteen years as a homemaker, she was left widowed, the only singleton amongst her friends. With more than sufficient financial resources left from my father, she took it upon herself to learn how to manage her investments. She sold and moved from our split-level home to an apartment, which she furnished anew with antiques and art she'd collected. After her first bout with cancer derailed her dreams, in her early sixties, my mother picked herself up and bought her first piece of real estate: a beach condominium in south Florida where, until the age of eighty-two, she lived part-time as a snowbird, managing its yearly rental from afar to offset the cost.

I feel blessed to be able to see my mother differently now, as a woman filled with grit and determination, independent of me and of what I did or did not do for her as a child. I see her agility and resilience, her devotion to doing her best to mother me and my brother, and to show us her love. My mother fought a courageous battle to rise above the pain of loss she endured and the extra suffering she brought on herself. Yes, she had shadows on her journey. We each do. I feel only the utmost respect, gratitude, and compassion for her.

• • •

Each of the three times I have visited the Holocaust Memorial Museum in Washington D.C., I've stood transfixed watching the video footage documenting Dachau's liberation. No matter how improbable it would be to see my father, my eyes searched over and over again for an image that resembled him. I wasn't sure if I could recognize him among the walking dead. My father was twenty-seven years old when, on April 29, 1945, the three U.S. Army divisions converged to liberate Dachau. Thirty-three years later, on that very same day, I gave birth to my first son, David, who, of my three wonderful children, feels the pull of his ancestral lineage most strongly.

I am intrigued by the mystery of this connection.

When I read about the 2015 United States Holocaust Memorial Museum anniversary gathering, I imagined what it might be like to attend. Could I learn anything about my father's experience by talking to another Dachau survivor or a soldier who liberated the camp? For several years, I had been part of a training program to teach U.S. Army personnel mental resilience skills. This work had been, in small measure, my way of giving back to those unknown soldiers who freed my father and to whom I indirectly owe my life.

On May 4 of that same year, my husband and I were at a party celebrating the engagement of our middle son Jeremy to his sweetheart, Cathryn Byrne-Dugan. We sat in the garden of her family home, talking with her parents and eighty-nine-year-old Irish Catholic grandfather, Art. I was careful not to broach any details about the upcoming wedding. Cathryn had converted to Judaism several years before she met Jeremy, and she'd warned me that it still might be a sensitive issue for her Pop-Pop.

Our garden conversation turned to discussing my need for a new car. I said I would not consider purchasing any vehicle made in Germany out of respect for my parents' suffering. My parents never allowed the purchase of German products in the home. Cathryn's mother informed me quietly that Art had been in the Army during the war, and that he too never allowed German merchandise in his home.

She motioned to Art to come over and told him, "Pop-Pop, Jeremy's mom won't buy anything German. Her parents were in a concentration camp during the war."

He nodded silently. "Did you see any of the camps?" I asked Art, and then quickly added, "My mother was at Stutthof, and my father at Dachau."

Art hesitated and when he began speaking, he averted his eyes from mine.

"Our unit went to Dachau. I will always remember that smell. When they gave us the assignment, we thought we were going to help transport some prisoners out of jail. I had just been shipped from overseas a few weeks earlier, all of seventeen years of age. I knew nothing about the camps or about war. On our way to Dachau, there was this terrible stench."

He paused for a moment. Cathryn's mother whispered beside me that Art had refused to ever talk about his wartime experiences.

"I couldn't believe what we saw when we arrived . . . dead bodies lying everywhere. You stepped over the corpses like they were roadkill. And those alive, I won't ever forget what they looked like. I don't care what the Germans say; the townspeople definitely knew what was going on inside the camp. With that smell, there was no way *not* to know."

I nodded in agreement. I knew about the complicity of silence and the pain it held for my own mother. Hearing this eyewitness account, I cringed not just for the suffering of the victims, but also for this young boy inside of Art. "I can only imagine how hard that must have been for you as a seventeen-year-old boy, green from Philadelphia, to face this horror. My mother told me how kind my father found the American soldiers who liberated the camp. I want to thank you for your service."

I paused for a moment to allow him to take in what I'd said. "Isn't it amazing, Art?" I continued. "If it weren't for you and your troop, in all likelihood, we wouldn't be here today celebrating Jeremy and Cathryn's engagement!"

A faint smile came to his lips. Art went on to talk more about his wartime experiences while Cathryn's parents sat motionless, grateful to hear him share what he'd never spoken about before. I was only half-listening, my mind filled with one word: *grace*.

• • •

On Center Street in Boston in August 2015, twenty of us gathered. The sky was a perfect shade of blue. Sparkles from the sun danced along our path to the tiny park across the street. Embraced by the trees and scattered sunflowers, we formed a circle. I stood beside Jeremy and Cathryn, soaking in the wishes each of our party expressed for their new baby, my granddaughter.

I wish for you to experience only peaceful times.

May you grow into your own person.

I saw tears well up in the eyes of my college friends; I listened to the catch in my brother's voice. The power of this ceremony felt immense to me. My granddaughter was honored with the name of my mother: Alice.

"I think of how my daughter came to be," Cathryn said at the ceremony, "and that it's a miracle. The great-granddaughter of a woman with such beauty and strength who survived the Holocaust."

I, who was unable to name my children directly after a family member for fear of the burden it might hold, now had a granddaughter whose parents saw such a name as a gift. In that moment, I sensed the sweet scent of Chanel No. 5 in the air. The gift of the old paving the way for the new: the gift of Alice.

6

Generation to Generation

Sassa Åkervall, daughter of Magda Wilensky (née Kahan)

Magda and Tore Wilensky's wedding, Copenhagen, Denmark, 1955

My mother and I rarely spoke about her trauma from the Holocaust, at least not in detail. It was a not-so-well-kept secret in our family that if you don't talk about things, they don't exist. So the story I have to tell consists of fragments, bits of memories that have faded in the distance due to time. I've also picked up a few things from speaking with my brother and my husband, who was a confidant of my late mother. If I don't get all the details right, at least I am doing the best I can to help her story come to life.

In 1997, my mother was interviewed for Steven Spielberg's Shoah Foundation Visual Library. Afterward, she gave me two tapes and was eager for me to see them. I think being interviewed for this project made her feel important—more important than just being my mom. I remember that I felt so awkward realizing this, to the point where I would push her request to watch the tapes to the very back of my mind. To me it seemed like she wanted to dwell on the past, whereas I wanted to not be reminded of things that had happened to my mother in the past. At the time I thought, why is this so important to her? How naïve I was. Needless to say, my mother and I had a very complicated relationship.

With a newborn son and a three-year-old daughter, my focus was on the children more than on my mother's story. I told myself I didn't have time to sit down to watch the tapes. I know I made up that excuse, maybe knowing it would be too painful for me—not even acknowledging how painful it had to be for her. Here I am, so many years later, and I still haven't watched more than half. What is my excuse now? Both my children, now young adults, have watched them. I think it would be something we could discuss together, so that we can remember

Grandma together. The older they get, the more distant her memory will be to them. They were both very young when she passed.

When our family had an opportunity to move from Sweden to the United States in 2004, we were very excited. I had planned to spend the last six weeks in my mother's house, as a sort of kick-off to our big adventure. But five days before our scheduled move, my seventy-nine year-old mother suddenly died from a heart attack. It was quite a shock for all of us, but especially to me. I knew she had her aches and pains but I never thought she would be gone just like that. My husband and I had planned to have her come visit us in the United States for long periods at a time so that she wouldn't be too lonely. I don't think I had realized how much we meant to her and how much she needed us until one day, just a few days before the heart attack, she told Isak, then just six years old, how much she was going to miss him. I remember saying, selfishly, "But Mom, we are still here for another five weeks." Looking back at that moment, I realize how immature and insensitive that comment was. I have oftentimes wondered if it was the defining moment when her heart decided it was time to just stop beating.

My mother was born Magdalena (Magda) Kahan, daughter to Sarolta (Charlotte) (née Kind) and Maximilian Kahan. Maximilian was an architect and a photographer, and Sarolta was a housewife. They both came from large country estates in Hungary (my mother told me that her grandfather owned mountains!), but the small family of three settled in Romania's Satu Mare district. There, Magda attended a Jewish school for girls.

With the war raging all over Europe, it was only a matter of time until Jews would be deported. Maximilian arranged for his family to flee to Switzerland. But when his elderly parents begged him to stay, they did. My mother, Magda, was nineteen years old and her parents were, of course, extremely concerned over what was coming. As a safety measure they sent her away to stay with one of the caretakers of their estate, hoping that her blond hair and blue eyes would help her survive. When the much-dreaded knock on the door came, my grandparents had to leave everything behind and enter the Satu Mare ghetto, which was established in the spring of 1944. Sarolta and Maximilian hoped that their only child would be safe. But Magda, facing the horrible fact that my grandparents were gone, was overwhelmed with grief and made the irrational decision that her place was with them. So, a few days after my grandparents were forced to enter the ghetto, my mother voluntarily entered as well. When they saw each other again, my grandparents cried grievously, knowing that all hope was gone for Magda to avoid being deported. And they were right.

A couple of days later, they were rounded up to get in the cattle cars for the transport to the concentration camps. Sarolta was already affected by fever. Magda, thinking she was helping her mother, asked the guards for a place for her mother to lie down. Of course, Magda didn't understand that such a request was a death sentence for her mother. As soon as the train arrived, Sarolta was pointed in one direction and Magda in the other. Magda never saw her mother or her father again.

My mother never spoke about this; I learned of it from watching the one tape I have been able to get through thus far. I can only imagine how hard it must have been for her to live with what had happened. I wish I'd known this years ago, when my mother was alive. Maybe I could have helped her heal. Maybe this would have brought us closer together. I will never know. My mother was busy trying to fit in to our lives in Sweden, and so was I. The traumatic war experience was not something I wanted to learn too much about. And my mother never offered to sit down to speak about it. It's only since her passing that I have learned a lot more about her and her time in the concentration camps. I will never know how she managed to get through. That is the burden I have to live with.

My mother was a prisoner at several camps: Neuengammen, Auschwitz, Weisswasser, Horneburg, Bergen-Belsen. She survived partly because she was selected to work in the Philip-Valos factories, as one of three hundred Hungarian Jewish women. This group was transported from Auschwitz to Weisswasser, via Horneburg, and then finally to Bergen-Belsen. She survived all of these horrendous places to some extent, I'm sure, because of pure luck, but I also suspect her will to live played a role.

At the end of the war, there was so much going on at Bergen-Belsen that Magda and a friend managed to flee to the woods, but it wasn't long until a German boy discovered them. He called on the guards, who dragged the two women back to the camp for execution. In the chaos of these last days of the war, however, the Germans were evidently too occupied with trying to get out of there to take care of executing two more Jews. While my mother was agonizingly waiting for her final moments, the British Army arrived and liberated the camp on April 15, 1945. My mother was free.

After the Brits' liberation, the Swedish government and the Swedish Red Cross rescued thousands of refugees from the camp by sending down what became known as the White Buses. Magda heard about these buses and was lucky enough to get onboard one of them. Once in Sweden, the refugees were gathered in a high school in the city of Lund in the very south of Sweden, where they were disinfected and quarantined until they were "safe" to go on to their next location. In my mother's case this was Stockholm. I don't know too much about the time she spent in Lund, but I know she made friends and that they traveled together to Stockholm. As an adult I came to live in the city of Lund. Every time I passed that high school, I would think of my mother and her first arrival in Sweden.

My mother and her refugee friends had a very hard time, not just because of the extreme circumstances of being alone in a country without knowing the language or culture. The Jewish community of Sweden was not very welcoming to the Jewish refugees. Perhaps the Swedish Jews saw the newcomers as lesser beings, or didn't want to connect with them because they feared becoming targets themselves. Even though Sweden, along with Switzerland, was considered a neutral country in Europe during the war, there was a lot of antisemitism under the surface, and sometimes out in the open. The Swedish King at the time, Gustav V, was very friendly with the Nazis, as was his wife, Queen Victoria, who was of German descent. The "neutrality" came at a hefty price; the Swedish government had to agree to let German trains with Nazi troops travel through Sweden on their way to invading Norway, and later on through Finland to the Russian front.

For seven years my mom worked as a maid for a Jewish family. She taught herself Swedish by reading cartoons in the newspaper and made some Swedish friends. One of them was a cousin to my dad, and she set my parents up on a blind date. This budding relationship was not looked upon with gentle eyes by my father's family. My dad's father was a well-known interior architect and designer; among other things, he designed all the old ornate and beautiful movie theatres around the country. He did not consider a refugee, a "slave" from the war, a suitable wife for his only son, even though she was Jewish. My dad's family never came to like my mom—and the feeling was mutual. I can't imagine coming to a new country, not knowing the language, having lost everything just from being Jewish, and then being considered *persona non grata* among Jews—one's own people! It must have been awful. Who can live like that? Well, my mother did, like so many others.

Growing up in Sweden, we never celebrated Shabbat, something I, as an adult, have tried to change with my own family. I love to make a beautiful meal, bake the challah, and light the candles. I wish that I had that tradition and memories from my childhood, though it wasn't something I longed for growing up, mostly because I had no concept of it. It became important as I became a mother myself. My Jewish identity grew very strong as I grew into my older teens and even more so after I had children of my own. I know that Shabbat was celebrated in my mother's family. She told me stories about this. But perhaps after the war she didn't want to be reminded of her parents and what had been. I will never know.

I do think that my mother wanted to soften the fact that she was Jewish for the world outside of our home. She just wanted to fit in and lead a "normal life." My father enabled her in this. He came from a secular Jewish family, even though there was a shohet, a Jewish butcher, on his mother's side. That never translated into my father's way of eating; I remember him putting pork steaks on the grill. He was certainly Jewish enough to go to shul and to make sure my brother became bar mitzvah, but Judaism wasn't something that permeated his life. At home we would celebrate Christmas with Santa, a tree and gifts, and the traditional Swedish smörgåsbord. I knew it was odd—and perhaps also "wrong"—but I enjoyed it and looked forward to it. The Christian holidays seemed so much more fun and easily accessible to me than the High Holidays.

Yom Kippur was always accompanied by the sound of my mother's weeping. Every year, the same grip of anxiety settled in our house. My mother weeping over the deaths of her parents, her family, and the loss of everything she'd known life to be as a nineteen-year-old in Hungary. She wouldn't explain exactly how she felt, but it wasn't so hard to figure out. She would light the yahrzeit candles and fast. It was always a somber time both at home and in shul. For me, a young girl living in Sweden with her whole life ahead of her as a blank canvas, this was beyond comprehension. Why dwell on the past when the future held so much more, so many promises and opportunities? There was no end to the feeling of unfairness I felt in being Jewish, with so much of life filled with anxiety and fears and tears. None of my friends seemed to have mothers who cried; none of my friends were Jewish because there were no Jewish kids my age in town. None of them could understand my family's incredibly sad history. The upbringing that taught me to always try to fit in kept me from discussing this with them, so I kept it to myself. I was alone in feeling anxious and fearful at the thought of Nazi boots stomping around in my neighborhood, looking to take us to the concentration camps. I was too young to comprehend and my mother was too overwhelmed with her own anxiety and sorrow. My father would switch channels on the television as soon as there was any war footage. We were never to remind my mother of her past, because we didn't want to cause her more pain.

My mother had a very unpredictable temper. She frequently had angry outbursts. When there were fights between my parents, I would always get a knot in my stomach. This anxiety, combined with the little bits and pieces of my mother's talk about the Nazis and her war experiences, filled me with fear sometimes to the point where I couldn't breathe. I heard fragments of how they starved in the camps, how sick she was. She talked about the kapo that hit her head with a rifle butt, causing a retinal detachment that scarred her for life. Of course, my young brain couldn't process all of this. I hated being Jewish and feeling so lonely and out of place.

My feelings about Judaism and being Jewish started to change when, at fifteen, I became a bat mitzvah at my own request. All of my classmates were being confirmed and went to summer camps. I really didn't like being different, though I knew I was. So I decided to be who I was born to be. I started going to shul to study Hebrew with Mr. Apfelblatt, who never thought I did my homework or read well enough in Hebrew. Slowly, I realized that this dark sanctuary— hidden away in a back alley in my hometown, where most people never even knew there was a shul—began to give me a sense of belonging. My initiative didn't come from my parents. This all came from me.

I realized I needed something to be real, to be mine. Maybe it was about God—my God.

Years later, coming to the United States was like finding the missing puzzle piece—how happy you get when you find it and it fits right in. I would hear words in Yiddish thrown around like they were part of the English language. I could proudly wear my Magen David, the star of David, around my neck and nobody would point or confront me about it. My husband Jan is not Jewish but he encouraged me to find my Jewish roots because it was important to me. We joined Temple Beth Emeth in Ann Arbor, Michigan. My children went to religious school and learned Hebrew. That not only created a feeling of belonging for them, it also created friendships that have lasted over the years.

At one point my daughter felt compelled to exult, "Hebrew is the most beautiful language in the world." I still remember how proud that made me feel. During her youth she was involved in temple life and was excited about visiting Israel. She blessed the candles with me every Friday night, and she said Kaddish at her grandmother's grave because she knows the prayer by heart, and I don't. I'm sad that she was so young when my mother passed, but they loved each other very much, and my mom adored my son too, whom she knew for the first seven years of his life.

Secure in her roots, my daughter also daringly questions them. Being a good person, living a responsible life, and caring for others, rather than religion, is what drives her and many others of her generation. She is widening her outlook on life, so that it includes everything that is important to her. How could I, as a parent, ask for more? These days both my children seem removed from Judaism. It bothered me for a while, until I let it go. During my twenties, I also felt removed from religion. There were far more interesting things to think about and do. I can understand a reluctance to say the prayers, to come to shul, to recognize being Jewish, because I have been there myself. For me, that changed when the children were born. As a parent you always try to leave a legacy with your children, whatever that may be. In my case, some of it is their Jewish heritage. Because if you don't know where you come from, how will you know where you are going? How will you know who you are?

A couple of years ago, I had a conversation with my son, then around nineteen, about Judaism. It turns out he understands many of the complexities of the religion, even though he never shared that with me before. He knows the history of the Jewish people and of Israel. And he sees this as it is, both good and bad. He is not afraid of discussing and even arguing his points. He identifies as a Jew. This makes me happy, even though our points of view can often differ. Especially as the children have grown older, I've felt alone in being Jewish in our family. At times I almost felt like I embarrassed them with our Friday night Shabbats, the lighting of the candles, the challah and the wine. But I have persisted, encouraged by my husband, hoping that at some point in their lives this will make sense and be a piece of the puzzle for them as it was for me. My son, who I see more often than my daughter because he lives closer, seems to want his girlfriend, who is not Jewish, to know and understand something of his background.

In spite of the complicated relationship I had with my mother, in spite of growing up in a society where I avoided all things Jewish, because I realized the pain that being Jewish had caused my mother, I have finally found a meaningful way to live a Jewish life. The realization that my children are so much more at ease with their heritage than I was at their age gives me hope that they will eventually find their own way to a life that will include Jewish traditions. As for myself, I'm still wrestling with uneasy emotions around watching the second tape of my mother's interview for the Shoah Project. I'll get there—in time. It will be important for both my children and myself, and for the conversations that will follow. Going forward, my hope is to inspire them to bring our traditions, both old and new, into their lives and eventually their families. Because as we say: *L'dor v'dor*—from generation to generation.

I am a mother. I have done the best I could.
My mom did the best she could.
And it brought me here.

Magda Wilensky celebrating Purim, Landskrona, Sweden, 2004

Memorize This Address

Ava Adler, daughter of Minna (Mindl) Adler

Minna and Ray Adler's wedding, Windsor, Ontario, 1948

As a child growing up in Oak Park, Michigan, I don't recall thinking a lot about how my family was different from other families. I knew my mom had an accent, but I don't remember feeling self-conscious about it. I was the eldest of three sisters and was a very good girl. I was happy, did well in school, and had a lot of friends. We sat alphabetically, and my name, Ava Dee Adler, usually placed me in the front row. When the teacher asked for a volunteer for anything, I felt compelled to raise my hand, whether I really wanted to or not. Did this sense that I had to be good, responsible, perfect come from my family's Holocaust legacy? I'm not sure.

Our house was always spotless, and house chores and meals were on a strict schedule. My dad worked several jobs to support the family and was not home much. My parents were distant cousins with the same last name of Adler, but my dad's parents had emigrated from Poland before the war and he was the youngest of five children, born in the Bronx, New York. He was fun and outgoing, with a passion for the arts, and had imagined a showbusiness career as a tap-dancing tenor before his life took another turn and he became a high school teacher, then a college professor and speech pathologist. He taught my sisters and me to sing in four-part harmony and gave me tap dance lessons in the basement. My mom, on the other hand, was quiet and shy. She did not have close women friends. She spent all her time keeping our house meticulously neat and clean, cooking, and doing laundry. We got along well, but I have no memories of her playing with me and my sisters. Perhaps we kids felt the undercurrent of our mother's anxiety that became more prominent as the years passed. We always felt more safe and secure when my dad was home.

• • •

In September of 1939, the German army stormed into the village of Pantalowice, Poland, my mother Minna (Mindl) Adler's birthplace. My mother's family was one of only ten Jewish families in their town. They owned a large, thriving farm where she lived with her grandfather, Moishe Adler; her parents, Chava and Meijer Adler; her sisters, Pesia and Dvora; and her brothers, Hersch and Aba. My grandfather died of a heart attack before the war. People said that it was a blessing because he never knew the horrors that were to come.

For the first three years of the occupation, Nazi officers took over half of the Adler farmhouse. My mother and her family lived in the other half of the house and continued to work the farm, whose harvest was handed over to the Germans. There were apparently two reasons why the Adlers were chosen for this "honor." The German officers did not speak Polish, and because Jews spoke Yiddish at home, a language very similar to German, they were the only ones the Nazis could communicate with. Also, their home was the nicest one in town, with a sturdy wooden roof and floor.

My mother, having painted an idyllic picture of prewar Pantalowice, never mentioned this shocking situation when she described her life on the farm. My one surviving aunt told her daughter about it, and that cousin only recently told me. It's hard to imagine what this experience was like for my mother and her family. I'm sure they must have been fearful. But it occurs to me, as I write this in safety and comfort, they never could have imagined the true nightmare of what the Nazis had planned for them.

One day in August 1942, the Nazi-controlled mayor of Pantalowice instructed the Jews to report to the village square the next day. My grandmother Chava was extremely worried about her family who lived in a neighboring shtetl. Heeding what they sensed was an advance warning, my mother, aunt, and grandmother decided, instead of reporting, to walk several hours to Chava's family to see what they were planning to do. When they arrived they were devastated to discover that the entire family was gone. They walked back to Pantalowice, only to find that Moishe, Hersch, Aba, and Dvora were also now all gone. Chava grabbed a small sack of jewelry and pressed it into my mother's hand, saying to her and Pesia, "Run! You have to run! But before you go, memorize this address." It was an address on Snowden Street in Detroit, where my mother's uncle Irving had gone in 1918 to seek his fortune. I find it incredible that, in this devastating moment of loss, my grand-mother had the presence of mind to try to save her daughters.

My eighteen-year-old mother and her fourteen-year-old sister managed to escape. My grandmother stayed behind, knowing she would only slow them down because of her poor health. My mother and aunt never saw her or their other family again. Only recently did an American-born cousin return to the village for the first time and confirm that the Jews who reported to the square were forced to dig their own graves and were then shot.

· · ·

When I was around ten, my mother had a nervous breakdown. She was admitted to Pontiac State Hospital. The only thing I remember about the episode is that she had been hitting her reflection in the bathroom mirror and that my mother's uncle, who we called Grandpa Irving, came over during the day, which was completely out of the ordinary. My dad was at work and must have called him. I assume there must have been other abnormal behaviors that led to her hospitalization. I felt confused and scared, and I have a memory of thinking she was doing it because she didn't like herself. But I'm not sure if I am reframing the memory from an adult perspective.

Minna Adler with daughters Ava Dee, Margo and Roxanne, Detroit Metro Airport, 1962

My father called his mother, my Grandma Celia, to come to Oak Park from the Bronx to take care of us. He described her as the unofficial social worker of her New York neighborhood, dispensing counsel and support to those in need around her. She didn't hesitate to come. Grandma Celia was an Orthodox Jew and brought her own glass dishes rather than use the ones in our non-kosher kitchen. On Saturday mornings she went into the living room, closed the door, and prayed from a prayer book she'd brought with her. But despite what struck us as these odd differences, she was very kind to us. She made both my dad's favorite traditional Jewish pastries and Toll House chocolate chip cookies. She baked challah and let us help roll out the dough. My sisters and I felt like things would be okay.

We went to visit our mother at the hospital. At the time, we understood it as a physical illness (my mother had contracted pneumonia while there), but as the years passed, and she continued to be hospitalized and take medications, we came to understand that she suffered from major depression and anxiety. Periodically, she would become fearful and paranoid, not wanting to get out of bed in the morning. This was alarming because she was normally up early, working hard all day cooking and cleaning, keeping our small 1950s ranch home in perfect order. I don't recall an explanation being offered to me and my sisters about what was going on. This was before the concept of post-traumatic stress disorder was identified and recognized as a reaction to trauma. In college, I remember having an epiphany that she was "damaged" emotionally by her wartime experiences and that her mental health problems were a direct and tangible manifestation of the Nazis and antisemitism.

• • •

When I was in high school, my father established strict rules about dress, dating, curfew, and homework. However, he also instilled a sense of confidence in me and actively supported my ambitions and goals. A high school teacher at that time, he encouraged reading rather than TV and offered help with tests and papers when I needed it. Even when my mother developed breast cancer during my senior year of high school, I focused on my future. I left for college at the University of Michigan, discovered a whole new world, and never lived at home again. My mother wished I hadn't moved "so far away" from her, although it was only forty miles. She seemed uncomfortable in Ann Arbor and said she felt like I lived in a "jungle," perhaps because campus student rentals never met her standards. I think she envisioned that she and I, her oldest daughter, would always have a close relationship like she and her mother had, spending time together regularly, if not daily. My decision to not only go to school in Ann Arbor but also to settle there, changed that and was a great disappointment to her.

As a young adult, I was confident and adventurous. Meanwhile, my parents struggled with their marriage and with my middle sister Roxanne, who had many behavior problems. But I was not aware until much later of the way things were falling apart at home. I was living my own life in Ann Arbor, starting my social work career and my marriage. Reflecting back as the woman I became, I felt some guilt at what seemed like a lack of empathy for my mother, especially at the time of her breast cancer diagnosis. I think this was both a lack of maturity and my coping mechanism. I needed to forge a new path for myself. Ann Arbor fulfilled a need in me that life in suburban Detroit could never have done. And with the knowledge I have gained about the deep-rooted reasons for my mom's unhappiness, I know that I was neither responsible for it nor could I have changed it.

• • •

After my grandmother Chava told my mother and her sister to run, and they escaped from their town as the Nazis shot all the remaining Jews, they hid in deep farmlands. For a few weeks they managed to live on vegetables they dug from the ground and blades of grass. Finally, they decided that they had to ask for help. They entered the next village of Siennów and reached the Chadala family, Catholics who knew of the Adler family from Pantalowice. My great-grandfather, a self-taught veterinarian, had nursed one of their ailing farm animals back to health. He was a generous and gracious man whose good name was held in high esteem in both the Jewish and Polish Catholic communities. The Chadala family hid my aunt, and when their grand-daughter Zofja Zięba, who was about the same age as my mother, was called by the Nazis to be transported to Germany as a Polish slave laborer, my mother went in her stead. She spent the rest of the war in Germany posing as the Catholic girl, Zofja Zięba.

During the day my mother worked at hard, heavy farm labor. At night she dreamed she was back home in Poland, on the farm with her family. On Sundays she attended Mass, sitting in the front of the church with the German family she worked for. She even took communion in order to carry out the charade to save her life. She longed for the day when she could reclaim her identity as a Jew, as Mindl Adler.

In April of 1945 when the war ended, my mother thought that perhaps all the Jews had been killed and she was the only one left alive. She was terrified to reveal her true identity to anyone. So she stayed where she was, hiding with the same German family, maintaining that she was a displaced Polish Catholic girl. The Russian prisoners of war, with whom my mother had worked side by side on the Chadala farm, were released. They roamed the countryside, often drunk, looting the surrounding homes. Eventually, they came back to the farm where she had spent three long years. The family my mother worked for pleaded with her to answer the door while they hid upstairs. They were afraid that they would be harmed. The Russians knew who my mother was—or at least who they *thought* she was. They asked her what she wanted them to do to her German "hosts." She told them "nothing" and said that her hosts had treated her well. My mother gave them some milk, and then they left. The German family credited her with saving their lives and their farm and they remained in touch with her for many years to come.

My twenty-two-year-old mother, who had lost everything she held dear because of the Nazis' hatred and persecution of the Jews, who didn't know where she was going or what her future held, was able to refrain from perpetuating hatred and destruction on others just because they belonged to the nationality responsible for her loss. I often wonder whether I would have been as kind or shown the same presence of mind as she did, under those same circumstances.

After liberation, my mother went to a displaced persons (DP) enclave in the British zone of occupied Germany. She remembered her Uncle Irving's address that her mother had given her, but it took her two years to write to him. In 1947, with Irving's sponsorship, she left Europe and settled in Windsor, Ontario, in order to learn enough English to qualify for American citizenship. Meanwhile, her sister Pesia had survived the war in hiding on the Chadala family's farm. She, too, ended up in a DP camp and met her husband there. Both sisters settled in the Detroit area.

My paternal Grandma Celia, who was a distant Adler cousin, wanted to lend support to my orphaned mother after the war, and arranged to meet her for a vacation at a cottage on the Lake Erie shore in Ontario. At the end of that vacation, when Celia's son, Raphael, came from New York to pick up his mother, he met Mindl. Within two weeks they were married.

• • •

As a young wife, I looked at my mother's marriage with new eyes, realizing that my American father might not have been the best match for her. Their whirlwind courtship led them to marry before they truly got to know each other. My father later told me that he adored his Polish-born mother and that, on first impression, my mother had reminded him of her. But unlike my grandmother, my mother did not walk confidently in her world; she was still grappling with the trauma of her losses and displacement.

I didn't gain a full understanding of the impact of my mother's wartime experiences until I was well into my thirties. At that time, she began to confide in me about her disappointment in her marriage. While my father was an excellent provider, he—like so many men of his era—was so busy working multiple jobs and rising in his career that he was hardly home and could not be present for her. My mother felt like he did everything for others and nothing for her. She became so focused on her grievances against him that she was unable to be proud of his many professional accomplishments, viewing them as competition for my father's time and attention. Although my parents loved each other deeply, they seemed unable to avoid hurting and disappointing each other—especially after I left home.

As I heard more of her stories, I developed more sympathy for her and empathy for her behavior. Being a social worker, I thought not just about what people did, but the why behind it. I began to realize the depth of my mother's sorrow over the loss of her family and home. As a child, she had been an eager student, like me always sitting in the front row and being the first to raise her hand to answer the teacher's questions. The few Jewish students in my mother's class did not attend school on Shabbos. The teacher refused to give them the Saturday homework assignments in advance, but every Sunday, my very resourceful mother would seek out the smartest Gentile in her class to get the assignment so that she could be prepared for school on Mondays. Eventually, the teacher moved my mother to the back row of the classroom. He was more interested in teaching the Polish students than the Jewish ones.

As a teen, my mother kept the financial books for the mayor of Pantalowice, worked alongside her mother in running the household, and could sew and tailor clothing without a pattern. It pained me to see how in America, my mother felt no sense of place, and was so socially isolated and dependent on my father. It now made sense to me why she became so depressed every August—it was the anniversary month of her leaving her mother and her home forever. I came to understand

that my mother's nervous breakdowns were directly related to the trau-
mas of her wartime experiences, her dislocation and immigration, and
the strain in her relationship with her Uncle Irving and his wife, Aunt
Dora. I think she'd imagined that they would become surrogate parents to her. However, they, along with my father and others in their
generation, did not understand PTSD. None of them were fully able
to give her the emotional support she needed to heal and adapt to her
new life.

• • •

My mother, the talented seamstress, appreciated quality fabric
and workmanship; when she went out, she dressed fashionably in
classic styles and colors. After I left home, during college and into
adulthood, my mother would offer me clothing and jewelry of hers
that she thought I might like or need. My taste did not always match
hers. Sometimes I turned her down and other times, in order not to
hurt her feelings, I would take things with no intention of ever wearing them and give them away to charity. One day, my mother asked
me if I still had something she had given me and I had to admit what
I had done with it. She was obviously upset and asked if in the future
I could return things to her rather than give them away. My first reaction was to judge this as selfishness. There were so many people in
need who would appreciate our belongings and put them to good use.
She then told me that she only had one thing of her mother's—an
apron. I was shocked but it made sense. In retrospect, I wish I had
asked her several questions. How did she end up with this apron? Was
she or her mother wearing it the last time they were together? Did
her mother offer it to her, or did she ask her for it before she escaped?
How did she preserve it while she was on the run, hiding in Germany,
in the DP camp?

This helped me see that I had not sufficiently demonstrated my appreciation and gratitude for what my mother gave me, as she would have done with her own mother's gifts, had she only had the opportunity to hold onto them. Now I find that I'm sentimental about stuff—things that belonged to my parents, my friends, my kids. I keep in mind that my mother had nothing from her childhood, from her past, from her own mother. It's hard for me to throw anything away, not necessarily because I think I will need it, but because it brings me comfort and emotional security.

In her later years, my mother attended therapy in Ann Arbor, and I was invited to join her for a session with Neal—a young Jewish psychologist, whom, I believe, my mom viewed as the son she never had. Neal said I was the glue that held my family together, and that when I left for college, things fell apart. I found this idea surprising; I'd certainly never looked at myself that way. But apparently it was the case that my parents' marriage faltered when I left home. My sister Roxanne's acting out increased, creating a great deal of tension in the family. She was overtly disrespectful, did not follow house rules, hung out with friends my parents did not approve of, and skipped school. By the 1980s Roxanne had married, and she and her husband were both struggling with substance abuse issues. Their children, ages three and six, came to live with me and my husband. It was supposed to be a temporary situation but ended up as a permanent arrangement.

Once again, my mother's therapist interpreted our family dynamics: "For you, kicking someone out of the family or rejecting them would be like throwing them to the Nazis," Neal said to her. I realized that was true for me, too. I never even considered not taking in my nephews. This was a part of my Holocaust legacy: the importance of keeping the extended family together. My husband and I didn't yet have any children of our own, and our nephews became our sons. At the same time, I have always made sure that my sister stayed in their lives.

. . .

Today, my parents and my youngest sister Margo are no longer alive, and the nephews I raised live out of state with their families. They are committed fathers and husbands, for the most part happy and healthy, although they both suffer from bouts of anxiety and depression. Both of my sisters struggled with their mental health, as well. I will never know whether this is an inherited predisposition or the result of trauma transmitted across generations. The possibility that the impact of trauma can be passed on to children and grandchildren is just now being realized and studied in the second and third generations post-Holocaust.

As for me, my motto is "Hope for the best . . . plan for the worst." I allow extra time to get to places that are some distance away in case of an accident or construction. I check and recheck numbers, especially relating to finances. I don't really trust others to take care of things; I'd rather do it myself and make sure it is done correctly. However, I don't let small anxieties stop me in any way. In my family I have always been the sturdy one. To this day, I am their sister, mother, confidante, and social worker all in one. I am still the glue. My family did not fall apart.

. . .

My mother always felt guilty that she had left her mother behind, even though that was key to her survival. Her mother had told her to flee, "throwing me out the door," my mother said. But she could not forgive herself. She also struggled with guilt over following her agnostic husband's decision to not keep a kosher home or belong to a synagogue. Although my dad was raised in the orthodox tradition, he never embraced it. As an adult he observed the hypocrisy of many Jews who attended services and prayed to God regularly, but did not live their lives righteously. This seemed to make a big impact on his belief system and he wanted no part of Jewish institutions. In the 1950s and '60s, it would have been unusual for a married woman to attend synagogue without her husband, and my mother would have been self-conscious and embarrassed to do so. So she never developed a relationship with the suburban Detroit Jewish community. I believe the guilty feelings she harbored about these matters contributed to her mental health and marital struggles.

When my mother was dying, this was the last thing that she whispered to us: "I have . . . I have . . . I have to find my parents." In death, she could leave her guilt behind. Perhaps she believed that she would see her parents again, and that she could face them.

• • •

I have come to realize that my mother's experiences and my family history have instilled in me a strong emotional sensitivity toward discrimination at every level. I deeply feel the divisive impact of "partisan politics" playing out in our country; it seems to drill down to my DNA. I am really fearful of the echoes of Nazi Germany reverberating in America, of those in power who pit the dominant white Christian American culture against Jews, Blacks, Muslims, immigrants, and the LGBTQ community—labeling them all as "other." Around the world we have seen the election of right-wing leaders who perpetuate the marginalization of these groups and increasing violence carried out against them. I believe the only way we can save our humanity is to be very purposeful in our efforts to get to know each other and our common struggles. Divide and conquer has been a strategy used by those in power for thousands of years. If we are to challenge the resurgence of white supremacy and authoritarianism, we must become allies for one another, despite our differences.

My mother had no choice in 1939 but to be a slave laborer, to flee and hide her Jewishness to save herself. She was one of the lucky ones who survived. Today we are reminded that while conditions of oppression and violence evoke echoes of the Shoah, we are not being forced to hide or flee; rather, we can stand together with other groups who are targeted, and show our solidarity and strength in our numbers. If we use our power to unite, we will withstand the challenge of this time.

I want to honor my grandmother for her presence of mind to save her daughters. I want to honor my mother for her bravery in navigating her way to safety and her grace in protecting the German family who'd created a safe haven for her, not knowing that she was Jewish. It is only because of these two Adler women that I am here to write this story and I honor them by telling it. I honor myself as the next generation of Adler women who provided a safe haven for my nephews when my sister could not. I kept my family together so Minna and Chava's great-grandchildren and great-great-grandchildren could thrive. The Adlers of Pantalowice survived. I will continue to honor my family through my efforts to be a bridge to the common humanity in all of us. I will always speak out in an effort to repair the world, honoring a basic tenet of Judaism: *Tikkun Olam*.

• • •

When my mother died, I sat with my rabbi to prepare him to deliver her eulogy. As I told him about the totality of her life, I came to realize that my mother was not a victim; rather, she was a hero. I wrote this poem shortly after she died.

My mom saved zippers, elastic, safety pins.
Nothing remotely useful was put to waste.
Her pots and pans were scrubbed to perfection, as if her
life depended on it.
But her hands were so soft, like the tissue paper she kept
between her things in her drawers.

I'm not like her . . .
Meticulous . . . attentive to detail.
I don't know how I can take good enough care of her things.
I want to honor her . . . I want to remember her
attending to the details, as if her life depended on it.

8

Lessons from My Parents

Natalie Iglewicz, daughter of Henry and Franka Iglewicz

Top row left to right: Franka (Weintraub) Iglewicz (in a vest that she knit) and her younger sister Mala (Weintraub) Mosenson. Bottom row left to right: Franka's older sister Lola (Weintraub) Schwartz, her younger brother Leon Weintraub, and her first cousin Franka (Weintraub) Charlupski, Lüneberg, Germany, 1946

I was a late-in-life only child born to Holocaust survivors. My parents met and married in 1956, when my thirty-five-year-old mother was visiting Detroit from Israel. She was introduced to my father by her cousin's husband. My father was a factory worker and my parents, wanting to provide all they could for a child, decided to have just one.

I was named Natalie after my mother's mother Nacha, who died in the gas chambers of Auschwitz with her sister Ava. My middle name, Libby, was from my father's mother, Liba, who died in childbirth when my father was two years old. For my parents, I embodied their loved ones whose names I was given. I was cherished.

Growing up I knew there were more names of the dead who needed remembering: my father's beloved brother Lazer, who died at fourteen of some unnamed illness before the war; my mother's sister Rosa who died in the camps; her Aunt Ava, gassed along with her mother; and her best friend Ava, who was shot at her home in Łódź while hiding with her family. I stored those names, thinking one day I would pass them on to my children, and eventually I did.

My father worked on the assembly line at a Ford plant, leaving the house by 5:00 a.m. for the 6:00 a.m. shift, and arriving home just before my mother left to work in the Jewish bakery in Detroit. Right after that hand off, one day during the summer after kindergarten, I asked my father if I could play with neighbors across the street. The neighborhood kids were playing Duck Duck Goose, a favorite activity of mine. My father told me I could go if I brought a sweater. It was July and hot but I didn't argue. I wanted in on that game!

I never made it across the street. The car that hit me never saw me as I darted out from between parked cars. Dragged thirty feet before the driver stopped, I sustained life-threatening head injuries. As a teen I asked my mother to tell me about the accident. She went into her bedroom and emerged with a short clipping from the local newspaper. It wasn't very descriptive, so I asked her for a detailed account from the time she arrived at the hospital. I could tell that she didn't want to recall this terrible memory of how she almost lost her child, but I persisted, and she relented. My mother told me that when I arrived in the ambulance at the hospital with my father, the doctors had to medicate him because he was in hysterics. My mother, having been driven from work to the hospital by her cousin Rosa, found us both on a gurney when she arrived. When my father gained consciousness, he was consumed by guilt and worry as I was being operated upon. After the operation, I awoke briefly. When I opened my eyes, I saw my father's tearstained face and told him I loved him. Then I closed my eyes and went back into a post-operation-induced sleep. Apparently, my words of love for my father gave him some peace and he finally calmed down. My mother also said something I never forgot: during the operation she prayed only that I would survive. She didn't care if I was going to be a vegetable for the rest of my life. She only wanted me to live.

When I was seven years old, I took to climbing the huge oak tree that grew in our front yard. Knowing that my father would forbid this activity, I waited until he took his afternoon nap before heaving myself up the first large branch. Every day in the spring and summer, I tried to climb a little bit higher. I got as far as the rooftop of our house, which probably wasn't very far up considering our home was a small one-story. Still, I felt on top of the world and loved looking out from my perch at the street and houses below, observing the comings and goings without being noticed.

One day, while I was enjoying my hideout, an elderly Jewish neighbor, Mrs. Marx, came walking down the sidewalk towards our house. She stood underneath the oak tree, wagging her finger at me. "You get down from that tree right now," she said. "Don't you know? Nothing else can happen to you!" I scrambled down from the tree and never climbed it again. I was beginning to understand that something terrible had happened in my parents' life and that nothing else terrible could befall them. They couldn't lose me. In my predominantly Jewish neighborhood, my neighbors felt the need to protect my parents from more loss.

From an early age, I understood that being loved by your parents was natural. But the idea that I was so cherished and precious that neighbors would intervene in my tree-climbing exploits did not seem normal. When I went to my friends' houses, I saw that their parents were devoted to their children yet still retained an element of themselves. They seemed to have their own dreams and desires. In my house, my father told me often that I was his life. My mother would say she was living for me. This heavy love felt like a burden, and since at times I was troublesome and disobedient, I felt undeserving. Why did they act this way? What had happened to them? Around the age of seven, I began to get a vague notion. Unbeknownst to my parents, I understood their secret language, Yiddish. When they spoke the secret language among their close-knit circle of survivor family members and survivor friends, their conversations began with the phrases "before the war," "during the war," or "after the war." So they had been in some sort of war, I thought.

Throughout my early childhood, I was periodically awakened in the middle of the night by my mother's piercing screams—"No! No! NO!"—and then her face suddenly appearing above mine. I would ask what happened and she would answer, "Nothing. A bad dream." In the morning when she was doing a household chore, I would ask her about the bad dream. It was always the same: "I dreamt you and I were behind a barbed wire fence," she would begin, "and the Nazis were coming for you." One morning I asked why she kept having this sort of dream. Without hesitation she told me, "In the ghetto, the woman who lived directly above me on the third floor had a beautiful baby boy. He must have been about six months old when the Nazis came for him. Knowing what the Nazis did to babies, she threw him out the window. She wanted him to die from her hand, not the Nazis."

"You saw that happen, Mom?"

"I saw that happen."

Somehow, I could see it too. Scared, I went into my room and cried.

By the time I was ten years old, my mother no longer screamed in the night. That was in 1968, twenty-three years after her liberation from Bergen-Belsen.

I wanted to understand more about the before, during, and after-war life of my parents. I eavesdropped on their Yiddish conversations with others, and I prodded them with questions when they opened the door to their past in English. Over time I learned their stories.

While I was in elementary school, I spent the weekday afternoons and early evenings and all day Sunday with my beloved father, while my mother worked at the Jewish bakery. Every day after school, I would let myself into the house and then, with my face pressed against the living room window, wait for my father's arrival about twenty minutes later. After our initial embrace and his short nap, he was ready for me. My dad and I spent our time in the family room together playing board games and cards; I was a mean poker player from an early age thanks to my dad. We would also sit on the couch reading side by side: my father studying Jewish commentary while I read my latest favorites by Beverly Cleary or the Nancy Drew series. He would sometimes stop what he was doing, look up at me, and say in his heavily accented Yinglish, "I have to tell you something."

One time while we were sitting on the couch together, my father put his book down and, peering over his glasses, told me that what he had been reading was very important. He said that the Midrash, Jewish commentary on Jewish law and thought, explains that when giving charity it is essential to give it in such a way as not to bring shame to the recipient. He proceeded to illustrate this point with a story from his childhood. When my father was a young boy, his grandmother lived with his family because his mother had passed away. Every Friday his bubbe would awaken him early, to accompany her as she delivered challahs to those in need in their community. "She put it on their doorsteps before they awoke," my father said. "That way, who had given the challahs was a mystery. Having no one to thank, they weren't shamed."

My father grew up in a very observant home in Ostrołęka, a small *Fiddler-on-the-Roof* type of village about seventy-five miles northeast of Warsaw, Poland. He was the youngest child of four. By the time he was ten years old, his grandmother and father had passed away. An orphan now, he was cared for by his older sisters, Sarah and Zelda. After completing the equivalent of high school in Ostrołęka, he continued his studies at a yeshiva in a neighboring town. He frequently told me this story about the generosity he experienced from the Jewish community he was a part of.

"Jewish families in the village took turns hosting the yeshiva boys. Most of the families were poor but felt it was an honor to take care of us as we were pursuing Jewish studies. When I came to eat the main meal at midday at one host family's house, I realized that I was receiving more and better food than their children. This made me feel terrible.

"The next day, I decided to stay and study during our meal break so the family would not have to share their food with me. Wouldn't you know it: about forty-five minutes into the meal break, the mother of the household came to the yeshiva looking for me. She asked me why I hadn't come and gave me the meal she had prepared. It was her mitzvah, she said, and she asked me not to take that from her. I understood then and never skipped a meal again."

My father embodied this lesson of generosity and kindness

throughout his life. When I was a teen and my mother no longer worked at the Jewish bakery, I went with my father on Friday before Shabbat to pick up a challah. As we waited in line, a woman in front of us was parsing out her coins to pay for two loaves of bread. My father turned to her and said in Yiddish, "Would you give me the mitzvah of paying for your bread?" Of course, she said yes. She had to, I realized. She was doing my father the favor!

Just about anything could trigger a memory of my father's childhood. As we sat on the couch eating cherries, he would tell me how he and his buddies would climb a neighbor's cherry tree and steal the cherries. Another time, putting a Band-Aid on a childhood scrape, he told me about gathering leeches for the local doctor from the Narew River that ran behind his house. While we walked home from Hebrew school, which I attended two evenings a week and on Sundays at the Jewish orthodox synagogue a couple blocks away, my dad would tell me about Jewish life in his shtetl. "We lived as a close-knit Jewish community clinging to the Gemara, Mishna, and Tehillim, studying like you are now," he would say. He liked to point out such moments of continuity for the Jewish people.

Or if it was a day to bring to Hebrew school the tzedakah I had set aside from money I'd earned, my father would say, "Ostrolęka was famous for its charity and the good hearts of its people. I will remember always the Jews of Ostrolęka."

On Sundays when my mother worked all day at the Jewish bakery, my dad and I would "go places" as he put it. Sometimes we ran errands to the grocery store or the mall, or did fun things like go to the movies, the zoo, or the beach. I loved these outings with my father. He was always generous and kind, and through his words and deeds he taught me to be the same.

When I was around five years old, my dad and I went to the Northland Mall, an outdoor shopping center back then in the early sixties.

It was my first time going to the mall, and I was excited. As we were walking around, I saw an African American man. Never having seen someone with dark skin before, I said, "Oh no, Daddy. That man is burnt."

"No, no," my father said, "he is a Black man whose ancestors came from Africa. Black people are fighting for their rights and many Jews are fighting with them. We are a minority in this country too. When one minority suffers, all minority groups suffer." That was my introduction to the civil rights movement and to understanding that I was a part of the struggle.

Another time at the mall with my dad, I saw a nun in full regalia. I said, "Look, Dad. A penguin." That lent itself to another lecture: "That is not a penguin, but a nun. Nuns are people of God, many of whom risked their lives to hide and save Jewish children during the war. They deserve our respect." This is how my father taught me tolerance.

I was interested in my dad's world and I asked a lot of questions. As a child and later as a teacher, I was particularly interested in his schooling. "What were your teachers like?" I asked in my early teens. "Shmuel, Reful, Echala, Moshe Galina: these were my rabbis," he said. "From seven years old until I went to yeshiva, these men were my teachers, my mentors. They gave themselves completely to us, their students. They were involved in every aspect of our lives. They called us 'my zinala,' my son."

That description left quite an impression on me. In the early eighties when I completed my degree as a special education teacher, I moved to Mesa, Arizona, to teach. While my parents were visiting me, one of my young students who lived nearby stopped over to chat and play with my dog. I told my dad this happened frequently, and he remarked that I had the heart of his teachers. That filled me with pride, and I thought of his comment often as I strove to make my students my sons and daughters for the thirty-eight years I taught.

While my father clearly told his stories with a lesson in mind for me, my mother would offer details about her life when I asked, but it was up to me to find the meaning. The second of five children, she was born in the city of Łódź, Poland, a large town known for its textile industry. When my grandfather died, my mother and her siblings were ages one through nine. As a widow, my grandmother, Nacha, had to support her young children. Never having worked before, she started a laundry business in her mid-thirties. She also went against Jewish orthodox traditions practiced by the Łódź Jewish community by removing her sheitel (the wig worn by orthodox women to follow the laws of modesty), and by serving customers on Shabbos through the back door. My mother described Nacha as "a modern woman who did what she needed to do to keep the family fed." My mother and her sisters loved and admired their mother for her strength and wisdom as she raised them alone, eventually in the Łódź ghetto where they were forced to live in squalor and starving conditions.

When I was sixteen years old, I read *The House of Dolls* by a Holocaust survivor known as Ka-tzetnik 135633. The author tells a fictionalized account of what happened to his sister in the Nazi "Joy Division," where Jewish concentration camp prisoners were forced to provide sexual pleasure to Nazi soldiers. In the end the main character commits suicide. I was sitting next to my mother when I finished the book, and asked her some specific questions. One of them was, "What happened to your mother?" When she told me how the last time she saw her mother was in line at Auschwitz when she was about my age, I sobbed in her lap. It was unbearably painful to imagine what it would be like to lose her like that.

I vividly remember the scene of my mother and her sisters Lola and Mala telling me in greater detail about the last time they saw their mother. It was the summer of 1983, and I was twenty-five years old. My Aunt Mala lived in Israel, and we were together for her daughter's wedding. After the wedding, when my Aunt Mala, Aunt Lola and her husband, and my parents and I were all staying at a hotel in Tiberias, my dad and uncle went downstairs to find a card game, and I was alone in one of the rooms with my mother and aunts. It was a rare opportunity to ask them to tell me from beginning to end their experiences during the war. I had never heard what had happened in chronological order, nor from the three of them together. They were sitting on the bed, shoulders touching, and my mother was knitting. From my chair by the window, I asked them to tell me what happened from the time the Nazis reached Łódź to their liberation from Bergen-Belsen concentration camp. Their voices interwove as they told the story. This is my attempt to recreate how they described the last time they'd seen their mother, almost forty years earlier.

"They liquidated the Łódź Ghetto August of 1944," Aunt Lola said. "They told us to take all of our clothes with us because we were going to a work camp. The devils, they gave us bread as we were loaded into train cars to Auschwitz. I remember how my mother dressed that day: in a silk blouse and a navy, red, and yellow suit. She was always neat. She was wearing high heels. She always wore high heels."

Aunt Mala continued, "The train ride was horrible. We were packed men and women together. Our bathroom was one pail that was soon overflowing. I can't remember how many days we were on the train. Three, four, five, without food or water."

Franka, my mother, said, "We were very naïve. We couldn't believe the rumors: that some people who left never came back. We thought the Germans needed us for work. We thought they wouldn't kill the people they needed.

"When we came to Auschwitz we had our suitcases packed with our clothes and some silver, thinking that we could sell the silver. The kapos came. They said, 'Leave everything here.'

"I said, 'What do you mean? How will we find our things?'

"They said, 'We'll find you. Leave your luggage here.'"

Mala continued, "Then they started taking us to the selection. It was daylight. The women went one way, the men another."

Franka said, "Lola stood with Mother. I was behind Lola, and Mala and Aunt Ava were behind me."

Lola said, "Mengele, in shiny, high black boots, was making the selections. This I'll never forget. Mengele. He said to my mother in German, 'How old are you?' She replied in perfect German, 'Forty-six years old, Sir.'

"Well said," he replied and sent her one way.

Franka said, "He asked Lola her age and sent her in another line. I was next. When he asked me, I said I was the same age as Lola so he wouldn't think we were sisters and separate us. He sent Mala and me with Lola.

Mala said, "Aunt Ava wanted to be with her sister and went to the other line."

After my mother and sisters were separated from their mother and aunt, they were held along the railroad tracks between Auschwitz and Birkenau for about two days and then stuffed on trucks to be taken to a concentration camp in the hinterland of Germany. As the truck pulled away, Franka told me she cried out, "How will Mother find us?"

Another woman said, "See that smoke? That's your mother."

My mother slapped her and said, "This is the twentieth century. People don't do that."

She and her sisters never saw their mother or aunt again.

• • •

Like her mother, my mother was an exceptionally independent woman. She insisted on working when other women didn't work. In addition to her job at Zeman's Jewish Bakery in Detroit, she had a side gig. She was a talented and skilled knitter, having learned to knit as an eight-year-old schoolgirl in Łódź. When she wasn't at the bakery, there was a group of women, usually relatives, over in the afternoon knitting at our kitchen table, getting instruction from my mother. Sometimes she was knitting with them. Oftentimes she was going about her chores, ironing or making dinner, while helping correct dropped stitches and instructing on how to make a desired pattern.

One day when I was about ten, while searching for the needles she wanted from her needle case, my mother showed me an unusual pair. Then she told me the story of these knitting needles, which had their origin in one of the smaller concentration camps she had been sent to in Germany.

"It was a good camp," my mother said. "The head of the camp was an old World War I German officer who wasn't cruel. Still, the Jewish prisoners, all of us girls, were starved and poorly dressed for the upcoming winter. My sisters and I worked in the ammunition factory nearby. Mala and I worked the day shift, and Lola the night shift. Wounded soldiers and local village women worked at the factory as well. The soldiers and villagers were forbidden to speak with us, having been told that we were criminals.

"One day, a middle-aged German woman who worked with me came up and said, 'Pretend I am fixing your machine.' I nodded. Then the woman whispered, 'They told us that you are criminals. You are such young girls. What terrible crime did you commit?'

"'Our crime is we're Jewish,' I replied.

"'*Sind Juden!*' the woman exclaimed, shocked. 'What can I do for you? How can I help you?' she asked.

"'It's cold and we have no stockings. If I had knitting needles, I could pull the threads from the blanket and knit my sisters and myself stockings.'

"The next day I found a pair of knitting needles at my workstation.

They weren't real knitting needles. They were bicycle spokes with cork on the end. I hid them under my clothes and brought them back to my barrack, where I knit stockings for my sisters and myself.

"This woman risked her life for me. And every day when I arrived at the factory, she would smile at me. That smile meant so much. It was the smile of a mother, and I missed my own mother so much."

Through several more concentration camps and the chaos of liberation, my mother managed to keep those knitting needles with her until she died in 2012, at ninety-one. After her death, I searched for those makeshift knitting needles in her many needle cases and finally found them, among the beautiful sets of real knitting needles my mother used.

I never thought to ask why she kept those needles. I hope they reminded her in the most terrible times of the smile and the gift, of how one nameless person can give hope and warmth to another. That's what the story taught me.

• • •

I really resented being an only child. I wanted someone to play with and to help me figure out my parents. Someone to ask if my parents' actions were normal, war-related, or a result of being immigrants. Some of my questions were silly: Why do I have sardine sandwiches in my school lunch and everyone else has peanut butter and jelly? (*Because your parents are immigrants.*) Why can't I sleep at anyone else's house? They always have to sleep at my house. (*War-related: my parents didn't trust other people and wanted to keep their own eyes on me as much as possible.*) One day when I was whining about not having siblings and telling my mother how lucky she was to have two sisters, she said, "I have three sisters."

"I know you had three sisters. Rosa didn't survive the war."

"I still have three sisters. We adopted Jadzia. I made my sisters adopt Jadzia and we did."

When I asked her to tell me more, she told me the story of how she and Jadzia came to be sisters. "In the spring of 1945, at Bergen-Belsen concentration camp, my friend Regina and I were dying of typhoid fever. I had known Regina for a long time. We grew up together in the same apartment building in Łódź. Her younger sister Jadzia was Lolak's age and was a friend of his."

Lolak was my mother's youngest sibling by six years, the only boy. In Auschwitz, he was placed in the line with the men although he couldn't have been more than fifteen years old. He was standing in line with his best friend and his best friend's father. That was the last time she would see him until they found each other after the war.

My mother said, "We had spent the last year traveling to hell together: first to Auschwitz, now in Bergen-Belsen. We were a family: me, Lola, Mala, Regina, Regina's younger sister Jadzia, and my dear Fricka."

Fricka was a German Jew who had been forced to leave Germany with her Jewish-Polish husband, who was from Łódź. Fricka was in her mid-thirties at the time, a good ten years older than my mother and her sisters. She also came from a prominent German-Jewish family and was well-educated. My mother and her sisters met Fricka in the ghetto where they worked together sewing Nazi soldiers' uniforms. Whenever my mother told me about sewing the uniforms, she made sure to let me know that all the girls discreetly cut every few stitches so the uniforms looked perfectly made, but would open at the seams after minimal wear.

Fricka was on the transport to Auschwitz with my mother and her family. A mother figure to the girls, Fricka stuck with them through this dark journey. They all encouraged each other's survival, protected each other, and divvied up their meager rations.

When they knew the war's end was near, Regina and my mother were lying next to each other, in and out of consciousness, feverish and suffering from starvation. When my mother awakened and shouted, "Regina is so cold, bring her a blanket," Lola knew that Regina was dead, and she was removed.

My mother awakened again to find Regina missing and asked Jadzia where she was. Jadzia turned away, unresponsive.

My mother cried out to her sister Lola, "Jadzia doesn't answer me!"

"Regina is dead," Lola replied in a hushed voice.

"Then I will die too," my mother said. "Promise me you will take Jadzia as your sister to replace me. She is all alone now."

"Yes, Jadzia will become our sister," Lola said.

On April 15, 1945, Bergen-Belsen was liberated by British soldiers and my mother recovered from typhoid fever. She learned that her sister Rosa, who was part of the Jewish Resistance, did not survive. Jadzia, at fifteen the sole surviving member of her family, became a part of my mother's family. After the war she was sent to Israel, where she lived on a kibbutz with other child survivors. She later married a fellow Łódź survivor and had three children.

They are sisters to the end of their lives.

My mother retold this story to me many years later, when I was forty. I married my first husband when I was twenty-seven and soon after discovered I had fertility issues. I went through the treatments available for infertility at the time, to no avail. Well-meaning family and friends of my parents, all of them survivors, would see me and say, "What are you waiting for, darling? Your parents and *you* are not getting any younger."

I know they meant well, but I was suffering the guilt of the only child of Holocaust-survivor parents who'd lost so much family and wanted desperately to see their family expand. I felt horrible and I cried a lot. Then I got divorced. At thirty-seven I remarried and went

Franka and Henry Iglewicz holding their grandchildren Rosa and Eddie Newland, Detroit, Michigan, 1997

through the whole process again, this time in Argentina where my husband and I were living for the first three years of our marriage. Extremely hormonal and bloated from the fertility treatments, I was miserable and terrified of being childless as I approached forty. My husband and I decided that if I wasn't pregnant by the time I reached forty, we would adopt.

My parents came to Argentina to celebrate my fortieth birthday with me, and we took a beautiful trip together to Iguazu Falls. After blowing out the candle on my birthday dessert, I told them that because I had failed to provide them with the biological grandchild I was sure they wanted, and we weren't going to pursue any more fertility treatments, my husband and I had decided to begin the process of adoption.

My mother shouted, "It's about time," and my father grabbed my hands and said he was happy.

Tears streaking my face, I said, "I thought you would be so disappointed."

My mother then retold the story of how she had adopted Jadzia as her sister. Afterwards she repeated to me a Yiddish saying that goes like this in English: "Your mother is not the one who bears you but the one who raises you." And then she added, "We will love your child."

9

Cutting Corners

Phil Barr, son of Harold (Chaim) Rayberg

Chaim Rayberg, 1947

He passed away in a bed in Haifa, filled with tubes and wires. My oldest sister Lana, with whom he'd been living, described him breaking down in tears a few weeks earlier, wondering aloud, "How could I have left my mother?" When my father was seventeen, his mother told him, "Run." Was that the first time he had cried since 1941? Possibly. I know I'd never seen him cry.

Growing up, I remember Dad coming home after dark, long after Mom and us six kids finished eating. After shedding his work clothes and boxes of papers in the front hall, he heads for the kitchen. When I come in and give him a kiss, he's leaning forward in his chair, hungrily slurping hot soup and laying slabs of butter on pumpernickel, his wool cap still on his head. He is already anxious to collapse into bed. In a ritual we have at the time, I ask for his change purse and go through it, looking for silver. If I'm lucky there might be a Mercury dime. By the time I'm eleven, dimes and quarters have already been clad for a few years, and silver coins are rare. I check the date and mint mark for my collection and toss the rest of the coins into the green sewing bag to put into paper rolls later.

After eating, he might kiss several of us good night on his way to bed, but there are few words. Perhaps he'll yell "Shahrrap-You" to silence an argument between us. The ongoing argument with Mom over money for household expenses would wait till morning.

Fifty years later, that green box with the rolls of coins is still on the bottom shelf of my office. My father, by contrast, had nothing left from his childhood home.

Despite my mother's efforts to stop him, he worked seven days a week. Going to the junkyard was both habit and an escape. Since he saw everyone there as a *ganif*, especially the workers, he may have gone to prevent theft as much as to work. Trust in strangers, or in his family, did not come easily to Chaim.

The double doors of the Rayberg house in suburban Oak Park, Michigan, were painted a deep orange, a loud sixties color. Fairly disheveled inside and out, we were that house on the block with a truck and three old cars in the driveway. Two more junkers waiting to be sold or fixed up parked in front. A bustle of kids and our friends, always coming and going. We grew up around the kitchen table. For dinner we had large bowls of fresh salad and a rotation of dishes meant to feed a hungry brood: spaghetti and meatballs, beans and franks, tuna noodle casserole, trays of Weight Watchers' baked apples with red pop. We sang, argued, pushed, and grabbed. Insults and retorts were mostly delivered in good fun, but they were cutting, nonetheless.

After dinner, food was left warming or on the table for Dad. His attitude about food was pretty basic: "A potato, boiled meat, and some fried onions. Now that's a meal!"

Thinking back now on those happy times, it's hard to try to reconcile our "typical" suburban American upbringing with the history that brought my father to America, and to reflect on how that history inevitably influenced us.

• • •

My father, Chaim Roijtburd, was born on Lag b'Omer, 1922, in Ludvipol, Poland. He changed his name to Harold Rayberg when he came to the United States, taking the last name of his Uncle Piniah Rayberg in Boston. Seven years after fleeing his home, he was united with relatives and a small group of Ludvipol survivors in Detroit in 1948, in the home of Libby and Ben Ross. Tante Libby, his mother's sister, had immigrated a generation earlier to Detroit and owned a small dress shop. During the war, she founded a mutual aid society to send food and blankets to Jews remaining in Poland, and she continued these efforts after the war. She also sponsored my father's immigration to the United States.

Chaim went to work immediately at Chevrolet Gear and Axle. After three years, he quit GM following an argument with his foreman. He'd already bought a truck and he began collecting scrap metal. This developed into the scrap metal business which became the junkyard that we grew up in. He had also met my mother.

Tante Libby instructed him not to marry a greener, but rather to find an American wife so that he would have more family around him and be less alone. Chaim met my mother Miriam, called Micky, in 1951, when her friend's car broke down at a dance. He towed them home with his truck. My mother was studying at Wayne State University, her parents having sent her to Detroit to break up a relationship she was having with a non-Jew. A second-generation American, Micky grew up in Cleveland and moved to Omaha during the Depression. She was the oldest of three siblings, from a family of devoted Reform Jews with socialist and Zionist leanings. Micky was fun, open, and trusting. My father was several years older: closed, withdrawn, and very patriarchal. They couldn't have been more different, but they got engaged and were married.

My sister Lana was born a year later, followed by Elizabeth, then me, and then Shuli, Reuven, and Gila. When I was born we lived in a big house on fifteen acres in what had once been a stately old house in the country. My father surrounded it with junk cars and piles of disassembled engines, tires, and axles. It was an amazing place to grow up for a gaggle of lively kids.

But of my father's past, we knew nothing.

One time at the dinner table, my sister, who was probably seven at the time, imitated what she had heard while playing that day with kids in the trailer park next door. In answer to being told to eat her dinner, she raised her arm in salute and chanted a *Heil Hitler*. My father impulsively lunged up and smacked her right across the face. My mother, normally nurturing and protective, dragged her from the room, shaking her and scolding, "Don't you ever say that again. Don't you know Hitler killed your father's entire family?"

But we didn't know. My siblings and I had grasped only fragments from overhearing family conversations.

My father had a trigger fuse of rage and, I think, survivor's guilt. A dark well of emotion and loss which he could not articulate. When he felt slighted or criticized, his face would turn red, and the veins of his neck would stand out as he shifted into defensive anger. There were few opportunities for calm discussion. In a sort of cry to be understood, he might recall men's lives he had saved during the war. It was as if he were saying: "How can you bring up such petty criticisms when I once risked my life to save others?"

To Chaim, people were generally crooked and untrustworthy. He got into continuous conflicts with customers and employees, tinged with no small amount of bigotry on both sides. He saw the township officials who levied zoning fines and court cases against his business as evildoers to be fought. It was a losing battle. Learning to fight and distrust are two lessons I know that my siblings and I absorbed, and I recognize that they have not served me well. Those impulses, combined with a feeling of inevitable doom, became toxic in my high school years.

I used to joke that for my father the world was divided into two groups: "No-good Goyim" and "Fer'shtunkena Jews." Customers would call asking to talk to Abie. It was years before I realized they meant it as an antisemitic slur. That was part of why, when I was in first grade, we moved to Oak Park to be near a Jewish community. Mom made herself comfortable in an open, chaotic home where friends were always welcome. Dad was not involved with the synagogue, though he could recite all the prayers by heart.

Chaim had no friends and he fought with his surviving relatives. A few days before he was to walk his sister's youngest daughter down the aisle, he was arrested for buying a stolen car and refused to pay bail. My mother had to beg the judge to let him out for the wedding. For us six kids, there was no instruction on the importance of morality or the value of education. It was right if you could get away with it.

• • •

From the time we moved, as the oldest son, I was pushed by my mother to spend more time with my father than my other siblings. If I didn't have something else on my schedule, I would accompany my father on the weekends to work at the yard. Usually, I would just do what he asked, but it was largely unstructured time. Though we were there together, we never talked and I never felt like I knew him.

When I was twelve, we were all surprised when he reached for a violin that my sister brought home from school. Without saying anything, he put it under his chin, placed the bow to the strings, and, smiling, played the Israeli anthem "Hatikvah" perfectly. I didn't know he could play, didn't know how he'd learned. We never saw or heard my father play the violin again. Other than at Passover Seders, I never heard my father sing.

But music became important to his children. Reuven studied conducting, Lana became a band leader and bassoon player, Gila a professional touring jazz trombonist, and Elizabeth and Shuli were always creating new repertoires of songs and mastering various instruments. Not as artistically inclined as my siblings, I've always been drawn to mechanical tinkering and figuring out how things work. I admired the "hillbillies" who came to buy at the yard and who were so adept at the use of tools, with their tidy, organized toolboxes.

• • •

Once, when I was already a father myself, just the two of us were alone in a car in the dark, on the way to see my brother Reuven's concert in Indianapolis. The time finally seemed right to ask Dad about life growing up in his village of Ludvipol, Selisht, in Poland. His father, Isaac, was a trader and peddler, which meant he went out to the country and bought goods to sell at the market and to individual customers: furs, grain, and later a specialization in dairy products.

The Roijtburd family lived in a small house, on the square of the Jewish marketplace. In the center of the house was the kitchen, and in the center of the kitchen was a big stone oven. This stone hearth was the center of family life. In the winter, the four children's beds were arranged around the warm oven, where they slept comfortably at night. My grandmother used to make Shabbat meals in the oven, and during Pesach she baked large matzoth that they took to poor families.

His village was a remote shtetl of approximately fifteen hundred souls, 90 percent of them Jewish. It was attached to another village, Lower Selisht, which was largely Polish and Ukrainian. The youth of my father's generation, schooled in *cheder* by rabbis from the age of three, became fervently Zionist. My father joined the Socialist Hashomer-Hatzair youth group, which in Israel formed the backbone of the kibbutz movement. His cousin Steve joined the militaristic Betar. All the students of my father's age were passionate about the creation of a Jewish State, and rallied the youth to swear off Yiddish and Polish and speak only Hebrew, the language of Jewish rebirth and renewal. They participated in building a Tarbut School, or Jewish

Cultural School, in 1930s Poland. Until his dying day, Chaim spoke a beautiful Sephardic Hebrew.

The students hiked and sang in the forest, skated on the Sluch River in the winter, and fought with the Polish and Ukrainian gangs. It was by no means idyllic, but it was a close-knit community and it was home. History, however, was closing in on the centuries-old Yiddish heartland of Poland's three and a half million Jews.

. . .

On August 23, 1939, in order not to have to fight a war on two fronts, Hitler signed the infamous Molotov–Ribbentrop Pact with Stalin, dividing Poland between them. Ludvipol was less than fifty kilometers east of the new Nazi-Soviet frontier border. Within weeks the military occupation was complete, Germany invading from the west and Russia from the east.

Life under the Soviets was a mixed bag. Stores and businesses were nationalized with no compensation, Hebrew books and language were banned, and only Yiddish was allowed. On the other hand, new investment in roads and infrastructure helped lift the region out of a deep economic depression. The Jews, being better educated, often held clerical jobs. For Poles and Ukrainians there were brutal dislocations as Stalin sought to impose Soviet authority and Russian culture. Successive waves of Jewish refugees fled east along with Poles and Ukrainians, trying to escape the Nazi-occupied region of western Poland, as the worst excesses of the SS savagely began to unfold.

My father was seventeen when the German Blitzkrieg, Operation Barbarossa, began. It was the start of Hitler's war on the Soviet Union, with the Nazis overrunning eastern Poland in June of 1941. At that time, Chaim had graduated high school and had started studying to be a history teacher at a seminary in Rovno, a town west of where he grew up.

In the confusing days of the Nazi invasion, he and his older sister Chana came home to their village and begged their parents to flee, to retreat east deep into Russia with the Soviet army. His parents Lana and Isaac refused. His mother, in Chaim's words, "sat" on his younger brothers Meir, fourteen, and Sholoma, fifteen, refusing to let them go. "Better to stay than starve in Russia," she said. Despite what they had heard, "The Germans are a civilized people." But she did tell my father and his older sister Chana to run in the hope that they would have a better chance for survival. They all understood that the Nazi occupation would be more than another pogrom. My father and Chana were never to see their beloved family and home again.

• • •

Chaim retreated alone on a bicycle to the east, taking only a small bag of food. Chana caught a Soviet transport. My father met up with his sister in Gorodnitsa, the next major city to the east. The authorities had ordered the large Jewish population there to destroy anything that might be of use to the invading Nazi forces before fleeing. What remained of the stores were being looted and burned. Amid the chaos Chaim and Chana were able to scavenge some food from the abandoned stores. Then they boarded a freight car, continuing east.

They joined with wave after wave of refugees fleeing east through Gorodnitsa, Zytomer, Kiev, Kharkov—eating in refugee soup kitchens, exchanging day labor for food, and traveling in freight cars opened by the Russian government to allow refugees to ride for free.

When they reached Kharkov, they spent a month of the summer harvest working on a collective farm near the Caucasus Mountains. Chaim worked harvesting hay, wheat, and fruit. Chana worked in an office. They were hosted by a religious Jewish family of the Sobotnickim sect; the family received rations for hosting the refugees.

With the harvest over, twin threats of winter and the Nazi front were fast approaching.

Continuing east they took trains to the Caspian Sea. At the port of Kratsonvotska, Chaim talked the longshoremen into a deal. He worked several days and nights, loading and unloading ships, in exchange for a pass for him and Chana to board a freighter ship across the sea. In the testimony he gave to Yad Vashem at the age of eighty-one, he recalled storms and huge waves battering their old freighter. On reaching the other side, they continued east by freight train to Almaty, the capital and largest city of Kazakhstan. Both Chana and Chaim were drafted into separate workers' battalions in Kazakhstan, where they worked throughout the remainder of the war. Chana was a secretary in an agricultural collective. Chaim was sent to an army base, where he described seeing huge stores of brand-new uniforms, tractors, and transport vehicles sent from the United States to aid in the war effort. He was put into an army uniform and sent to work at a zinc mine. The zinc was used in bullets, artillery, and explosives for the war effort.

The history of the Soviet-era Gulag is one of horror: political banishment, ethnic cleansing, unfathomable state terror, terrible conditions for prisoners and refugees. Workers building the Soviet empire "earned" a bowl of soup a day. Life and death was in the hands of camp commanders. Along with tens of thousands of Jewish and non-Jewish refugees, Chaim was drafted into the system. At some point, he became a quartermaster of sorts where his job was to procure and distribute food rations to his list of workers: 700–1000 grams per worker per day. More if you were a good worker. Apparently, he had some discretion in the food distribution. Perhaps this was the period he was referring to when he made those remarks we heard as kids—that he'd saved men's lives. He also contracted typhus and was able to make it to the beet collective where his sister was interned.

Chana nursed him back to life and he returned to his assignment at the zinc mine.

In his testimony, Chaim does not sound bitter toward the authorities or his non-Jewish comrades. One gets the feeling of a day-by-day toil to survive in a brutal system in which he had next to no control. Learning about how my father survived these years, it made more sense to me the way he lived his life so reactively. Why plan when you had so little power? Best to wait, watch, and be ready to react from a defensive posture. I think he was proud of my mother's openness, her spirit and vitality, but couldn't see how his oppressive need to defend and control slowly grounded her down until she'd had enough.

• • •

When the war ended in May 1945, Chana, who had been released earlier, wrote to my father about what happened to their hometown and community. At first all the Jews from Ludvipol and the surrounding area had been confined to a fenced-in ghetto, where the young adults were assigned to work. The older people were sent to dig a large ditch in the forest. On August 26, 1942, the Germans finished off the whole population. There was no need to go home, Chana wrote. It was too dangerous. They never went back.

It took Chaim about two weeks to meet his sister in the ancient, largely abandoned, city of Bytom, Poland. Chana got married and her older daughter, my cousin Lana, was born there.

In postwar Poland, the various Zionist movements competed to recruit survivors of the camps and Jews like Chaim who were emerging from the Soviet Gulag. Chaim joined a kibbutz commune of Hashomer-Hatzair, where he was assigned to go to the refugee center and pick up rations for the kibbutz members. After six months in Bytom, he joined a Hagana smuggling operation that moved people, weapons, and goods legally and illegally to Italy. From Italy, the refugees were put on boats trying to run the British blockade to Palestine. His testimony is somewhat unclear, but it seems that Chaim was active in these pre-state Zionist efforts over the next three years.

In 1948, the Israel independence war was imminent. From a refugee camp in Brindisi, Italy, Chaim made contact with his family in the United States. His mother's sister Libby in Detroit and brother Piniah in Boston made sponsorship requests that he come to America. He signed up with HIAS, the Hebrew Immigrant Aid Society, and waited. There were rumors about how to beat the American quotas, so in filling out his application, he made himself seven years younger, back to being seventeen. Since records had been destroyed in the bombing, he also claimed to be a German citizen, despite the fact that he had never been to Germany.

After some time he received permission to immigrate to America. He arrived in Detroit with a falsified identity and history, and lived with some fear of being deported. Finally, in his eighties, I was able to get the record corrected and get him a corresponding bump in Social Security, as he was really seventy-two when he went on Social Security at the official age of sixty-five. Chana, because of immigration quotas, settled across the river in Windsor. When her husband passed away, she raised her two daughters, Lana and Mildred (Milly), on her own, and they were like two older sisters to us, frequently coming to stay with my family in Michigan. Chana eked out a living with a fruit and vegetable stand in the Windsor market. According to my cousin Milly, Auntie Chana shared even less about the past than my father did.

· · ·

My father never gave me any advice or direction as to how I should think about my future or prepare for college. Maybe this was because, during the Holocaust, he couldn't plan beyond the present. Fortunately, my first-generation American Bubbie and Zadie, my mother's parents, strongly valued education. My mom's younger brothers, both successful professionals and academics, served as role models for me. Mike was a successful mathematician, at one point chair of the University of Wisconsin-Madison math department. Sam, a Harvard-educated lawyer, worked in both the Ohio and Federal EPA on environmental justice issues. Their lively political and social justice debates every Pesach and Thanksgiving were great fun and all the young cousins looked forward to spending time with them.

My mother saved money so that my parents could take me and my two older sisters on a two-week trip to Israel and a week-long cruise in the Aegean Islands after my bar mitzvah. We toured Israel and met relatives, landsmen, and former teachers of my father, as well as a host of relatives from my mother's side. The last day of the cruise we watched the first moon landing on a grainy black and white TV in an Athens bar.

The trip made a strong impression on me. In an interesting parallel to my father's early experiences and also to my mom's family's Zionist activism, I found my social life in the Socialist-Zionist youth movement in Detroit. It was there that I that I first met my future wife Julie.

• • •

In high school, it was hard for me to stay focused and interested. I felt like school was meaningless. In the middle of eleventh grade, I decided to skip classes with my sister Elizabeth, who was a year and a half older. Jane Fonda was scheduled to speak at a local college and we wanted to hear her. But the day morphed into us deciding to get our backpacks and hitchhike to California, where Elizabeth had a friend. Three days later, when I called my mother from a friend's place in Chicago, she convinced me to come home and drove out to get us. Very soon though, we took off again, this time hitchhiking to Omaha to see my grandparents. Elizabeth decided to stay in Kansas City, where she had friends, and eventually received a fine arts degree from the Kansas City Art Institute.

I continued on to hitchhike to Los Angeles. When I called home, my father's only response was, "You're going to end up in jail or dead." Indeed, after five months of hanging out, traveling around, and working some, I got picked up for shoplifting in LA. I was taken into detention until my parents sent a ticket back to Detroit, and I ended up finishing high school on schedule with my class.

I also continued to work at the yard. One day, my father wanted me to drive a truck loaded with engines down to Detroit. His trucks were not in good condition, or well maintained. Safety was one more corner to be cut. When I got in, I felt the truck lurch forward, its front wheels coming off the ground from the weight. After I refused to drive it into the city, my father jumped into the truck, yelling that there was no problem, and took off down the road. A few hours later, we received a call that the truck had tipped over on the freeway. Fortunately no one was killed or hurt. My father never apologized for or even acknowledged this error in judgment that jeopardized my safety.

• • •

A few years after high school, Julie and I moved to San Francisco, as Zionist *shelichim* (emissaries), and spent two years there. We organized a group of thirty kids to attend Zionist summer and winter camps in the L.A. area. I got an associate's degree in electronics at the City College of San Francisco and worked repairing construction power tools. In 1979, we made Aliyah to the Kibbutz Gvulot in Israel and were married a year later. We took the last name Barr בר, which is a concatenation of ב (Bet) from Julie's last name, Bennett, and ר (Reish) from my last name, Rayberg. It carries the lovely connotation "of the place; indigenous; native, as in a weed." I sometimes felt that was how I experienced growing up: like a wild weed. Both of our kids, Maya and David, were born in Israel, where we lived for nearly seven years before coming back to the United States.

Upon returning, I naïvely thought I could work with my father in the yard again. I tried, but there was no way we could make it work. For instance, I used my own money to have a large roll-off box built, so that steel could be loaded directly into the box and trucked out without double handling. I thought my father and I had a deal that we would split the proceeds from each load. But when the checks came in, there was always some reason that I would not get my half. Sadly, it was impossible for Chaim to trust anyone, even his own son. In hindsight, it was for the best that I moved on. Working with my father brought out a rage that I realized could destroy me.

It took a while to settle into a career path. Like so many in my generation, I rode the electronics/computing/internet wave. My niche expertise is in backend database systems, a field that continues to engage and challenge me every day. In my personal life, I struggle with uncertainty and tentativeness. They tend to undermine me. Like my father, planning does not come naturally to me and basic rules of empathy have to be practiced and learned.

• • •

It wasn't until my children were grown and had moved away from home that I formed my first relationship with anyone German. Michael and Dorothea, a German couple, rented the house next door to Julie and me. They were about our age and we shared common interests, among them taking long walks.

Growing up it was a given in my family that we would not buy German products. The sound of the German language conjured black and white images of savage German Shepherds. My Uncle Mike would joke about avoiding travel in Germany, saying he would only briefly stop there to urinate. There was a deep well of unexplored emotion around the Holocaust. Once while I was studying electronics at the City College of San Francisco, a young Palestinian dropped a flyer with a Star of David printed next to a Swastika on my table in the cafeteria. I jumped up, tore the flyer to pieces, and began shouting obscenities at him like a crazy man. It took me hours to calm down, even though on a rational level I was sympathetic to his cause, if not his tactics. I would have liked to be able to carry on a calm discussion with this activist, but it was too charged of a subject for me at the time.

On our first walk together, Michael confessed that his father had been in the SS, in part excusing him for it by explaining that he was an orphan who had grown up in the Hitler Youth. Michael, a manager and engineer, was more closed off and theoretical than Dorothea, an educator, who worked to teach children about Germany's history. I'll never forget Michael's question, "Why do they keep writing so many books about the Holocaust?" It was as though he saw it as something that should have already been dealt with and moved on from. Michael's was the generation that had pushed back the silence, speaking about their deeply-embedded sense of personal responsibility for Nazi atrocities.

We are still in touch today and I'm trying to figure out how to broach the subject with him of whether, as a German, he would help me research the SS officers who directed the atrocities in Ludvipol. I know that he is interested in trying to find out more about the activities of his father in the SS during the war. In getting to know this couple, I was surprised to see that, like me, they too were struggling to come to terms with their past. While it took a decade to make Europe fertile ground for mass genocide unseen in human history, it will take generations to heal.

• • •

In the summer of 2007, Julie and I visited my father's village of Ludvipol in what is now Ukraine. We also visited with Michael and Dorothea, who had returned to live in Germany. In preparation for traveling to see my father's village, I read *Babi Yar*, a book by Anatoly Kuznetsov, which describes surviving the war in Kiev from the point of view of a ten-to-fifteen-year-old Ukrainian boy. The book gave me a wider perspective on the suffering during World War II beyond the horror of the Jewish experience. Needless to say, I did not grow up with sympathy for Poles or Ukrainians. In every story I'd ever heard, they were helpers of the SS—vicious and enthusiastic in rounding up, dehumanizing, and murdering Jews. From *Babi Yar*, I learned that they too suffered and died by the millions, both under Stalin and in the war.

Ludvipol, still a tiny rural village in the province of Volyn, is located in western Ukraine. The terrifying thing about visiting Ludvipol was how normal the village seemed. It was not the dark, scary place of my nightmares, but a place of serene natural beauty with rivers and forests. Jews had survived and built a rich culture in the region for more than 300 years. When the Nazis arrived, each religious leader met them with gifts. They took the Catholic and Patriarch's gifts, but they threw the rabbi to the ground by the beard and spat on him: a signal to the local population of what to do with the Jews. That night, homes were ransacked and Jewish neighborhoods were set on fire.

On the evening of August 25, 1942, the elderly women and

children were ordered to dig their graves. The vicious Commandant, with reported sadness in his voice, gave a final speech to "his Jews," saying that he would allow them to die as a family, together. The Commandant left as the machine guns began to fire.

In just over a year, the entire Jewish community was buried in the ditch in the forest on the other side of the Sluch River. Ludvipol had rid itself of its Jews, who had once made up most of the population. Walking through the forest after visiting the fenced-in memorial site built by the survivors, I picked up some charred birch sticks from a campfire. I still have those charred sticks, one of my few souvenirs from the trip. They act as a link to that past, reminding me of my father and his lost family.

The people I was able to talk to in the Ukraine, who had endured the war, didn't ask me how my father had survived. They each had their own stories. They mostly asked, "How did he get out afterward?" This gave me respect for the initiative and effort that my father had demonstrated—in spite of his limitations—not only to survive, but to make it to the United States and accomplish all that he did.

· · ·

How does healing occur? Certainly it never happened for my father.

He managed to start a new life and had six kids, but he never recovered himself. He didn't seem to understand how to negotiate American life. He retreated into his scrapyard sanctuary, surrounded by towering piles of automobile engines and vehicle axles which were too heavy to be stolen. It was a simple, effective calculation, but it came at a cost of isolation and suspicion.

Throughout my life, I continued to vacillate between embarrassment, anger, and resignation at my inability to get through to him. But no matter his rage (or mine), I found I still felt protective of my father. Only recently have I come to realize how much my father himself was a lost child of the Holocaust. What if he could have carved out a few moments each day to reflect on the good in his life, on how far he had come? To breathe freely as a man no longer being chased and persecuted. To not feel he had to cut the next corner to gain some small imaginary advantage. How much of a difference that would have made for himself and those he cared about.

I am now a grandfather to three beautiful girls: Evie, Margot, and Sylvia. It's amazing to me that I don't recall my father ever playing with my own children when he visited my house (he was only a forty-five-minute drive away). I see him just sitting on the couch, not doing or saying much of anything. My kids, when asked, have only the vaguest memories of him. I realize now that when Dad visited, I was always defensive, angry, or on edge about when the next insult or embarrassing action would occur. These feelings made it difficult to make space for him with my family and children.

In his last years, my father lived in Israel near my oldest sister Lana. On a trip to visit him in Haifa's RamBam Hospital, where he was recovering from cancer surgery, we had fallen into the familiar pattern of bickering and silence. I desperately wanted to break through the annoyance and embarrassment. To create a moment for us. On my last evening there, I wrote something to share with him. It was based on a meditation template suggested by a dear friend, a psychologist who lived on a nearby kibbutz.

Dear Dad,

- Thank you for the rich family life you've given us and for all you did for me.
- I'm sorry for the unfathomable loss of family, community, and normality which you endured. For the

pain you've endured and for my lack of compassion for you.

- I forgive you for holding your sorrow and rage inside. For the sorrow you caused to Mom, and not being able or willing to express your love for us or to forgive yourself.
- I love you and know you cared and continue to care. I will never stop loving you.

And then I wrote "Goodbye," since I was flying home the next day.

As I began to read it aloud to him, I started sobbing. Chaim tearfully begged me to stop crying. I am not sure I got through all that I wrote. He held me, kissed me, and told me he loved me.

I regret that this affectionate connection didn't last long. Neither of us handled showing or seeing emotion very well. Nonetheless, it is a moment that I cherish. This turned out to be one of the last times I would see him.

• • •

Piecing my father's story together has taken a long time. In 2004, I found the Generations After group at Temple Beth Emeth in Ann Arbor. Being a seeker of sorts, I had joined many groups in my effort to understand myself. Over many discussions and good food, my self-mocking acceptance of my ignorance of my father's past gradually turned to curiosity, a drive to know the history and gain an understanding of its implications for me. One of the gems I found in my search was the book *Kaddishel: A Life Reborn*, by Aharon Golub, one of the only witnesses to the massacre of Ludvipol's Jews in 1942. Aharon was a few years younger than my father.

I also listened to video testimony by Chaim's cousin, Steve Golden,

Rayberg Passover Seder 1988. Photo taken at the home of grandparents Rachel and David Bleicher. Top row (left to right): Phillip Barr, Julie Barr, Dario Cabib, Lana Cabib-Zin. Middle row: Delilah Raybee, Adina Cabib, Miriam Rayberg, Gila Rayberg, Harold Chaim Rayberg, Shuli Rayberg, Reuven Rayberg. Front row: Elizabeth Raybee, Amethyst Frech, David Barr, Maya Barr, Iris Cabib

who grew up across the Jewish courtyard from my father in Ludvipol and survived the war in the Soviet Union, arriving at Tante Libby's home in Detroit. Then, while writing this chapter, I found out by accident about an interview my father did at Yad Vashem in Jerusalem, where the interviewer had coaxed out many of the missing details of my father's history from the years 1941–1948.

If part of growing is forgiving, I'm able to say that, painful and scary as it is, I have grown. I am learning to forgive not only generations past, but also my father, and myself. In raising my kids I have made many mistakes, but I know I've been guided by an overarching desire to provide a delicate balance between protectiveness and nurturing, and to help them realize the open-ended possibilities for creating a life. My greatest fortune has been Julie—my wife and life partner—who models for me how to treat every person with respect: a respect that goes deeply into every aspect of how she conducts her life. At times she's been bewildered and even shocked at the ease with which my family members and I have lapsed into a sort of forgetfulness, have demonstrated an ignorance of the basic rules one should follow in interactions with others.

The Generations After group has been a safe place for me to let down my guard, to confront unexplored feelings, to realize that beyond the black well of my emotion was much I didn't know about the wider history of the Holocaust period, about our parents' stories, and about myself. I am on the healing path.

• • •

Recently I asked my sister Elizabeth if Dad had ever shared particular memories of his experience with her, as I'd had so few such interactions with him. "Only once," she said, "did he volunteer any information on his own. A couple of years before he died, I took him to see the movie *Titanic*. After the show, in the parking lot, he looked confused. He said to me, 'You know the part when the boat is sinking? That's what it was like when I was leaving home. Only without the water.'"

10

Always an Outsider

Cilla Tomas, daughter of Ruzena and Jakob Tomashpolski

Jakob and Ruzena Tomashpolski, Prague, Czechoslovakia, 1948

I have often felt like an outsider. I spent my childhood in a very homogeneous white Christian society. My parents were both Jewish and immigrated to Switzerland after experiencing persecution in their countries of origin. They were both overprotective of my sister and me, especially my mother, who was very suspicious of people and taught me that I should be wary since most people were "bad" or even "evil." As a consequence, I was shy, insecure, and suspicious of other people's intentions. I didn't feel comfortable in my own skin and saw myself as an outsider at school, among my classmates, and even in the Jewish community, where most of the members hadn't been directly affected by the Holocaust. I had few friends and mostly only related to schoolmates who weren't popular, like me.

I was born and grew up in Bern, Switzerland. My father's family escaped after the pogroms in Kishinev, in present-day Moldova, and moved to Switzerland when he was about nine years old. My mother and her one sister, originally from Kosice (then part of Czechoslovakia), were the only ones of her immediate and extended family who survived the Holocaust.

I remember my paternal grandfather, Pinkas, who died when I was three, only very vaguely, as a loving man with a beard and a great smile, who talked to me in Hebrew. He had joined the Zionist movement in Russia after the pogroms in the early twentieth century. He travelled to Palestine and lived there for a few years, but didn't stay because my grandmother wanted to move back to Switzerland, since life at that time in Palestine was dangerous and lacked certain conveniences. My grandfather lived with us and worked as a textile merchant selling wholesale fabrics and yarn, which we stored in our basement for a long time, even after my grandfather's death. My sister and I often went into the storage room and played that we were selling those colorful fabrics and yarn.

When I was growing up, my mother rarely talked about her experiences during the war. She died when I was a teenager, and I was never able to pursue a discussion with her about her family and what had happened to them in the Holocaust. My guess is her experience in Auschwitz was so horrific that she didn't have the words to talk about such trauma.

I remember once we went on vacation with some friends and they asked her why she had a number tattooed on her arm. She told them she got it in the concentration camp during World War II. Right away, they wanted her to sit down with them and talk about her experience. My father, who was very protective of her, came to her aid and said it would bring up too many bad memories. My sister and I knew, too, that we shouldn't upset my mother because she lost her temper easily, and upsetting my father would apparently affect his heart. When I got into an argument with my sister, he would tell us to stop, and if we didn't stop immediately, he would demonstratively squeeze drops from a medication bottle into a glass in front of us. This was an effective strategy, since I was afraid that he might have a heart attack and die. Later on, I found out that those drops were harmless over-the-counter medication to calm him down.

My father never expressed how the pogroms had affected him and his family, nor did he say whether he had any family left in his homeland. Otherwise, my father was a good role model for me: hardworking, honest, and ethical in his profession as a lawyer. He was highly intelligent and well-educated. He had many interests, including reading books and newspapers in different languages, listening to music, hiking, travelling, and socializing with a small group of friends, mostly related to his work. He was a leftist when he was young and even read Karl Marx's

Capital, though he became more conservative later in life. My sister and I discussed world events with my father. Whenever we expressed any left-leaning ideas, he told us we should really educate ourselves first with the basics and read Marx before we thought about changing the world. He was suspicious of how successful political change in different countries would turn out. He told us that he believed in the French saying by Jean-Baptiste Alphonse Karr that translates as "The more things change, the more they remain the same."

We went on hikes almost every weekend, often skied together, and spent wonderful vacations in different mountain resorts in Switzerland. I have the distinct memory that once, as a family, we went on a very adventurous hike across a glacier by foot! But our home life was subdued. Our apartment in Bern, sparsely furnished with secondhand furniture and very few pictures hanging on the walls, appeared as if it was not really lived in. It looked like we could pack up our suitcases quickly and be ready to move at a moment's notice. My parents had few friends, and very rarely did anybody come over to our apartment to socialize or share a meal with us. My mother explained that she didn't want to invite anybody because she was ashamed of having such unattractive furniture. I believe that their social isolation was largely self-imposed, as they never felt really integrated into Swiss society, perceiving that almost everybody around them was their enemy because of what they'd encountered in their country of origin. In addition, they were fed stories by a monthly Jewish magazine that frequently focused on antisemitism within Switzerland and other countries. I personally encountered antisemitism a few times in Switzerland and also while travelling in Austria.

My father sat me down one afternoon shortly after my mother's death, when I was approximately seventeen years old, and explained, "We left Russia because there were persecutions, especially during and after the pogroms in Kishinev. Your grandfather Pinkas had

175

to bribe officials in Russia in order to be able to leave and move to Switzerland. This is the reason I am keeping gold coins and diamonds in the bank, so that you and your sister could use them for emergencies, or if Jews in Switzerland would be persecuted, even though this is very unlikely." I didn't put much thought into what my father told me at that age, but it seemed somewhat odd to me to be preoccupied with the danger of being persecuted, so different from what my Swiss friends' parents were concerned about. I regret that I never asked him for more information about the pogroms in Kishinev in 1903 and 1905 and how those events affected his family.

• • •

When I was about to start school, there was an outbreak of polio. While there were vaccinations against polio at that time, my parents didn't want me to get one. Later, I read that in 1955 there were some cases of severe side effects, like paralysis, from this vaccine. I assume, since my father was well-read, that he knew about this and didn't want to take the risk. They were no doubt very protective of me because of their own circumstances. My mother lost so many of her family members in the war and her first child was stillborn. I was my father's first child, born when he was already fifty years old. My parents kept me at home rather than enroll me in kindergarten, where I might be exposed to polio. I could barely leave the house or play with other children because of this epidemic.

When my parents finally permitted me to go to first grade, I was completely unprepared. Despite the importance my parents placed on education, they were so socially isolated they hadn't learned that a child should start school knowing how to count and spell her name. Nor did they know the basics of what a student should wear to school. My mother, who always made my clothes, sent me to school in my best

Shabbat outfit: a fancy red dress and black patent leather shoes with white socks. Everyone else was dressed more typically in regular everyday clothes, their backpacks filled with school supplies.

• • •

In Switzerland, the school year started in spring, and despite an official separation of state and religion, every Christian holiday was integrated into the curriculum. In my first weeks there, we had to count Easter eggs. I had no idea how to count. Every other child was counting off the colorful Easter eggs on the blackboard, and I felt utterly intimidated. Advent and Christmas were also celebrated extensively in my school, with decorated Christmas trees, candles, handmade decorations, songs, and religious plays. I didn't want to sing Christmas songs because my mother had told me, "It is not appropriate for Jews to praise Jesus in songs and poems because we don't believe that he was god." She only allowed my sister and me to sing "Oh, Christmas Tree" because in German we translate it as "evergreen tree." My teacher got angry at me when I refused to sing the songs and I felt excluded and lonely during the Christian holidays. Everybody else had extended families with whom they celebrated the holiday season. I had few Jewish friends, and we had a very small Jewish community living in the city of Bern.

My mother made my envy of what the Christians had even worse for my younger sister and me. She had grown up in Slovakia (at that time part of Czechoslovakia), whose population had strong Catholic beliefs and was very antisemitic, even before World War II. When my mother, my sister, and I were walking through downtown Bern, with the famous arcades and shop windows with beautiful Christmas decorations and Christmas music, she told us with a sigh, "Oh those goyim with their Christmas! Don't look at this—we don't celebrate it. Instead, we have Hanukkah!" But Hanukkah was much less of a big deal than Christmas: just us four in my immediate family, celebrating by lighting one additional candle every evening for a week, saying blessings, singing, and playing dreidel. We exchanged only a few simple gifts. My father was against giving and receiving gifts since they hadn't done it in his family. His attitude was that receiving a gift meant that he owed something to the other person.

I didn't like eating the food my mother cooked because it was so different from what my friends ate at home. Every week a lady came to our house and brought us kosher chicken. We always had the same typical Jewish food: gribenes (fried chicken skin), schmaltz (chicken fat) with bread, chicken soup with noodles, chicken schnitzel, gefilte fish, pickled herring, matzo ball soup, and chremsel (small fried pancakes made with matzo meal or potatoes). Sometimes, I ate at my friends' homes and we ate regularly on Saturdays and sometimes on Sundays in restaurants. We had two wonderful bakeries close to our apartment, and almost every day we bought fresh crispy bread, plus a variety of delicious pastries on the weekend. Frequently, my mother went downtown to a bakery where they had a wood oven, and bought the dark rye bread she was used to eating during her childhood in Kosice. Still, I missed out on baking and eating the delicious Swiss Christmas cookies other families had during the holiday season. Nowadays, I rarely cook Jewish food, but sometimes I bake Swiss Christmas cookies.

My parents reacted strongly against Christian symbols. If they saw a cross somewhere, as jewelry, or even in a fabric pattern or on a carpet in somebody's house, my mother would say, "Ohh, there is a *kreyz* (Yiddish for cross). Don't look at it or touch it!" Unfortunately, there were many church towers with crosses in Switzerland and even the Swiss flag has a cross. We were different than 98.5 percent of the Swiss population and we couldn't trust the Christians, in my parents' view. Christians used to believe that the Jews, instead of the Romans, killed

Jesus and put him on a cross. During the Holocaust, some Jews had to carry crosses when they were sent to the gas chambers.

Throughout my childhood, my parents continued to be very protective of my sister and me. Often, they didn't let us play with other children or do certain activities they considered dangerous. As a teenager, I wanted to take a train to visit a good friend of mine, but my parents forbade it. Only later did I realize that they might have been fearful of me travelling alone by train; it would have reminded them of Jews being transported to the concentration camps.

• • •

It has been very difficult for me to be objective about my mother. I always idealized her, especially because she died young. How could I criticize her or be angry at her since she had experienced so much suffering in her life? During one of her darker moments, we sat in the kitchen of our apartment on the fourth floor. My mother looked out of the window and said with a sigh, "Sometimes I feel like jumping out of this window, but I keep thinking about you and your sister and that keeps me alive." Until now, when writing this memoir, I have kept this painful incident out of my mind. I felt tasked with a heavy responsibility to please her, to prevent her from hurting herself. I tried very hard to read her emotions and to make her happy. This was almost impossible because she criticized almost everything I did.

One day, I had the good intention to help my mother prepare dinner and I started cutting carrots. Instead of thanking and encouraging me for helping, my mother criticized me for how I was holding the knife and cutting the carrots. She immediately took the knife away instead of showing me how to do it differently.

My sister was even more oppositional and didn't follow the rules, such as when we were supposed to be home and when she was allowed to go to friends' houses or not. At times, when she yelled at us for not picking up after ourselves, or making our beds, or doing our homework, we were quite disrespectful of my mother. We said "Stupid cow, I hate you," and other mean things.

My mother lost her temper easily, and in those moments, she became verbally abusive and said horrible things to us, repeating the same language the SS had used in the concentration camp. She called us *mamzers* (Yiddish for bastards) and said, "You should burn in hell and somebody should cut off your tongue." For some reason burning in hell was not a concept that frightened me. Perhaps because this would only happen way in the future, after my death, and we never talked about the concept of hell and heaven in Jewish religious school. Also, I was not very religious. Imagining my tongue cut off really frightened me a lot, though. I was not aware of what *mamzer* meant until later in my life.

Not long ago, I found out that my cousin Nurit had experienced similar abuse from her mother, Elisabeth (my aunt), who also survived the Holocaust. I have been in denial for a long time about my mother's verbal abuse. Expressing anger and being assertive has been difficult for me. I became a very shy and insecure person, perhaps because of my mother being so critical and unpredictable and having such angry outbursts.

I was a poor student and hated school with a passion. Swiss education at that time was run like a military school. The focus was on intimidation, discipline, memorization, and at times corporal punishment if you didn't follow the rules. My father would often suggest that we check out my homework and study together. Sitting on a heavy chair in the dining room, I would respond, "I can't come and study with you because I am glued to the chair and can't move."

My father would say, "Studying for school and acquiring knowledge is the most important thing for us Jews. The goyim took most of our belongings, but one thing they cannot steal, should we be perse-cuted again, is our education and our knowledge."

At that time, this argument was not strong enough for me to go study. I didn't learn easily and might have had an undiagnosed learn-ing disability. I can still hear my father say, "*Brett vorem Kopf*," a Swiss German expression for "thick as a brick." I took it as a joke but also started to believe that I was not smart. Much later in life, after both of my parents' deaths, I finally became more confident. I wanted to pur-sue an advanced degree in social work, but I knew only one instructor at the School of Social Work in Zürich, Switzerland, who had a mas-ter's degree, and it was from the United States. I decided to study for my master's in the United States, where my aunt and her family lived, since we didn't have any graduate studies in this field in Switzerland. I intended to go for just two years, but it has now been almost forty years, since I met my husband, got married, and decided to stay here.

Growing up, my poor school performance was a big disappoint-ment to my mother. She had very high standards for me as her first-born. My mother even had a nervous breakdown after I failed an exam. I felt tremendously guilty, but it also felt impossible to excel because she always criticized me. On top of academic subjects, I was never good enough at cooking and baking, or sewing and knitting, because she prevented me from doing those tasks. As a result, I became dis-couraged and unmotivated.

My mother was a professional seamstress and made beautiful clothes for us and herself. She knitted artful sweaters, hats, and gloves for us children. She was a very good baker of tortes, cakes, and strudel, and was known by the other members of our synagogue for making the best challah bread. She baked all those delicious sweets without ever using a recipe. I missed out on learning how to sew and how to bake all those Eastern European specialties.

Life in Switzerland, a well-functioning democracy, was peaceful and prosperous. We never even went on vacation in a foreign country because my parents always insisted that Switzerland had so much natural beauty, we didn't have to leave it. With all our advantages, though, my mother was sometimes overtaken by melancholy, by her anger at the world. I can still hear to this day her frequent sighs and the Yiddish word *tsouris* (meaning troubles or suffering) coming from her lips. Many times, she would warn my sister and me to remain aware that most human beings were bad and cruel.

Despite my mother's angry outbursts, she and my father were also very loving and affectionate to my sister and me. I believe this helped me to grow up as a relatively normal adult in spite of all the dysfunction: to become resilient, to be curious about improving my knowledge, and to be interested in increasing my self-awareness. I am still working constantly on my personal growth. Our family dynamics helped me develop skills like reading other people's feelings and being sensitive to suffering and injustice in the world. The fact that my parents and their families suffered from the consequences of hate and prejudice motivated me to become a social worker and to be politically active. It made me committed to participating in *Tikkun Olam*, to repairing the world.

• • •

I have never felt nationalistic or patriotic about the countries in which I've lived. Even in Switzerland, my country of birth, I felt like a stranger. I didn't put any effort into learning the words of the Swiss national anthem, which at first had the same melody as the British anthem. Later they changed the words and melody, but it still doesn't sound melodious to my ear. I could not identify with my country of birth since my parents made me believe that we were outsiders and could be driven out of Switzerland at a moment's notice. On the other hand, I loved to sing the Israeli anthem when I participated in

Jewish youth groups. I identified myself more with the Jewish state of Israel, though when I tried to live in Israel for half a year, I found life too stressful. I was twenty years old and was full of idealism about "our" country. I lived in a kibbutz of several hundred people for five months. We shared work and income and learned Hebrew at the Ulpan for intensive study. Unfortunately, though, the kibbutzniks were not very friendly with the "foreigners" and we ended up organizing a protest against them. I only made friends with foreigners, not Israelis. When I took public transportation or went to the movies, I often encountered Israelis' aggressive behavior. They were not willing to stand in line and wait without an argument breaking out against somebody cutting the line or throwing bottles and other objects around in the movie theater.

When I travelled to Israel forty years later, I had the same experience in a museum and at a food stand. Pessimistic about ever having peace with their neighbors, Israelis live in constant fear of being attacked, and thus their aggressive behavior is no doubt linked to their coping within a hostile environment. I am proud of Israel's accomplishments as a young country that is economically prosperous, with advanced technology, good social programs, excellent schools and universities, and a relatively well-functioning democracy compared to other countries in the Middle East. But I prefer the more relaxed lifestyle in the United States and not having to live in constant fear of being attacked by neighboring countries.

When I first arrived in the United States, though, almost forty years ago, I felt like a wandering Jew. After so many years living in this country, I still haven't made any effort to learn how to sing the American national anthem. I cringe if anybody says that the United States is the greatest country because we have the strongest military and have great influence in the world. The frightening authoritarian tendencies of the forty-fifth president and Donald Trump's propensity to ignite hate have sounded to me like echoes of pre-Nazi Germany, of a history that may be repeating itself. During the Third Reich, the intelligentsia—people like Theodor Adorno, Hannah Arendt, Sigmund Freud, and others—escaped the Nazis just in time. They were aware of the danger that the rise of National Socialism posed to freethinking intellectuals, leftists, Jews, and others. But in pre-Nazi Germany, ordinary people were not able to educate themselves about politics as easily as we can today.

In my own family, it was fortunate that one of my cousins was intellectually curious, interested in politics, and well-read. He made sure that he and his brothers left Czechoslovakia in 1938. They immigrated to the United States and escaped Nazi persecution. On a rare occasion of talking about the past, my mother told me that because her family was very orthodox, they heeded their rabbi. He warned them not to immigrate to Israel because the majority of people there were not religious enough. Unfortunately, they listened to this authority and never left Czechoslovakia. The rabbi himself was eventually convinced by his friends to immigrate to Israel just in time, before the Germans invaded. Of my mother's entire family, the only ones who escaped death in the Holocaust were my mother and one of her sisters, and their cousins who educated themselves. My mother credited her survival to her sister, who was a very strong, optimistic, and clever person. She worked in the kitchen in Auschwitz and was able to smuggle food to my mother when she was sick and weak and wanted to give up living.

My mother also related to me a very positive picture of the American military. Both the Russians and the Americans liberated the concentration camp, but in contrast to the Russians, she said, the American soldiers tried to help the concentration camp survivors. My mother particularly credited one American soldier with saving her life. She was ready to die after surviving all those horrors, but this soldier encouraged her to fight and eat. He gave her a piece of chocolate that he saved from his rations. My mother always believed that her sister and this soldier were the main reasons why she survived the Holocaust.

• • •

I only remember a few instances when my mother talked about her experiences in the Holocaust. We didn't have much time to discuss it since I was only sixteen and a half when she died. I continued to also be mostly silent about it until several years ago, when I talked about my family's history in a self-awareness group and later to an old Swiss friend. She was very surprised since I'd never mentioned before that my mother was in a concentration camp. When I joined the Generations After group at our temple, I gained more awareness about the effects of my mother's experience and trauma on me. During these meetings, we discussed how Holocaust survivors, and possibly their children and even grandchildren, may suffer from permanent harmful changes to their brain structure. These findings concerned me a lot and I did not want my son, who was at that time twenty-three years old, to grow up with the same insecurities I had. The first step to healing should involve being open and honest with Jacob, not continuing the pattern of silence and denial in my family.

One night when my son was twenty-four years old, he joined us in the kitchen for dinner. For a change, he even liked the food I prepared. Jacob is a kind, introspective, and opinionated young man, who has acquired a lot of knowledge about history and politics from reading about it on his own since he was approximately thirteen years old. That night he was open to relaxing and interacting with us, so it was a good moment to talk with him about the Holocaust. I got up the courage to ask Jacob about his feelings and concerns as a third-generation descendant of Holocaust survivors.

I began by saying, "I don't remember all the things I've told you about my mother and her experience in the Holocaust."

"You told me that your mother rarely spoke about what happened," Jacob said. "I also remember you said that she had a short temper. Did she ever talk about her specific experiences in Auschwitz?"

I told him she didn't talk much about the horrors she'd experienced, but that she had mentioned a couple of encounters with Nazis who spared her life.

"Your grandfather was an orthodox man, a rabbi, right?" Jacob said.

I explained, "He was a *Melamed*, a teacher in a *cheder*, a Jewish school where the basics of Judaism and Hebrew language were taught. He made a very meager income and sometimes the parents of his students bartered food for the fee for school."

Jacob, who is attentive but doesn't express much emotion, told me that he also remembered this: "Your mother had five sisters but only one sister, Elisabeth, survived the concentration camp."

I asked him, "Do you remember much about Aunt Elisabeth?" She had died a few years before.

"Yes, I especially remember her two children, my cousins, who used to live in Israel and then moved to the United States. I like my cousins Moti and Nurit! Unfortunately, we have not much family left from your side, Mom."

"Does this bother you?" I asked him.

"Yes, and also, you are older parents and I worry about you dying."

Since middle school, he has mentioned this fear of being left alone without any family. It is one of the fates of Holocaust survivors that we have little family left.

Since March 2020 when the pandemic started, Jacob has been living with us because he lost his job. One evening I showed him a YouTube video by the Jewish musician Tom Lehrer, singing "National

Brotherhood Week" in 1967: "The Protestants hate the Catholics and the Catholics hate the Protestants . . . the Hindus hate the Moslems. The Moslems hate the Hindus . . . and everybody hates the Jews."

We both believe that these lyrics might be partly true. We wonder aloud together, why have the Jews been persecuted, over and over again, for thousands of years?

Again, I bring up my mother's experience in the Holocaust. I let Jacob know that I regret never finding out the details of how my mother's family was murdered. I imagine that most of them died in the gas chambers in Auschwitz. After my mother's death, my sister told me that Mom's oldest sister Miriam had survived the concentration camp and was brought to Sweden, but died shortly afterwards. I always wondered why my mother had never told me that, and only shared it with my sister.

Jacob agrees with me that under the Trump administration, with the rise of right-wing extremism, antisemitism increased significantly. It is his belief that Israel exists mostly because of the Holocaust and that it is a bulwark against antisemitism. The proof for him is that there haven't been any pogroms or massacres of Jews since the State of Israel was formed. Israel's presence makes him feel more secure. He supports the country at any price, in spite of all its flaws, and even thinks of making aliyah one day. He has never expressed much interest in Judaism as a religion, so I am surprised how strongly he identifies with the State of Israel after spending just a couple of months there. Three years ago, he travelled with the Birthright Israel program that allows Jewish young people from all over the world to tour Israel free of cost. In addition to this experience, he also travelled by himself and stayed for a month at Kibbutz Lotan.

In the past, I hadn't put much thought into how my being a second-generation Holocaust survivor could even impact my son. Now, I know that I was continuing with a similar pattern of denial as my parents. I felt so much better after being more open with him about what it means to be the next generations of Holocaust survivors, and I want to keep having this conversation. I feel good that Jacob is not reluctant to talk about our family's history and am reassured that he identifies with how important it is for Jews to have their own state, that he is inclined to protect it in some way or other if its existence is threatened.

Sensitive to other groups' suffering too, he tells me, "It is not only the Jews who have been persecuted and murdered! There have been other genocides and mass killings since the Holocaust: the killing of 1.5–3 million Cambodians by the Khmer Rouge, the massacre of eight hundred thousand Tutsis by the Hutus in Rwanda, the genocide of eight thousand Muslims by Serbian soldiers in Srebrenica in Bosnia-Herzegovina, and the destruction of a country and their people in Syria, which is happening right now."

Jacob reflects, "The difference is, perhaps, that for the Jews it has been happening again and again over thousands of years because they were considered parasites. They didn't have their own country and couldn't defend themselves. They were also forced into the money business. The fact that some people owed them money made them very unpopular."

I'm proud that my son is so thoughtful and continues to educate himself. Discussing these events with him has made me even more aware of the importance of learning, remembering, and sharing our history with one another. I've come to believe that if we acknowledge our discomfort with our past, and if we speak out about the cause and effects of those horrible genocides, we can create powerful actions to prevent the terrible consequences of hate and future massacres of people. The third generation is our hope!

• • •

Perhaps my aversion to feeling patriotism—for Switzerland, the United States, or any other country—is a result of my underlying fear of being "the other." For a long time, I felt helpless that as a member of a minority I could be persecuted, and that antisemitism could rear its ugly head again. I finally decided I did not want to be a bystander and started becoming politically active. I participated in both Barack Obama's and Hillary Clinton's presidential campaigns. I became aware of how much my state of Michigan had been gerrymandered by the Republicans and got involved in the successful initiative by a grassroots organization, "Voters not Politicians," to establish a citizen-led independent commission to redraw the district lines. The 2020 presidential election was the most important work to me for saving our democracy. Being elected a precinct delegate forced me to do everything I could to play an active role in the campaign: texting, leaving door hangers with voter information, sending emails, serving as a greeter at the polls.

My school friend from Switzerland, who saw me again after twenty years, assured me that I was more outspoken than I used to be, not anymore the shy wallflower I'd been in high school. I told her, "I realized that I did not have to stay an outsider, that I could overcome my denial and discomfort by speaking out." With the awareness passed down to me from my parents of how devastating it is to live as part of a minority group under an authoritarian leader, I told her, "I cannot be silent!"

11

Chesed

Simone Yehuda, daughter of Walter Juda

Renée and Walter Juda, Paris, c. 1940

My full name is Simone Naomi Patoute Juda Press Yehuda Shapiro. Each of these names carries a history from my families' cultural, psychological, and religious heritage. In relating some of that history here, I've included some of my poetry because I found early on that the intensity of my emotions could best be contained in verse. As a victim of massive psychic trauma, I needed to express unbearable pain in an acceptable way so as not to fall apart or alienate others.

Simone comes from my French Catholic mother, and Naomi from my German Jewish father. My nickname Patoute is a result of the first words my father uttered when he first saw me at the hospital: "*Mais elle n'est pas toute*" [But she's not all there]. Because of the many ways I was treated differently from my three brothers, I came to realize that, from my father's point of view, because I was a female, I wasn't a whole person. This was no doubt due to my father's Orthodox background where, in many ways, women barely register on the radar screen. Unfortunately, my American and French families, friends, classmates, teachers, and neighbors called me Patoute until I graduated from college, when I first realized what this name meant:

Not Whole.

EXILE

a sonnet with an interruption

At birth I was cast as anti-matter.
    "She's a girl.
    My child's a girl,
    not the wild-eyed boy
    of alchemy, posterity,
    my loins had promised me."

The projectile of my name flew from white
rose lips to my new limbs, binding anger
with sheer frail sight so well: a dizzy light,
became the cure for flight as remedy
for false smiles. Steps taken in sleek *galut*—
exile of Jew from self, the slow journey
toward certainty, rare earth's floor—took root.
So I turned my back on flight, the frowning
life preservers of everlasting song,
silver bracelets, amethyst wings crowning
the sweet rare salute to right over wrong.
Until my lungs bled black as newborn hair,
I couldn't stitch the robe I was meant to wear.

    Juda is my father's last name and thus my maiden name. Press is my kind and generous first husband's last name, and the last name of our twin daughters Corinna Nicole and Valerie Gabriella. I took the Hebrew version of my maiden name when Steve and I were divorced. Shapiro is my second husband Barry's last name. How fortunate I am to have met my soulmate, whose passion and depth have brought me so much happiness.

While in graduate school in New York, I realized I was crying every time I was alone and that this was unusual behavior. How could I have been unaware that I had been living with unbearable pain for so long? I sought the help of a therapist, the first of three, as it turned out. She helped me hold it together until I received a Master's degree in English and Comparative Literature from Columbia University.

I was well into my thirties, married with children, when I began to work with my second therapist. A strict Freudian, he allowed us some leeway in trying to assess the extent of my issues. However, a lawsuit had been filed against Blue Cross Blue Shield on behalf of Detroit's Psychoanalytic Institute (DPI) in an effort to retain coverage for its patients. My analyst asked me to testify on its behalf. This was the first time I ever spoke publicly about being the child of a Holocaust survivor and the devastation imposed on me by my family history.

IN CAMERA[1]

In a judge's chamber for the first time,
I speak aloud in company of the law.
The private recorder takes down
all that is private and public, her eyes
Startled, anxious, moving from face to face.

And I, the witness to my own promise,
confess fully before her, watch her type
the beginning of my story.

I came to tell you this really happened:
a child outside of the horizons of all
horizons, any moment spent beloved.
I am not sure yet why I have
decided to stand arm in arm
with life itself.

Although, in our work together, we examined everything in excruciating detail, we never discussed the impact testifying had on me. And, although the judge's final determination included grandfathering in those already receiving coverage, this ended any further help from him. I still had a long way to go in the healing process.

It had been important to my father before he married her that my mother complete her conversion to Judaism. A full ceremony conducted by an Orthodox rabbi took place in Jerusalem so that their children could be raised as Jews, and thus ensure a "generation after." My mother's mother, Blanche Devaux Molino, used personal connections to secure safe passage in late 1939 for my father and her youngest daughter Renée (my mother) on one of the last boats to leave from Le Havre en route to the United States. They settled in Cambridge, Massachusetts, where my father obtained a position at Harvard, having received his PhD in Chemistry from the Université de Lyon. My mother found work as a teacher at Wellesley College. They married in 1940 and started a family of their own. I was born first, then my three brothers: Daniel Peter, David Eric, and Benjamin Robert.

Not only did my French grandmother braid radiant silk bows in my hair, but she had been an important leader in the French Resistance in Lyon. She protected and saved my dad's life and many others, including Marc Block, the famous French historian. Thanks to her, and due to research currently being conducted by such scholars as Carole Fink and Cindy Biesse, new information is coming to light about the

Grandmother Blanche Molino with Simone Juda, South of France, 1953

participants in the French Resistance, their methods and the obstacles they encountered while combatting the vicious antisemitism of the Vichy government.

My grandmother damaged my mother in many ways, most of which I still do not understand. Nonetheless, I feel blessed to also possess some of their best qualities: a joy of life, a sense of humor, a passion for social justice, and the need to attempt, in whatever ways possible, to fight for the most vulnerable among us. When I visited Blanche's home in the summer of 2018, I saw for myself the intricate web of alleyways and safe houses that were used to protect and hide so many, at great risk to herself and her family. In a 2019 trip to Israel, I was able to witness Blanche's name inscribed on Jerusalem's Yad Vashem Wall of Honor as one of the "Righteous Among the Nations." I am extremely proud of her and this heritage.

Blanche and her family had suffered great loss when both of her sons (my uncles) died, possibly by suicide, initiating a series of suicides that occurred over the years, first with the suicide of my cousin Jean René Molino, then my youngest brother Ben, and finally my mother.

LESSON LEARNED

for Ben

What is it about death that makes its
way through sleepless hours, the daily threads
of bliss now soiled because he's gone? And soon,
yes, memory will melt like children's sight,
the roughage of years' and years' delight now
submerged, wasted, lost as night's withdrawal
into day then lost again, swallowed by
his silent, secret, shameful loss of breath.

While he was with us, the effortless rhythm
of our limbs clung to a well-being which
now, in hind-sight, was either undeserved
or blind, even weary without measure;
Remember, then, once and for all: each and
every one of us, today sure-footed,
can lose the balance upon which we place
our hopes, the fabric of dreams, our lives.

• • •

My father, Walter Mendelssohn Kempinski Juda, came to know
my maternal grandmother because she ran a school under whose aus-
pices she assisted those in need during World War II. One day in 1933,
my physician grandfather, Adolf Juda, received word that a patient's
son had been stoned to death in a schoolyard. Fearing for the life of
his own son, that very night, and against his wife's wishes, he put my
seventeen-year-old father on a train to Switzerland. From there, Walter
traveled to Lyon, where Blanche sheltered him, helped him complete
his education as a chemist, and managed to extricate him from a trau-
matizing French detention camp where he and other detainees were
slated to be returned to Germany and the camps. My father told me
stories about how he and another man had to bury themselves underground and breathe through reeds of straw when German guards
arrived to round them up.

My father's career soared. He built his first company, Ionics, where
he developed the award-winning membrane process of changing salt
water to fresh water for Israel. Though my father was much more successful professionally, his scientific inventions a legacy unto themselves, my mother's gifts of wit and insight graced all who knew her. Yet

my parents' legacy of exile and grief, survival and despair, resulted in an odd identification with both oppressor and oppressed. This marred their remarkable accomplishments, their capacity for happiness, and their children's well-being.

In a horrifying echo of the use of gas in the camps, my mother would sometimes punish me by putting me in the shower and turning on fiercely hot water followed by freezing cold water. She would also sometimes attack me in my sleep and, like the Germans who watched the Nazis do their grisly work, my father would witness what she was doing to me and simply walk away.

In other words, both my parents suffered from unacknowledged mental illness. Whether this was due to their upbringing, the nature of the personalities they were born with, or the after-effects of Holocaust-related trauma is unknown. Suffice it to say, my father was a narcissist incapable of loving anyone other than himself and my mother was quite possibly a schizophrenic. My childhood and my brothers' childhoods were severely damaged as a result.

THE YEAR OUR MOTHER DIED
for my brothers

The wind on the hill of our birth
blew low on her last night on earth.
Our hands could never quite reach her.
Hers, around our throats, never stirred,
though our eyes, ever rising moons,
swept down, up and around like spoons
digging, digging for swells of air
that just once might have kept us there.
We learned too late what could have been:
dizzy shelters for us to win.

She could have found a strong belief,
chose instead to choke the gift of grief.
So we still endure her boundless blows
and long for all she shunned, for love's repose.

It was as an adult that I first began to be aware of how the Holocaust had affected me. Like many children of survivors, I was suffering from the toxic effects of unresolved trauma caused by the Holocaust: for my father directly as a refugee from Hitler, and for my mother indirectly as a refugee from Hitler, as she was forced into exile from her beloved France and family.

As is often the case with post traumatic stress disorder (PTSD), I was in no way aware of the causes of my grief—nor of its debilitating and too often misunderstood effects. Thanks to my ability to dissociate, I had always somehow achieved a very high level in school, had many friends, published books of poetry, performed in a dance company called Mass Transit, played the flute with a New York City symphony orchestra, produced plays, married and had beautiful twin daughters. However, it was not long after my daughters left for college that I realized I was feeling alarmingly self-destructive. In desperation, I made an appointment to meet with a doctor in the Detroit area, himself a survivor of several concentration camps and death marches. When I first walked into his office, Dr. Henry Krystal took one look at me and said, "You've come to the right place."

I knew Dr. Krystal was an expert in massive psychic trauma and had treated hundreds of survivors. When I first heard him speak at a conference, I'd noticed that his face had the same frozen mask of pain that I had seen on Elie Wiesel's face when I invited him to the university where I taught. But when I entered Dr. Krystal's office years later, his face displayed no traces of the severe damage I had witnessed earlier. I could see for myself that he had successfully healed himself.

My work with Dr. Krystal over the next several years saved my life in more ways than one. His compassion, generosity, and expertise helped me to identify the serious impediments to reconciliation with my thus far unspoken heritage. I learned that trauma has its own detrimental effects independent from whatever psychological difficulties plague us. It was such a shock when he told me that I was the worst case he had ever dealt with. I should have asked him what he meant. I assumed it was that the severity, depth, and thoroughness of the trauma I experienced over the course of my entire childhood had resulted in a kind of brainwashing that was unusually difficult for him to help me recover from.

He taught me that it's love, and love alone—*chesed*, loving kindness—that can heal the wounds of soul murder. His desire and ability to heal himself and others after unimaginable cruelty and torture embody my highest ideals, and have made it possible for me to work toward being the kind of person—woman, wife, mother, friend, and citizen—I most aspire to be.

RABBI

a sonnet for Henry Krystal

When I first saw you speaking long ago,
the paralyzing pain which numbed your cheeks
reminded me of rescue far too slow,
sinking into history's eyes, like weeks,

no, years of sorrow etched in ancient grief.
Much later, when I came to you alone,
the thorns of my internal war's beliefs
had swamped my arteries with hearts of stone.

My lungs, akin to drowning, cramped within,
were chasms of a judgment dark and grim.
Determined that I was a child of sin,
My life's sad cup had overflown its brim.

Never, never will I forget your face:
Your voice, your eyes that healed me with such grace.

For the first time in 2016, I was able to visit the home of my father's childhood in Berlin. We stayed at the astonishing Adlon Kempinski Hotel, which had been established by my father's maternal grand-mother, Amalia Kempinski, as a family business many years earlier. Though the hotel and restaurant were stolen by the Nazis, it miracu-lously retained our family name. We were treated like royalty. Thanks to my father's one and only return to Berlin in the 1980s, a plaque was placed on the front wall outside the Kempinski Bristol Hotel (the Adlon Kempinski's sister hotel in Berlin).

I am grateful I could finally go back to visit my father's home without fear of the pain I suffered at his hands, or my prior paralyzing awareness of Germany's role in the Holocaust. The heroism and drama of my parents' Holocaust histories had resulted in incredibly tragic consequences for my family. My brothers and I bore the brunt of my parents' unresolved anguish.

A RONDEAU TERCET FOR MY PARENTS

Because the walls of my home were lined with grief,
since from birth to marriage and motherhood
exile's currents overshadowed the good,
I well understood the world without peace

my dear parents endured, fled, and withstood,
struggling to keep hold of strength and belief,
fighting hard for the hope, however brief,
of the dream of love tangible as wood.

I prayed for their souls, did all that I could,
left nothing unturned, not a single leaf,
but the wound had done its job as a thief
so even sharing my protective hood
would alas, for them, provide no relief.

In raising my daughters, I was fortunate to have learned from my abusive childhood not to repeat the damage done to me. Although I am sure that having a mother in unbearable pain a great deal of the time was no picnic for them, I have always loved and supported them with all my heart. Most importantly, I have always done—and will continue to do—everything in my power to seek all the help available to me. I wanted to heal, I fought to heal, and I still wish to heal. I have learned that healing is possible and that it is my life's work.

This is what Dr. Krystal taught me. It is thanks to him, in part, that I now have a wonderful life. I am happy and in love with my husband Barry. I'm the mother of two beautiful and thriving daughters. I'm a writer of serious poetry, with two published books. Several of my plays have been produced, and two of my screenplays have been recommended to producers and managers. Blessed with friends, I'm active in a variety of social action groups, sing in two choirs, and teach creative writing and French to those who wish to elevate their skills.

What I most want to honor is that we, the "generation after," have the blessed and miraculous opportunity to serve as antidotes to the "grief beyond measure" caused by what is forever lost. By facing our own sadness and loss, we give ourselves and others the opportunity to heal. By coming together in community, we show ourselves and others that yes, we are really here. And because we remain, because we try to connect with each other, we can embody the joy of joy, survival, and prayer in the face of all odds. We are living proof that it is a true gift to celebrate, witness, and remember the past, as well as face the present and future, together.

RECIPE FOR SURVIVAL

"A labor of love is what's called for,"
my grandmother said because of my tears.
"Think of this and what you adore,
not the memory of the countless jeers
you and your ancestors faced each time
no mercy was shown at your enemies' hands.
Holding fast to hope, its sweet light sublime,
is all you'll need, what survival demands.
Hear me now and forever. Hear me well.
Think of the stories you will tell."

12

If Only

Eszter Gombosi, daughter of Julianna (Juci)
and István (Pista) Gárdos

Juci and Pista Gárdos, Pécs, Hungary, 1962

My father used to say: "If only the Americans had been more helpful, the family could have survived." It almost sounded as if he blamed the Americans for the murders of his parents, in-laws, and child more than he did the Germans, or the Hungarians for that matter. I think he considered the complicity of his fellow citizens and the atrocities committed by the Germans as a given, but held the Americans responsible for not taking a more active role in rescuing and helping the victims. I would agree, and history agrees as well.

I don't have any statistics for this, but my belief is that the vast majority of Jews who survived the Holocaust did so by accident, sheer luck, by totally random circumstances, not because they were helped by righteous people. The masses were Nazi sympathizers, and even if they didn't openly cheer the grave fate of their countrymen, they turned a blind eye or agreed silently with what was going on. This is well documented in the literature. While there are examples of people saved in monasteries or other religious institutions or hidden by brave Gentiles, for each saved Jew there were many who had been betrayed and sent to their death by their Nazi sympathizer neighbors, former business partners, and others.

In their hometown, my parents' friends had a newborn baby just when the Nazis overtook Hungary. The mother, in her desperation, took the baby to the nuns and begged them to take her, but the head nun slammed the door in her face. The mother, the baby, and their older son perished in Auschwitz. The father survived and was a deeply scarred person for the rest of his life. When I was growing up, I heard this story from my parents over and over again. They also told me the story of how the population of the town lined the streets cheering as the Jews were herded into the ghetto. Before all this happened, these people had been their fellow citizens, clients, business partners, and acquaintances. Nobody stepped up to say anything, let alone offer a glass of water or a piece of bread.

There is no positive or uplifting message to be taken from the Holocaust. It happened to millions of Jews, to our families, for no reason other than that they were Jews. I worry that some of the sentiments that allowed the Holocaust to happen are present today, are present in America. It is of utmost importance to stand up against the forces of discrimination and persecution, the vilification of groups considered "other." So, here is another chance, America. Let no father rightly tell his child down the road that if Americans had acted to stop the pain of someone considered "other," everything would now be different for their family.

• • •

According to my father's cousin, Vera, my brother Miklós was all smiles. Vera was eighteen years younger than my father and survived Auschwitz as a nineteen-year-old girl. As a toddler, little Miklóska had pronounced cheeks, and looked very much like my father. Vera often played with him while my mother gave private French lessons to her students.

In May 1944, my mother with Miklóska, her mother, and my father's parents were herded into the ghetto. By that time my father had been in forced labor for two years. He only saw his son for two months when he was able to return home in the spring of 1943 before he got conscripted again. My maternal grandfather, a prominent lawyer, was deported to Mauthausen earlier, together with other leaders of their community. He perished there by the time the rest of his

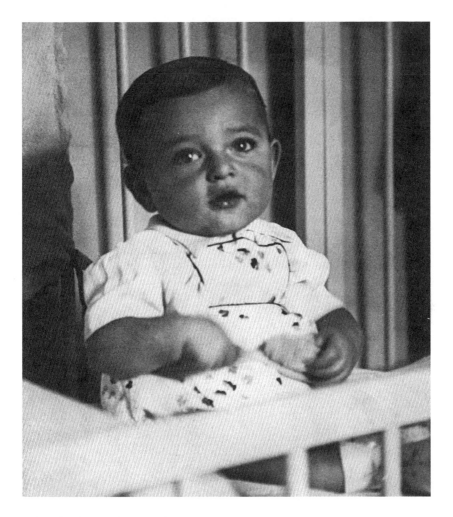

Infant brother, Miklós Gárdos, Pécs, Hungary, 1943

family was packed into the cattle cars to Auschwitz on the fourth of July, 1944. Upon arrival on the platform in Auschwitz/Birkenau, the kapos told everyone with young children to give them to the old. My mother gave her firstborn, Miklóska, to her mother, who, she learned later, carried him in her arms to the gas chamber. My mother never talked to me about Miklóska, other than to share how he perished. She referred to him as "the child," never by name. My parents' tragic losses didn't seem to completely overtake their lives, but I am sure they never recovered. My mother became an excessive smoker, seemingly wanting to harm her health, attempting to drown her grief in this self-destructive behavior. Smoking damaged most of her internal organs and she had an untimely death at age seventy-six.

My father survived forced labor and returned from the east in the fall of 1944. Shortly thereafter he was deported to Dachau where he was kept as a prisoner until a day before liberation. When he spoke about his wartime experiences, he always concentrated on the humorous incidents of his forced labor service and very seldom did he mention anything gruesome. This was his way of dealing with his losses. In one such incident he recounted, the whole battalion suffered from dysentery after eating crab apples. They all got sickened until one of the more humane guards shared some spicy Hungarian salami with them, after which they all got cured.

Along with a few other prisoners, my father was commanded to dig his own grave when an air-raid came and the guards ran away. My father escaped to the farm of some peasants, who gave him shelter and food. He kept a little diary, where he described in great detail the food he got, how much of it he ate and how happy it made him. He weighed about eighty-five pounds when he was liberated. He showed this diary to me once, toward the end of his life, completely out of the blue, and we never discussed it.

I have often wondered what it would be like to have an older brother. Perhaps he would be the doctor or lawyer who could have fulfilled my parents' wishes. They wanted me to study medicine or law so that I could stay home, as the small Hungarian town of Pécs only had a medical school and a law school. In order to study mathematics and physics I had to attend university in the capital, Budapest, where there was a school of natural sciences as well.

If I had an older brother I might have nieces and nephews now, and my children would have some cousins on their mother's side. I imagine my brother and I would have a keen understanding of each other, based on our common background and genetic composition. He might tick the same way I do, have similar ways of reacting to life's challenges. We might like similar things: the same music, books, and people.

• • •

My mother had a brilliant mind. She would have liked to be a chemist but because of the policy of *numerus clausus* (the number of Jews accepted at universities had to be proportional to their number in the general population) and later *numerus nullus* (no Jews were accepted at most Hungarian universities), she had no chance of attending the Technical University. So she settled for German and French literature; and she was lucky to be able to study at all. Most of the Jewish youth had to go abroad in the thirties because no Hungarian university would accept their applications. My mother got her PhD in 1939. She spoke German almost at the native level and also spoke excellent French, having studied at the Sorbonne. While in Paris, she had a British roommate who invited her to spend some time in England. That's how she picked up English, though it was her weakest foreign language.

Upon liberation by American troops, my mother gave a talk to them about her experiences. My assumption is that the troops questioned the liberated prisoners for testimony, and my mother, as studious as she was, volunteered to write up her vivid memories of the atrocities. Not many of her peers would have known enough English to do something like that. A copy of her essay now resides in the United States Holocaust Memorial Museum. This excerpt from it describes the three weeks my mother spent in Auschwitz-Birkenau:

Upon arrival, we were unloaded onto a platform lit by strong floodlights. There stood a tall and good-looking German officer and I suddenly felt him grabbing my shoulder and throwing me to the left, almost causing me to fall. My mother holding my baby son remained on the right and disappeared. I tried to return to them and felt only a shock on my head as I was slung back.

From this moment, things happened quickly and like in a factory. We went to a building, where we had to undress and leave everything we had, and then some girls shaved our hair. We arrived in a shower and after that we got some ragged clothes and got a red stripe painted on our backs. We could not recognize each other when we met again.

Three weeks followed then, what I can hardly remember. All of us were almost crazy. We slept in barracks, where it was raining in, on the naked earth, without blankets, crowded, about twelve hundred women in one room. At three o'clock in the morning, we were awakened and had to line up immediately. It was a hard climate at this place, in the morning everything was frozen, by day hot to suffer. In the morning at the first *Zaehl-Appel*, we were standing in lines for three or four hours and were counted over and over again. After that we sometimes got some drops of coffee or vegetable tea. At ten o'clock, we had to stand again, and got our only meal. I cannot describe what it was. Some raw vegetables in water, cold, little, tasting terribly. The first days we could not eat it at all.

As we heard afterwards, the bad taste came from medicine, bromide used to tranquilize us so we would not go crazy and make trouble over the loss of our mothers and babies. As a result we always felt to be half in a dream. When we did not have to stand, we were lying on the ground, in the dust, just lying, without speaking or thinking.

My mother was shipped to the German town of Lippstadt, where she was made to perform forced labor in an ammunition factory. She described how the workers sabotaged their products—endangering their own lives to assert an act of resistance against the Nazis, to hinder the war effort:

> We learned our work in one day, but we learned how to sabotage it in two hours. Quickly we discovered the weak points of our machines and tried to break them down so that the repair lasted through the entire workday. The munitions we manufactured we tried to sabotage, too. They were a little bit too long or too short, the holes in them were not at the right places. It was not too obvious, but it rendered the ammunition useless. The Russian, Polish, and Italian workers in quality control cheated for our sakes so we wouldn't be discovered.

• • •

After nine months of hard labor in the ammunition factory, the war ended and my mother was liberated. I often heard her share this story of her liberation to friends and family. "A girlfriend and I were walking down the main street of the little town soon after we had just become free, when a tall Black American soldier came toward us with a huge butcher's knife pulled out of his pocket. We were incredibly scared, having never seen such a large man, nor a Black man. We thought that after we had survived the horrors and hardships of deportation, hard labor, and starvation, now we would have to die when we had just been liberated."

Every time she repeated this story my mother seemed incredulous about what happened next. "The American soldier walked up to us smiling. He cut the yellow star off our shirts with the big knife and gave us chocolates and cigarettes."

With this small act of kindness, they felt the soldier gave them back some of the dignity that they'd been robbed of throughout their darkest years of persecution and torture.

• • •

My parents' journey out of the darkness of the Holocaust started when my father, Pista Gárdos, having been liberated from Dachau, found my mother's name on a list of survivors in German displaced persons (DP) camps and set out to find her. This was in May of 1945. My parents had been married on December 24, 1938. Their marriage ended up lasting for almost fifty-four years, until the passing of my mother on September 24, 1992.

When they were reunited, my parents made the fateful decision to return to Hungary so they could wait for their parents and child to come back home. They made this decision in spite of the fact that they were residing in the American Zone and had an affidavit to immigrate to America from an uncle in New York who had lived there since the early 1900s. When I heard this as a young person I imagined that, had she come to the United States, my mother would have become a professor at Columbia. In Hungary she ended up earning two additional university degrees to become employable in the communist regime. German and French were not desired at the time. She learned Russian quickly, memorizing more than sixty new words a day. Her first job was as a librarian at the library of foreign language books. While on the job, she enrolled at the College of Library Science and earned a degree. This position, however, did not satisfy her ambitions, so after working for a decade as a librarian, at about the age of forty-five, she enrolled in the College of Literature and the Arts and earned a master's degree in Russian literature. This enabled her to take a position as lecturer of Russian at the Teacher's College. She retired as vice president of the Teacher's College at age fifty-eight. At the time the official retirement age for women in Hungary was fifty-five.

My father was a lawyer which is not a portable profession, and I don't believe he would have had the motivation to start his studies over again had he immigrated to the United States. His language skills were not great. If he had come to America, he said, he would have become a painter. He added that he meant a house painter, not an artist. I always suspected that my parents used the fact that my father would not have been able to work as a lawyer in America as an excuse for not immigrating. I don't think they ever really considered it, not even during the darkest days of communism.

After the war my parents returned to their apartment in Pécs, only to find that other people were living there and using their furniture, their dishes, all the possessions they had left behind. My father threw them out, and he and my mother settled back in to their apartment and waited.

Neither their parents nor Miklóska ever came back.

And they experienced yet another trauma before I was born. In 1946 they had another son, Gyuri, who, as a result of medical malpractice, died at four months. This second son was mentioned even less than the first one—all I know is that he existed and died almost immediately. After this my mother was said to have been ill with fever until I was born two years later.

In the late 1990s, after I had already been an American citizen for some years, and after both my parents had passed away, I went back to my town of birth and obtained the birth certificates of both brothers along with the death certificate of the second son (there are no death certificates for the victims of the Holocaust), so that there is proof of their existence. These documents, residing in the safety deposit box at my bank, now complement the birth, marriage, and death certificates of my parents, thus standing as an official record of our family.

• • •

The next phase of my parents' journey was another unhappy chapter, as they had to live under communist rule and put up with continued antisemitism, though it was more covert. My parents went from being apolitical to becoming believers in the Soviet system, and that's how they raised me. Since everything before had only brought devastation, they felt that the only way was this new way. Perhaps this coping mechanism completely closed their minds off to all the faults of the new regime and the atrocities it committed, allowing them to become productive members of the society they had to live in. This is the only explanation I can find since they both were highly educated, very intellectual people, and they interacted with many friends and acquaintances who were critical of the Soviet era. Even when the Berlin Wall came down in the late 1980s, they had a very hard time seeing it as a positive change. It took coming to the United States for me to fully see all this and try to make sense of it from their perspective. Before that, I had never known anything other than communist propaganda and didn't have the opportunity to think for myself about the ills of society behind the Iron Curtain.

• • •

On the surface, in Hungary, my parents were able to give me a more or less normal upbringing. Our family life was warm, nurturing, and intellectually stimulating. At the same time, my parents always acted as though they were anticipating something bad would happen, to one of us or in life in general, where their livelihood could be endangered or they could be displaced again. They had no doubts about the "if," only about the "when." Though understandable in light of what they had gone through, this constant fear cast a deep shadow in my parents' home. A veil of sadness and anxiety enveloped our family.

Eating, for example, was a constant subject of lament when I was young. I was a naturally slender child with a slight appetite. My parents worried that I was too thin and never wanted to eat. I regularly brought my school snack home untouched. Though they gave up saying anything about it after a while, my parents still packed me a snack every single day of school. At home, as afternoon snack time approached, I remember making my way out to our garden and climbing high up in the branches of my favorite walnut tree, hiding where no one could see me. This tree was supposedly my age, planted when I was born, and I felt a certain kinship with it. As a child, I always wondered why the tree grew so much taller than I did. I vividly remember hearing our house-keeper hollering at me to eat my snack as I deliberately ignored her call.

For some reason I particularly hated hot chocolate. I could be seen pouring my hot chocolate into the sewer; it didn't fool anyone when I went back into the house and triumphantly showed my empty cup to a grownup as proof that I had drunk it all. My behavior bordered on criminal, since in postwar Hungary cacao was virtually non-existent, and we possessed this treasured food thanks only to occasional packages from my mother's uncle who had immigrated to the United States. My distaste for hot chocolate has stayed with me to this day.

To my parents' credit, they did not make me dread mealtimes or force me to eat. But they constantly expressed their views on my eating, or rather, not eating and my low body weight, to me and to anyone who would listen. They were terribly afraid that the lack of nutrition would make me susceptible to deadly illnesses, and they would lose me. Interestingly, though, I was a very healthy and sturdy child. I was sick much less often than my well-nourished classmates, and I did exceptionally well in school, so my brain must have been getting enough nutrition at the time. This whole eating issue was completely physical for me, and not at all any kind of resistance or rebellion on my part. I was a very obedient child and had only a handful of arguments with my parents, which they always won. But I remember that often I felt so paralyzed during a meal that I was unable to chew or swallow. I just sat there holding food in my mouth until it felt completely sour. I still get goosebumps when I think of this.

My parents' protectiveness toward me verged on the hysterical. They did not permit me to do the kinds of things that other children could do. When I progressed in ballet class to a session that ran until 9:00 p.m., I had to leave at 8:00 because my parents insisted that I be home by then. They were constantly petrified that I would catch a cold. On the March 15 holiday commemorating the 1848 Revolution, it was already spring weather, and every other girl wore a skirt and knee-high socks. My mother never let me go in a skirt; I had to wear long pants to protect against the weather. I was very upset, but never did anything behind her back in defiance.

I explain all this behavior in terms of intergenerational trauma. I often thought as a young adult that even though I was born several years after the end of the war, my genes were somehow in Auschwitz and in Dachau. Now we know that epigenetic research shows trauma can be written into DNA and carried down to the next generation.

As a result, I carried a similar fear with respect to my own children's well-being. I got overly agitated when they were sick, which happened all the time when they were little. We called the pediatrician at every sniffle—doctors made house calls in Hungary. I was also overly concerned with their hygiene and dressing for the temperature. I still have this problem with my grandchildren, which my children and their spouses find laughable. They joke, "Our child put on a sweater because Grandma is cold." My eating habits did normalize during my pregnancies and after the birth of my two children. With them and with my grandchildren, despite my worries, I came to be more easy-going, as I did not want to expose them to my traumatic experience.

• • •

My parents did not have many friends, and almost all of them had been touched by the Holocaust in one way or another. When they got together with the few fellow survivor friends they had, the conversation among them was almost exclusively about their experiences with deportation. As a child, I overheard these conversations constantly and it made a strong impression on me. One friendly couple with a little girl my age (her father was one of my father's colleagues), visited on most Sunday afternoons. The parents had coffee in the living room and exchanged notes about their experiences. The girl and I played in my room with the door open and I remember that my ears were long, drinking up the adult conversation while we played with dolls. I can't remember the exact content of these conversations, but I recall the frequent references to life in the *Lager* (concentration camp) and my father's accounts of forced labor. They made a big impression on me, and I am sure that's how I learned some of the details I've described here.

My parents let me make friends with other children, but there was always a certain apprehension about whether it was safe for me to trust people outside of our tiny family circle. I felt enormous pressure to do well in school. In second grade, I brought home a report card with Bs in penmanship and physical education, and my mother exclaimed, "We do not get Bs!" I grew up to put that pressure on myself in all kinds of things that I did, even in my adult life. I didn't do well with the slightest failure in my work or everyday tasks. During my school years, I was completely unable to handle criticism from my teachers on mistakes made in schoolwork.

My mother told me that on fast days, her father had to eat, because he had Type II diabetes. I didn't know what a fast day was; my mother never said the words "Yom Kippur." My father always bought matzo during Passover. He would crumble it up into his coffee and when he gave me a spoonful, I thought it was delicious. Since it wasn't sold in stores, he would have had to go to the Jewish congregation to buy it, but I never knew the story behind the matzo. I only found out about its significance after coming to the United States at age thirty and learning about Jewish holidays and customs through new friendships and joining a synagogue. My parents raised me mostly unaware of my Jewish heritage out of "protection." We did not observe Jewish holidays; like most Hungarians and many assimilated Hungarian Jews, we celebrated Christmas. I did not receive any religious education.

My parents' wishful thinking was that hiding my Jewishness would erase other people's memory about our family's origins before the war. This did not work though, and everybody always knew and identified us as Jews. We lived in a small town where people knew each other and remembered very well who the Jews were and who came back from deportation. As early as age five, one of my preschool classmates told me that I was stinky. I went home and asked my mother, "Why did she say I was stinky? I take a bath every day." Obviously this child had heard the phrase "dirty Jew" at home. I was always somewhat of a loner and felt that people were looking at me with inquisitive eyes. At the time I thought it was because of my eminence in school. I was always first in my class, with an impeccable report card. I won or placed high on district competitions in mathematics and physics. Now that I am conscious of my Jewishness, which I was not as a child and young adult in Hungary, I know this wasn't the only reason people seemed to look at me differently. They put us Jews under a magnifying glass, examining how we lived, whom we were friends with, and what the secrets of our successes were, probably thinking that those stinky Jews were getting ahead again.

• • •

I think I see my parents' lives in a sadder light than they did. They considered themselves to have successfully integrated into Hungarian society. On the surface they seemed to have overcome the trauma they experienced. Even after my father was imprisoned in the early 1950s over false charges filed against Jewish lawyers by gentile members of their lawyers' association, my parents did not acknowledge the antisemitism rooted in communist Hungarian society. They made very strong efforts to fit in but I think they always looked over their shoulders for warning signs of imminent ostracization and persecution. They led me to believe that they never suffered discrimination because they were Jews. I now know that this was not entirely true. My mother was passed up for promotion a couple of times and, in spite of her excellence, she had to have very strong and influential political supporters (some Jewish friends who were in the position of power) to be able to get ahead professionally.

In retrospect, I view their entire life experience as double jeopardy: first wronged by Hitler, and then again by communism.

• • •

It took the journey of the next generation, namely, myself and my family, to make the move that my parents should have made thirty-plus years before. My husband and I came to the United States in 1979, after he spent an extended period of time at the Soviet Institute of Space Research in Moscow, observing the first spacecraft to orbit a planet other than Earth (it orbited Venus). Based on his achievements, he was invited to the University of Michigan to join a team of scientists who were working on the competing U.S. mission—the Pioneer Venus Orbiter. We were in our early thirties and our children were four and six years old. I found a temporary position with the University of Michigan doing data analysis at the Space Physics Research Laboratory, where my husband had his postdoc position. Our daughter entered kindergarten and rode the school bus with delight without knowing a word of English. Our son started preschool. Six months later they were talking in English to each other. In Hungary, they'd both cried every morning when I dropped them off for day care; here they both smiled and were very happy in school. We always attributed this to the way educators here handle children—with kindness and by welcoming and respecting their individuality—as opposed to the strict and non-personalized treatment of children in Hungary. A child there could never be right in opposition to the teacher, and the punishment for disobedience was swift and harsh.

Everyday chores seemed way simpler in the United States than what we were used to in Budapest. Grocery shopping could be done seven days a week and into the evening; in Hungary, the stores were open only when one was at work. People we encountered in the United Stateswere generally polite and helpful. I remember the Kroger employees had a pin on their uniforms that said, "We are happy you are here." This would have been unheard of in Hungary, where it often seemed that the store employees were only allowing us to shop there as a favor. When we returned to Hungary fifteen months later, I was heartbroken because I'd realized that the United States was the place where I should have been born. Our stay in the United States opened my eyes to the real world beyond the Iron Curtain. I especially liked that in America, people mostly did not seem to judge you because you were not a native-born person with an accent. You could argue your case and reasoning worked. If you were wronged, an apology followed. In Hungary, you were often blamed for other people's mistakes, small or big, and nobody apologized. You could not speak your mind freely either.

We spent the following summers in the States so that our children could stay acclimated to American culture and the English language, and we immigrated to the United States permanently in 1983. This was a bittersweet experience for my parents. They knew by then that the right decision for me was to live here, but this move also separated them from their only child and their two beloved grandchildren. Abandoning my parents left them essentially all alone in their old age. They never said so, but I am sure this amplified their feelings of loss that stemmed from the Holocaust. I will forever be torn by this decision, but in the end, it was the right choice to make so future generations could continue their journey to live freely and have the opportunity to be successful. My two children are both accomplished professionals and have great families with six of their own children between the two of them.

• • •

Once my husband and I made the move from Hungary to the United States, I found my way back to my Jewish roots. Here it seemed everybody had to have a religious identity. Close friends influenced me in identifying myself as Jewish, which I had not really done before. My children had friends in Ann Arbor public schools who belonged to Temple Beth Emeth, and they pushed for our family to join. I struggled for many years to reclaim my identity as a Jew. It was difficult for me to learn so many new things that I had never known before, that I'd discovered were part of my heritage. When I first started to attend Jewish religious services, I had severe anxiety. I was not sure whether I should enjoy the experience or feel ashamed that I'd betrayed my a-religious upbringing. It took me a long time to feel more comfortable and rid myself of the chains of the communist dogma that said any kind of religion was wrong and practicing it was considered criminal. I struggled with understanding that attending services did not have to mean believing in God. It was a tradition that made me part of the tribe, regardless of my personal feelings about religion. When I finally accepted this, it opened for me the rich realm of customs, stories, historical background, music, and other aspects of Judaism that I wanted to belong to.

One year when my parents visited us over the high holidays, I convinced my mother to come to services. There, to my great surprise, she chanted all the prayers. Her heritage was still a part of her. Afterwards no questions were asked, but the experience spoke for itself.

My husband grew up openly Jewish, in the Jewish center of Budapest, mostly sheltered from antisemitic incidents. His high school class was 40 percent Jewish and his parents raised him to strongly identify as Jewish. He had a bar mitzvah in Budapest in 1960, which was a strong political statement at the time. Since my husband grew up in a family that kept with tradition, to him it was nothing special to engage in Jewish life. After we got married and while we still lived in Hungary, we did not keep any of the Jewish customs or holidays. He didn't feel a strong need to pursue his parents' way of life. When we came to the United States, I realized how important it was to give our children some background about where they came from and who they were. I made a special effort to learn about the Jewish holidays and to start building some traditions at home. For our first Passover Seder, I enlisted a colleague of mine to conduct it in our house.

Once we had a number of grandchildren, my husband decided to write a family history for them. He engaged in two years of research, had a lot of conversations with the very few relatives we still had left, and sorted through family photographs and documents. He wrote a book titled *Phoenix*, after the bird that rises from the ashes of destruction. It goes back two hundred years on all four of our ancestry trees and finishes with the new generation of our children's children, representing the rebirth and multiplication of our families after the Holocaust. The book contains about four hundred family photographs and many family stories, all against the backdrop of Hungarian history, in general and with respect to the Jews in particular, over the last couple of centuries.[1] The interpretation of the events reflects my husband's personal views. The historical remarks I make throughout this chapter are well explained in this book and can be referenced there.

• • •

The Hungarian writer Kálmán Mikszáth wrote in a newspaper article in 1884, "The definition of an antisemite is one who hates the Jews more than necessary."

This about sums up the attitude of many Hungarians today as well, although it's not limited to Hungary. You can find this attitude widely present in Europe and in the United States among some segments of the population too. Antisemitism can probably never completely be eradicated, as humans seem to need scapegoats to blame their shortcomings on, and the Jews are a good target. In 2014, I traveled to the town of Pécs in southern Hungary, where my family came from and where I was born and raised from the ashes of the inferno. There were fifty-six hundred Jewish souls in Pécs and neighboring areas before the Holocaust and only 200 survived, my parents among them.

I returned to Hungary to attend seventieth anniversary commemorations of the Holocaust. Every ten years, the local Jewish council organizes a three-day event, including a symposium with talks about the role of the Hungarians in the annihilation of their fellow citizens, and other historical analyses of the times. An interfaith memorial was held at the local Jewish cemetery. What stood out at these events was that while some speakers openly acknowledged the complicity of the Hungarian people and even asked for forgiveness, others, mainly those associated with the Catholic Church, were still in denial. They promoted the canard that only the occupying Germans were at fault and that the Hungarians were merely victims, not active participants in the atrocities. Forgiveness requires repentance, and the Hungarians have never faced their guilt. To this day, they are trying to make excuses and put the blame on others. I remain very cynical about the sincerity of any Hungarian officials who make statements about the Jews in general, and the Holocaust in particular.

In the United States, although there was systemic antisemitism at the government level during World War II and in its aftermath, when Jews tried to get visas to enter the country, attitudes and policies toward Jews evolved. At the present time, there is very strong support for Israel, and antisemitic fringe groups are vastly outnumbered by the mainstream. My father would be glad to see this, and so am I.

It is very important to me that my children and grandchildren identify as Jewish. In light of their family history, these grandchildren of four Holocaust-survivor grandparents need to consciously carry the torch of survival for the Jewish people. My daughter always said she was only going to marry a Jew. Her sons have a strong identity as Jews. The two older ones had their b'nai mitzvah in January of 2021. My son also has a strong identity though he does not practice. His wife isn't Jewish, and although they sent their children to Jewish preschool, they are raising them in both Jewish and Christian cultural traditions.

It is a miracle to know that my parents' lineage continues in my children and grandchildren. My eldest grandson carries the middle name Miklós, in memory of the brother I never knew.

13

Please Remember

Myra Fox, daughter of Henry Fox and Rachel Najman Fox

Our dear friend Myra passed away before she could complete her chapter for this book. She was an essential part of our group, and her prose and poetry belong in our anthology. What follows is a selection of the pieces Myra wrote for our services over the years 2004–2018.

Henry and Rachel Fox's 50th wedding anniversary, Florida, 2000

Odd that I miss so much now what sometimes felt burdensome then.

And then again it's not.

Our living room was filled with those worn familiar faces almost weekly.

They settled on the white brocade sofa with extra chairs brought in to form the circle.

They seemed ancient to me then,

though most were younger than I am now.

This was our family.

Not by birth were they my parents' sisters and brothers, but by the inconceivable losses that they shared, by the guilt and wonder of their survival, by their desperate need to create normalcy and new families and community.

Few blood relatives had survived the camps.

I did have a very special aunt—my Cha Cha Regina—who often called screaming both day and night, certain that the Nazis were outside her door.

And an endearing Uncle Moniac who came to visit when relationships were stormy at his house.

And two aunts—only to be imagined, in Israel—a place only to be imagined.

But there in our living room, gladly sacrificing the flesh of their limbs to my mother's plastic sofa covers, was a family of survivors that were bound to each other—eating together, reading books, arguing politics, reciting poetry, singing, celebrating life's cycle. Did I mention eating together?

And here was a family of survivors who longed to embrace me.

That, in fact, was my burdensome job. To be their well-loved child.

My yoke was to be the new generation, the children of survivors—who need never suffer, who are guaranteed happiness, liberty, protection.

And so I moved from lap to lap to accept the warm hugs, and lipstick kisses from the women, to marvel at tricks with nickels disappearing and reappearing in ears, and to beg for my nose back between giggles, when captured by the men.

All this amidst the telling and retelling and re-retelling of stories filled with death, torture, fear, loss—told in a Yiddish I wasn't supposed to attend to or understand yet.

After they treasured and adored me, I might be enticed to play a song on the piano.

Then I was permitted to escape.

But sometimes I would remain there leaning up against Libel, Henia, Duvid, Mendel, Bronca, or Jash

to banish their grief for a little while longer.

• • •

"You will sit at the table until you finish your food. Don't you know there are children starving in Europe?" The rhythm of my mother's too-familiar anthem beat on my unwilling belly. I was a very skinny little girl. My parents called me "Skinny Skiducie." Food just held no appeal to me, except for candy and chocolate cupcakes.

No, I didn't really have an inkling of who was starving in Europe at the time. But I had seen glimpses of the shadows of those who had in the past. I heard about them in the hundreds of Yiddish conversations I wasn't supposed to have understood. Conversations told in whispers, in sorrow.

"We had it good at our camp," my mother would say, "compared to how it was for Henry in Buchenwald. Ours was not a death camp. But we were always hungry. Some of the girls would let the Germans touch them for an extra potato. I never did."

And there were the stories that wouldn't be uttered in their entirety in any language. The desperate acts over a crust of bread. Prisoner against prisoner. Jew against Jew. My father would always tire in the middle of those stories and the details were never fully revealed.

I was not supposed to comprehend these recollections as I sat, a young child, amidst this community of survivors. They counted on my protected innocence. They needed me to eat heartily, to never ever suffer like they had. My charge was to move happily from lap to lap to lap, spreading love, receiving their praise, rekindling their hopes. That much I could do obligingly.

But it was not so easy being full.

My sister, I'm told, kept the food in one side of her mouth for extended periods of time, until she was liberated from the table. My brother, I hear, stuffed his pockets with meat in order to escape. I discovered that the spare leaf hanging below the kitchen table was a fine location for food I was unable to consume. Sure, it was eventually discovered, dried-up, discolored, with who knows what kind of life-threatening organisms growing on it. But desperate times call for desperate measures, and those were moments of incredible boredom, entrapment, loneliness, desperate fullness.

It was not so easy being full.

I sat next to my father at the dinner table once I was the only child left at home. It was not a refined experience. I knew this was a manifestation of having lived too close to starvation, but he consumed his food with such ravenousness. When my mother served up the chicken, my anxiety rose tenfold. Yes, I had practiced the Heimlich maneuver on my pillow many nights, but I had to wonder if I could actually perform it adequately on a man the size of my father.

As a young adult, I engaged in many long fasts, sometimes lasting up to ten or twelve days. Purification, I explained to my friends. Looking back, I know it was just not so easy being full.

I appreciate being spared the experience of hunger quite a bit these days.

And I understand now what this community of survivors knew: that Hope, Empowerment, and Human Dignity were far more possible on a full tummy.

However, with this gift of fullness, I think comes great responsibility.

And with responsibility, opportunity.

While there is hunger on our planet, may it never be easy to be full.

• • •

WE HAVE HEARD STORIES

We have heard stories
with our young half open ears
of childhood recollections
of innocence
of beloved family

How idyllic they sounded
at first
how warm and contained

how unfamiliar
these ancestors were

There was once a mother
whom we would've called
Grandma

But how could we fully
listen to stories told
in softly breaking voices

How do we offer comfort when our young ears hear
the quiet howls

Our young eyes witness
the broken hearts
the unappeasable
longing for
a past obliterated
a family destroyed

How could we bear such
discomfort from the
mouths of our Protectors

What does one do about
the cries in the night

We lay awake hearing
screams in sleep
haunted
unable to enter our
parents' chamber

So hard it was
to be an adequate child

And now we are of riper age
desperate to see
the street that was their home
to translate their words
to find living connections
to their past
to read words written by their young hearts and hands
to discover their likenesses
among the few
published books
of recovered photographs

To embrace
the black and white
image
of the once
less troubled face

that in a world apart
and decades later
bent to kiss us

Our fingers
touch the images
caress the
creased parchment

And then our lips

• • •

KIDDUSH HA'SHEM

Radogoszcz Prison
My father breathes in darkness
Breathes out time
With no other way to measure the passing of
Fetid moments

It was a pogrom that they had protested most recently
My father's job was to protect the other marchers.
He did his job well.

Wasn't he
just a moment ago
young tall and strong?
Brimming with justice, righteousness, social equality?

From where within,
Father, does this courage come?
To oppose the persecutors who surround you in hateful
    organized masses
With no weapons but your voice, your arms, your beating
    heart?

Radogoszcz Prison
Breathing in darkness
Breathing out time
Three in a rank cell

But it is his turn to remove the excrement from their cage
What a moment of foul fortune
A chance to move his legs and stand almost erect

To be reminded by a shadow that light exists somewhere
That maybe he was a man once
Whilst he carries in his hand the feces of friends

Radogoszcz Prison
My father emerges not quite dead thirteen months later
Swollen with hunger
Blinded by even an overcast sky
He collects this favor—to live longer
Wishing his brother martyrs life or was it peace
He is thrown back to Łódź—now a ghetto
To a world where suffering can at least be measured by the
       passage of time

From where within
Father, does this conviction come?
The days of protest are over, you insist
But in that ghetto you hide a scroll
for others to borrow
In observance and prayer
At the risk of losing Life
While you swear the voice of God
Speaks not to your ears?

Kiddush Ha'shem

• • •

He sat on his recliner, in the den of the Florida condominium, rub-
bing his head in the way I've seen him do a thousand times or more.
But the comfort he usually got from this act was nowhere evident on
his face.

"I never would have believed," he said, "that such technology would be devised for the purpose of mass murder like this."

There was a long pause in his storytelling. A bit of uncertainty on his face. "Turn off the tape recorder," he directed me.

Then he said, "I was married once before. Her name was Alta Rosenzweig. It was before the war. We had a daughter together. They died in Auschwitz."

I didn't know if I was shivering or sweating. Here I sat, a grown woman, nearly thirty, hoping to record pieces of this man's history, but this . . . ? Another marriage? Another child? How little did I actually know of my father, of his losses?

My mother could be heard in the kitchen, clanging the pots and pans together as she began to prepare for Shabbat. Her daughters were visiting from Michigan. A chicken soup was warranted.

He continued. "Bluma was two when they were taken away. From what I understand they were in line at Auschwitz for the selection. The Nazis tried to separate Alta from Bluma. Alta would not permit that. She would not let go of Bluma, so they walked into the gas chamber together."

The grief on my father's face was as immediate as if he had lost them just a moment ago.

He never spoke of this again.

I know nothing else of Bluma, just that my father loved her. That she died in her mother's arms. And that she was my sister.

• • •

My father pulled me near him. "Don't try to deceive me," he whispered from his hospital bed. "I know what's going on outside the window. I can hear the tanks in the street."

My father's delirium, albeit brought on by a UTI in this case, emerged from a reality that lived forever in his brain. In his younger years, we ran in terror from his unpredictable temper and his knee-jerk reactions. In his later years, his unresolved trauma showed itself in unexplainable tears, or in his wondering if I shouldn't wear the Star of David necklace he and my mother had years before given me.

Getting my father's story was no easy task. I didn't find out until my twenties about his first wife and infant daughter who were selected for extermination. Nor until then did he talk about his arrest after demonstrating with the Resistance, or his year of punishment in solitary confinement in Radogoszcz prison. He was brief and selective in the stories he shared about his four years in Buchenwald. The stories of the prisoners' inhumanity to each other . . . well, he acknowledged that they existed, but he could never, ever bring them to bear.

I was terrified of my father. And yet, his emotional predicament spoke to me. It still does. The world is an unsafe place. Humans can be pretty bad news.

Thus, I struggled with this theme of forgiveness. After all, I think I'm supposed to do it. It allows us to love ourselves and others, to treat ourselves and each other with kindness and compassion. But forgiveness as related to the Holocaust? I had to look into that.

First I studied the research. There was Philip Zimbardo's Stanford Prison Experiment, in which nice Stanford students assigned the role of prison guards degraded and dehumanized their classmates who were assigned to be prisoners. The experiment was stopped after six days; five of the students had emotional breakdowns.

Then there were Stanley Milgram's studies of people's willingness to blindly obey authority. Subjects assigned the role of teachers ended up giving what they believed to be dangerous levels of electric shocks—450 volts!—to subjects who, as learners, gave incorrect answers.

But really, I thought, why am I looking at experiments? Real life vividly demonstrates our capacity for evil behavior. Remember the Reverend Jim Jones, who convinced 912 followers in Guyana to commit mass suicide? What about the photos taken with the cameras of our own American soldiers, sons and daughters of other Americans like us, who tortured and humiliated their captives at Abu Ghraib?

And of course, can't we look at the calculated extermination of our own families, of the Jewish people during the Holocaust?

Dostoyevsky said that nothing is easier than to denounce the evil-doer, nothing more difficult than to understand him.

I can get with that. But what I think is even more essential is that we understand and be alert to the system that encourages that evil.

Philip Zimbardo, in his book *The Lucifer Effect*, discusses the social processes that grease the slippery slope to evil:

Mindlessly taking the first small step

Dehumanization of others

De-individuation of self (anonymity)

Diffusion of personal responsibility

Blind obedience to authority

Uncritical conformity to group norms

Passive tolerance of evil through inaction or indifference

We humans are easy prey to these processes when we are in new or unfamiliar situations.

So, yeah, I'm going to try to understand the evildoer as well as the social processes that make it easier to treat others with cruelty. But without bitterness, I believe resolutely: there is no forgiveness for acts of genocide. There is no forgiveness for the Holocaust.

For the slavery, the ghettos, the starvation, the death camps, gas chambers, crematoria, mass graves—these things were and will always be unforgiveable.

I'm pretty sure that if my father were here, he would agree.

• • •

Who is that? My mother asks.
Her finger points at the man in the photo.
My throat clenches.
I try to answer in a ho-hum kind of voice

"It's Pa. Your husband, Henry."

"Henry? We were married?"

"Yes, sweet Mommy, for almost sixty years!" I say.

She thinks for a moment.
"I don't know what happened to him."

"He passed away, Ma.
More than two years ago."

I turn to the window allowing my face a brief moment of spasm.
Brief silent bursts of grief.

"We should never forget!"
And then we do.
The memory of my father is lost to his most precious life-long companion as she loses her battle with neurons that no longer fire.
Will I follow my mother into this world of not knowing? Will both of my parents' stories of survival, determination, and love vanish into nothing?
I wrote notes here and there as I gathered my thoughts for this very reading.

Pieces of paper lost.
Ideas forgotten.

Will our children grow tired of our stories? Disinterested?
Too detached to care?
"We should never forget!" A mantra that I hated as a child.
I'm just a kid, I would complain to myself,
Why must being a Jew mean acknowledging how violent
and debasing human conduct can become?

My mother wrote poetry in her teen years during the war.
When I was younger she suggested that we translate the
poems together.
I didn't pursue the offer.
I keep her notebook of poetry close by now.
Loosely Bound, Browned Paper, Polish words.
But the chance to translate together has passed.

"Of blessed memory," we say of our beloved who have
died.
The Pirkei Avot claims the crown of a good name sur-
passes the crown of Torah, priesthood, and kingship.
Zachor . . . zachor . . . remember . . . a word we find
throughout the Torah.
How can we remember when we are destined to forget?
Of what value is the crown of a good name when we all
become nameless?

Oh, but before I forget:
My father's name was Henry Fox.
He says that as a child he taped the Rabbi's beard to the

desk at school. He also claims to have ridden a goat around the classroom.

I choose to believe both stories.

He left his Orthodox home at twelve, joined the Jewish Socialist Party, survived Buchenwald after a year of solitary confinement in a Polish prison. But he remained funny and caring to his dying day. A day before his death, he turned to his hospice nurse and inquired if she was happy with her job.

My mother's name was Rachel Fox. She was sent to a work camp in Czechoslovakia, choosing to take the place of her youngest sister in an effort to save her. Her sister was later taken to Auschwitz, where she perished while my mom survived. Once in the United States, my mom cared for her older sister, my Cha Cha Regina, who survived Auschwitz but lived in fear of the Nazis, in a state of schizophrenic paranoia and depression. My mother brought Cha Cha's daughter, my cousin, to a safer harbor—our home. My mom's warmth always drew people in. Even when she could no longer carry on a conversation, she was well loved by those who knew her.

Please remember Henry and Rachel Fox.

But also know that when you do forget them, I understand.

• • •

My mother had a pet dog in her apartment at Rose Schnitzer Manor. Whenever she was helped back to her room, she would go to her dog who sat on the coffee table and greet him. He barked a "Yap! Yap!" whenever his head or tail was touched—as long as the batteries were in good working order. It delighted my mother, who would then carry on a conversation with the stuffed animal: "Yes! Yes!" she would say. "Good boy!" "Oh!" "Yes! Yes!" This could go on for quite a while, if not interrupted. My sister hated that dog. The dog, I guess, was something tangible she could despise in this period of loss.

My sister visited my mother much less often than I did. She never could forgive our parents, and most especially my mother, for what they were unable to give her. My sister was born in the American sector of occupied Germany, in a displaced persons camp in Landsberg. She was a baby and a toddler while my parents were recovering from their own horrors in Buchenwald and Oberstadt, and while they mourned the murders of my father's wife and child, all four of their parents, and the nine sisters and brothers between them. My sister was not yet in kindergarten when they left to start over in a new country. When God was passing out normal childhoods, she knew she got a raw deal. And she made sure the rest of us knew it, too.

Sometimes though, my sister showed amazing compassion and grace. After dinner in the dining room at Rose Schnitzer Manor, during what would be my sister's last visit, the three of us returned to my mother's apartment.

We unlocked the door for her.

She called to her pet dog.

We helped her to sit on the couch.

"I think I had dogs once before," my mother said, as her battery-operated pooch yapped in her lap.

"Yes, you did," my sister confirmed. "They protected your father's leather goods store."

"My father? Where is he now?"

"He died, Ma," my sister explained.

"Oh . . . and my mother? Where is she? I want to go there."

"Ma, she passed away too."

"But what happened?"

"Well," my sister said, "they were very old. So they died in their sleep peacefully. But they lived very, very long and happy lives. And they loved you so, so much."

I sat speechless, my throat a giant immovable lump.

"Okay," my mom said.

She was still a little sad, but she was comforted.

In this moment of her life there were no death camps, no gas chambers, no war.

When my brother and I cleaned out my mom's apartment, we decided to give the dog to my sister with fully-charged batteries. She winced when we gave it to her.

But she still keeps it in her den, even today.

• • •

IS IT ESSENTIAL?

I wake in the night and curse yet one more time that what
    my own mom told me is true
Once you are a mother, the worry never ceases
But
My son lives in a liberal paradise—a city of Beauty and of
    Tolerance.
He is working long hours
enjoying praise for his creativity and skills
        arriving home tired
                enjoying time in the company of friends
And he is happy it seems.

He gets bits of information from friends and coworkers
No time to read the newspaper between jobs
No time to focus on the Madness

And I wonder

Is it truly essential that he recognize the trouble we're in?
That he too lay terrified in the night?
That he worry about who will next
be impoverished
     imprisoned
          openly mocked and hated
               deprived of the most basic human rights
Exterminated?

He has already listened to the stories his grandparents
   have shared
And he has already heard my retellings.

Ghettos
concentration camps
        hunger
           torture

Loss.
He knows why our family is so small.
So, Please, can't I instead remind him of the Lullabies I sang
To soothe him to sleep?
Remind him of Rozhinkes mit Mandlen
Dem Aleph Beis?

Is it essential?
Is it truly essential?
I mourn the reality
That the unlikely miracle of my parents' survival
That the unlikely birth of my sister brother and myself
Make it so

Myra and her young son Joe, San Francisco, 1998

14

Osmosis

Fran Lewy Berg, daughter of Alfred and Irene Lewy

Alfred, Irene, Jules, and Fran Lewy, Montreal, Quebec, 1954

My life is shadowed by a history I am supposed to know nothing about. My parents did not talk about the Holocaust. It was in the air that we breathed. My brother and I absorbed it by osmosis.

I don't know a lot about my parents' experience during the war. But I can tell you what I lived.

Alfred Lewy

My father, Alfred (Fredek) Lewy, used to call me Lalka, which is Polish for Doll. When I was no longer a child, we continued to indulge in a ritual that went back to my infancy. Both of us standing, he would sway me in his arms to an old Polish lullaby about two noisy kittens. I remember it as:

> *Aaaaaah Aaaaaah*
> *Kotki dva*
> *Shara boo-a*
> *Ovid va*
> *Dola chowa*
> *Nara sue*
> *Naro bewa*
> *How-a sue*

Even though it was more fitting for someone much younger, my father and I would rock to the melodious chant, and I never squirmed away. I knew enough to cherish it.

My parents talked between themselves in Polish but never to us children, as they wanted to purge themselves of that country and not contaminate the next generation. Polish was reserved for my father's lullaby and for names of endearment. My mother called me Francheska and Francelina Pumpalina. But the nickname that most warmed my heart was when my father called me Lalka.

After the war my parents left the small town of Jarosław, where they'd grown up, for the promise of a new life in Canada. My father arrived in Montreal with two gold coins sewn into the waistband of his pants. The first notice for work he came upon was "Leather cutters wanted. Experience necessary." My father had none, but he took the job. The food he put on the table he paid for with badly cut up hands. Thirty-five years later he established The Irene and Fred Lewy Youth Center in Jerusalem for disadvantaged youth. Supporting Israel meant everything to my father. He would say if it had only existed earlier, there would have been a nation to welcome the Jews of Hitler's Europe. If there was a next time, Jews would have a homeland to escape to. In Montreal, my father achieved the life of a successful real estate developer. As president of B'nai B'rith, he won humanitarian awards.

A large man with shockingly thick hair, my father was handsome in a European sort of way. There was a quiet elegance to him. He always rooted for the underdog. While he was capable of red-faced rage, he had a softness and tenderness that belied his imposing, at times intimidating, exterior. I saw his eyes melt sometimes when he looked at me.

He was an enthusiastic and colorful storyteller, his tales punctuated by a twinkle in his eye. Yet, as gifted a storyteller as he was, he could not tell me his own story.

When I became a doctoral student in psychology, I wanted to write my dissertation on children of survivors. My father bellowed, "I forbid it!"

Irene Lewy

The phrase most often used to describe my mother Irene (Irka) Lewy's essence was "joie de vivre." When in public she was a beauty, made up impeccably and dressed to the nines. She was animated and abundantly charming; people were enamored with her incredible spark. At home she did not make the effort, and often seemed despondent. I frequently found her midday lying on our couch with a blanket pulled up over her head.

Extravagantly extreme, my mother was passionate about traveling, feeding family and guests, playing bridge, and appreciating the beauty in nature. She wasn't just passionate about the freshness of ocean air— she made it a mission to have my brother Jules and me breathe it in deeply. When we were on vacation at the seaside, she would instruct us to join her in an enormous inhale. This was followed by a dramatically extended and hugely satisfied "Aaaaaaah," which started at a high note and descended the musical scale. As we stood on the shore, my lungs were full of the salt air and my mother.

Her audacity and tenaciousness knew no bounds when it came to looking out for her family. When my father became severely depressed by the death of Vucho Muti, his uncle, I was ten and away at sleepover camp. My mother decided that seeing me would cure my father's depression. But parents were strictly prohibited from entering Camp Navarac on any day other than Visitors' Day. Making exceptions to that rule would understandably create havoc. Nevertheless, my mother was undaunted by the camp director's loud and insistent protests. She was louder and more insistent still. I do not know if her persistence in accomplishing her mission lifted my father's spirits. I was too young to understand what they were doing there. I just know that her will broke the director's will. Years later my husband and I would call examples of that fervent assertiveness "Pulling a Mrs. Lewy."

Unlike most of her peers, my mother rejected the familiar comfort of the companionship of other survivors, or even other Europeans. Wishing to divorce herself from her past, she surrounded herself with Canadian friends. To her frustration, though, her accent was thick and she was constantly asked where she was from. In response, my mother would puff out her chest and declare, "Cah nah dah!" citing the country in which she was proud to have citizenship.

My parents wanted to hide their past and their wounds from themselves and from their children. As if they and their children could then emerge unscathed. They were determined that their children would not be affected by the Holocaust. They would not, or could not, see the myriad ways we soaked it up.

When I was twenty-five, my mother discovered me reading Helen Epstein's *Children of the Holocaust*, the first book to examine the intergenerational transmission of trauma. My mother declared shrilly and with a vengeance, "There is no difference between children of survivors and other children!"

The Phone Call

The summer before I turned thirty, Jules and I were making plans for a celebration of our mother's sixtieth birthday. Our family was going to gather in Stowe, Vermont. My parents had a favorite inn there with a gourmet restaurant. The surrounding mountains and meadows appealed to my mother's love of nature, a love that is deeply ingrained in me as well. When she spotted something of beauty, she would stop us, regardless of what she was interrupting, and exclaim "Oh! Oh! Look at that!"

But before my parents could make it to Vermont, while they were on vacation in Switzerland, my brother called to tell me they had been in a car accident. With horror I imagined them badly injured in a hospital. With dread I wondered what extensive care they would need, and then with self-centered apprehension, what would be required of me. "How badly are they hurt, Julie?" I asked.

Silence. And then the words, "They are dead."

No.

God no.

Please God no.

But God did not take it back.

Outside it was pouring, syntonic with my heartbreak. Nature held me to her bosom.

It would be an understatement to say that my parents were well-loved in their community. At their memorial service the attendees were too numerous to fit into the funeral home. They spilled out into the street. I overheard a woman say, "What a waste to survive the Holocaust just to have this happen." I was incensed. She was discounting the richness of the lives my parents lived after the war. This included my birth, and that of my brother, and all the generations to come.

I remember days after my parents' death, swimming laps in a pool under a cloudless sky. With each stroke I willed myself not to feel. If I just lock it tightly away, if I don't think about it, I won't have to feel it. I can bypass the pain. As I cut through the water, I decided that was my plan.

Such a plan has echoes of my parents' strategy for dealing with the unbearable pain of the Holocaust. Push it down. Bury it. For me, as for them, the sorrow leaked out sideways.

For a full year after my parents' death, I had a repeated dream that I came upon them in a crowded train station acting quite ordinary. They said dispassionately that the announcement of their death was nothing more than a terrible error. Oh, the joy of that nocturnal reunion. The depth of the relief that replaced the depth of grief. Then, upon awakening, the stark realization, the losing them all over again. Again. And again. The silent howling that became part of my waking.

What had been the substance of my parents' dreams? What had evoked their cries in the middle of the night?

COVID through a 2G Lens

Some thirty-five years after my parents' death, I find myself viewing the pandemic through a lens that reflects the darkness of my parents' story. My friend speaks of vaccines. I speak of the limitations of vaccines. She speaks of the virus's duration in months. I speak of its duration in years. I lament the coming winter when we won't be able to gather outdoors. She exclaims, "Are you kidding? It's eighty-eight degrees outside. How can you think about winter?" I think, are you kidding? How can you not? Her thought is we don't know what will happen. Why go to the worst scenario? She insists she can't live that way. I insist I'm being realistic.

Why such different-colored lenses: hers of hope, mine of dread? I grew up in a home where "Be on the alert for something bad" was a code we lived by. Post-traumatic stress ran in my family's veins. How could it be otherwise?

Epigenetics informs us about the intergenerational transmission of trauma. I imagine a fetus floating in the womb of my mother's distended belly, her anxiety and her sorrow permeating some membrane that is me.

"Catastrophe lurks" is in my bones. Yet when imminent catastrophe was pervasive in Jarosław as Hitler's plan began to unfold, why didn't my parents recognize it? Time and again I have made that silent accusation, "Why didn't you leave? There were so many signs. You could have spared yourselves. You could have spared your family. You could have spared me." Days before the 2020 election, the news is full of fears, hatred, and lies. Are there actions I should be taking now? If the political situation got worse would I move back to Canada? How could I give up the satisfying life I've built here? Seen through this lens, it's easier to accept my parents' inertia.

Why do all roads lead to the Holocaust for me? Maybe because it's the most significant determiner of my identity. No. It must be otherwise. It's too dark to be at the core of who I am.

My parents embodied an unexpected combination of global pessimism and personal optimism. I grew up on the dictum, "You can accomplish anything you set your heart to." My parents personified this philosophy, as did their children. My brother is, in my father's words, "a big-shot lawyer," and I'm a PhD clinical psychologist. My father's career as a real estate developer was a true rags-to-riches story. When she wanted something, my mother's perseverance was Herculean. She was determined that my husband-to-be have an *Aufruf*, the Jewish custom of a groom being called up in synagogue to recite a blessing over the Torah. Mark declined but she kept repeating the request, till finally she pulled out all the stops and implored, "Mark. Please! Do it for your parents." And so, recognizing an unstoppable force, he did.

Despite what my parents went through, they found a path forward into love, hope, and generosity. If they could hold onto all that— through and after the war—then I can trust myself to make my way through this pandemic and whatever follows.

Long-Distance Phone Calls

My parents knew each other as children growing up in the same small town. When the war broke out my father was eighteen, my mother sixteen. Both were in forced labor camps, my father in Siberia and my mother in Poland. Like so many survivors, my parents entered

Alfred and Irene at Fran and Mark's wedding, Montreal, 1979

into marriage hurriedly after the war. Having lost everything and finding themselves alone, marriage was a way to retrieve a semblance of normal life. Anyone who did not live through it could never understand their world.

They married in a courthouse. There were no wedding guests. To fulfill the requirement of a witness, in my mother's words, they "grabbed someone from off the street."

Years after my parents' death, a family friend, Olga Koretz, told me she was in the same concentration camp as my mother. Somehow, I blocked out the camp's name. It was in a town that started with a B and I have not been able to place it. When I try to determine which camp it was, I notice a resistance in myself. I look at the lists of Polish concentration camps on Wikipedia, and none of the names jump out at me. I quake inside—wanting to know and not wanting to know. As I write this, I become aware that I am doing to myself what I protested my parents doing to me—withholding information.

Another friend of my parents, Rena Linhart, offered me sympathy years after their deaths. She said, "It must have been very hard for you to lose your parents that way. During the war it was easier for us because it was commonplace. Almost everyone's parents were dead." How horrific to think that the murder of parents could be normalized. As for whose loss was harder, I don't know that you can—or should— even compare such a thing. I didn't tell her that for me those calculated deaths seemed harder to bear than an accident of fate.

I know hardly anything about my mother's parents, who perished in the war. Rena said she had memories of them walking down the street, hand in hand. This image of their love for each other is precious to me. I'm not sure what happened to them. I have been told several disparate versions by relatives. One version is that my mother had written T Y P H U S on the front door, hoping this would discourage anyone from entering, but on her return from the black market, her parents were gone. I was also told they were shot while my mother hid behind a door. In yet another version, they were arrested and taken to a holding area. My mother went there at night with the purpose of helping her parents escape. But her father was in such a precarious emotional state he could not be moved and her mother would not leave without him. She never saw them again.

I am left with a fog.

I know my father's father died in a Siberian labor camp weeks before liberation. He was so weak that my father had to hold him up during inspections so that he would pass. My father shared his measly daily portion of bread with him, as my grandfather, not being able to work, was given nothing.

My father's mother survived that Siberian labor camp and lived out the rest of her years in Montreal along with my parents. She was famous for being the only woman with an outdoor newspaper stand. In her day she had spunk. Shortly after coming to Montreal she was interviewed by *The Montreal Star* at her kiosk. Her stance in the accompanying photo is markedly self-assured. Her presence dominates that of the male reporter. I imagine her smile reflects her satisfaction with herself at having an occupation practically unheard of for a woman.

My father was my grandmother's only child. My mother's experience growing up was largely that of an only child as well. Her sister Marysia was thirteen years older and left home when my mother was quite young. I do not know Marysia's story, merely that she and her daughter Danuta survived, and her husband did not. When the war ended, Marysia set out on foot to look for my mother and her husband, not knowing if they were alive or dead. She made arrangements for a neighbor woman to provide food for seven-year-old Danuta, who she left with only the company of their German shepherd. I don't know how Marysia found my mother. But the sisters' heartrending reunion is something I have imagined many times. I see them catching their breaths as they catch sight of each other, struggling between disbelief and the will to believe. An elated embrace. Not letting go till they've come up for air. Weeping from the depths of unspeakable grief. The joy and sorrow interwoven, raw.

As a child, I witnessed shades of this emotion in their rare long-distance phone calls, which neither family could afford. Through the background of overwhelming static, what passed between them was almost solely unrestrained weeping. They could barely manage words.

Heaping Piles of Food

Even though my parents tried to shield us from the Holocaust, they were constantly providing us with its lessons. One such lesson was the preciousness of food. My mother would tell the story of going into Steinberg's, one of Montreal's largest grocery markets, for the first time after leaving Europe. Row upon row of canned goods, meats, and savories, heaping piles of fresh fruit and vegetables. Endless food as far as her eyes could see. She took in the abundance and wept.

Even when my parents were financially successful, my mother could not throw out food. She consumed stale bread. She encouraged me to eat the fat on my steak.

When my brother turned thirteen, he implored my father to raise his allowance by twenty-five cents. My father flatly refused. Jules proclaimed he would not eat until my father changed his mind. This was probably the worst form of protest he could have devised for a Holocaust survivor. My father was incensed. How could Jules take food for granted? His response to my brother's hunger strike was to deny him and raise my allowance by a quarter. As far as I can recall, this was one of the meanest things he ever did. The only way I can understand it is that, in this moment, the cruelty once directed at him was transformed into a harshness he inflicted on his son.

Many years later, when showing my husband and me our prenatal ultrasound, the ob-gyn commented lightly that the fetus's stomach was full. My satisfaction was immense.

As empty nesters, there are just two of us at home now. Yet my fridge is full to brimming. When I entertain, there is enough food left over for a second gathering. I unconsciously but routinely leave a tiny amount of beverage in my glass. I imagine this is just to be sure I have some for later, to ensure that I do not run out.

Scalding Water

I used to carry my small gray teddy bear most everywhere. I slept with him pressed safely between my chest and the bars of my crib. He was as ratty as he was well loved. His scruffy fur lay in uneven tufts from being rubbed with abandon. His vision was limited to the benefit of one button eye. The small mound of black thread that was his nose was fraying.

My mother kept an immaculate house. Having endured filth, lice, and disease in the camps, she now surrounded herself with order and cleanliness. She asked my permission to throw out my dirty, smelly lovey. "Absolutely not!" She dragged him from dry cleaner to dry cleaner, but they refused to do her bidding, explaining he was too fragile to be subjected to their chemicals. She would have liked to take bleach and scalding water to him, but Teddy would not survive that either. Again, she implored me to let her throw him out. A flat "No!" She tried to bargain to replace him with a bigger, swankier teddy bear. I assured her and my Teddy that I was not that fickle. She enlisted my father's support to attempt to convince me. I remained steadfast.

When I awoke one morning, the unthinkable had happened.

She had disposed of Teddy. My meltdown would not be appeased by cartoons or candy. My father, the voice of reason, instructed my mother to retrieve the thing from the trash. She could not, she said. She had thrown it down the apartment building's incinerator.

This was one of my earliest experiences of separation and loss. I was to have many in my lifetime. I can imagine my mother thinking she was giving me a lesson, strengthening me by not letting me get too attached to love objects. Loved ones can be taken from you instantaneously, incomprehensibly. They can be torn from you as you stand powerless. The unfathomable horror of loved ones going up in smoke. I wonder what went through her head when she disposed of my lovey. Did she experience what it felt like to be agent instead of victim?

• • •

One day when I was five, I was playing tea party in front of our apartment building, filling the tiny pink cups with snow and having a lovely time. How could my overprotective mother have allowed me to be out there by myself at that age? Years later my therapist told me overprotectiveness goes hand in hand with neglect.

A man came by and asked where my mother was. I knew I was not supposed to talk to strangers. But this wasn't a stranger. He was someone who must know my mummy because he was looking for her. As I led him into the apartment building, I felt pleased with myself, important. I wanted to call Mummy from the downstairs intercom to let her know he was there. "No," he said. "Take me to her." And then, "We'll take the stairs instead of the elevator." That was strange because I lived on the sixth floor. We passed a neighbor going up the stairs. My eyes said please help me but she did not see. My legs were tiny, so climbing was very hard. In the stairwell when I couldn't climb anymore he said, "Put your hand in my pants pocket." I did. "Now rub." I did.

I didn't fully understand what was happening but I knew this was something horrible. When it was over he said, "Wait for me here while I go get you some candy." I didn't want his candy. I just wanted to go home. But I was afraid when he came back he would catch me leaving and that would make him mad. I stayed for the longest time, scared and sick feeling, till I finally got up the courage to leave.

When I told Mummy what had happened, I lied by adding he had a knife. I needed to explain why I had done such an awful thing when he hadn't "forced" me. I did it because he was big and you are supposed to do what adults tell you to. I was being a good girl. But in being good I had done something awful. Surely it was my fault.

Without a word, Mummy took me to the maid's bathroom which was never used by anyone in our family. She washed my hands with water so hot it felt scalding. Then she looked me in the eye and said, "You must never tell anyone about this. Never."

I forgot all about it for years until one day, as a teenager, I was traveling on a bus for a school ski trip. I have no idea what triggered the memory but there it was, clear in every detail. I thought about raising it with my mother but decided not to because it would make her uncomfortable. Instead of sharing the memory or, even more pointedly, confronting her, I assumed my role of protector.

To this day I wonder if she ever told my father.

My neighbor, who is in her seventies, recently told me how a stranger had put his hands in her pants when she was little. Upon being told, her mother immediately called the police. Not only was it not a shameful secret, she went public with it. I envied her mother's reaction. How appropriate to protect her child and other children to try to find and punish the perpetrator.

For me, it was another secret. Child molestation. Holocaust. Bury that which is too ugly to reveal. Tell no one and hopefully you can make it disappear. But burying breeds shame. That which is unspeakable has tremendous power, I tell my psychotherapy clients. Giving it voice takes away much of that power. Shine light on it and you can start to deal with it.

All the Beds in the House are Made

At nine, I had to get an eye exam because I was having trouble reading the chalkboard at school. Dr. Morgenstern reported that I needed glasses and my mother broke into body-wracking sobs. He tried to calm her. "Glasses will fix it, Mrs. Lewy." Continued sobbing. "Lots of children her age wear glasses." Breathless gulping. "She can wear contacts when she's older." His attempts to console my mother only intensified her outburst. Dr. Morgenstern was mystified. I wanted a hole to disappear through. It was only when I was older that I understood. I couldn't have anything wrong with me. Any vulnerability, any frailty meant death in the camps. It was the survival of the fittest. Charles Darwin had no idea. Neither did Dr. Morgenstern.

In the service of having nothing wrong with me, I did not miss school unless I was seriously ill. Staying home for a stomachache or bad cold was a luxury I was not generally permitted. My mother liked to quote her mother, "I'm not happy till all the beds in my house are made." This referred not only to a tidy household but also to no one being sick in bed. In fourth grade I was awarded a cardboard medal that proclaimed me "Least Absent from School." Wearing it on my chest, I felt furious, not proud. My being sick made my mother decidedly uncomfortable. She would wring her hands and ask frequently—too frequently—if I felt better. Often prematurely she would assure both of us that I did. To this day having something physically wrong with me makes me markedly uneasy, at times even afraid. I question whether I am "ill enough" to permit myself not to go to work, or even more exceptionally, to stay in bed.

In my mother's household, it was also not acceptable to be depressed. Some days she yelled at me to "Smile more!"—a self-defeating command. Forcing my lips to turn upward failed to satisfy her need, as there was no corresponding light in my eyes.

Even though I was not supposed to be sad, my parents carried sadness beyond measure. A tense atmosphere permeated our home. My father had considerable expectations of his firstborn son that my brother rebelled against. Jules was expert at igniting my father's short fuse.

One day when I was seven, I matter-of-factly announced to my mother that things were not very happy at home. She glared at me with barely contained fury. "How dare you say you're not happy when you have food, a roof over your head, and a family that loves you! You have no right!" I never voiced anything like that again.

When I was young the tension in our home seemed normal to me. It was all I knew. When I was old enough to visit friends' houses, I was amazed at how easily their parents laughed and how light the air felt.

• • •

During the Israeli Six-Day War, my father grew increasingly depressed. Never one to lie on the couch, he took up residence there. He said he couldn't bear that young Israeli soldiers were dying. I believe he was also grieving the threat to the Jewish homeland and all that it represented to him. Not ever talking about the Holocaust, never truly processing any of it, must have contributed to this spilling over of emotion that, once tapped, was incapacitating. My mother dedicated all her energy to getting him, in her words, "back to normal." She was beside herself, yelling at him to get off the couch, demanding that he go to the office. Alternating between ultimatums and sobs, eventually she succeeded in getting him out the door. Depression was not to be tolerated in Mrs. Lewy's immaculate household.

Don't Ask

Starting at the tender age of five, I was sent to camp for two months every summer along with my older brother. My mother wailed every year while I boarded the camp bus. I, a bewildered child, had to comfort her about a separation she chose and I dreaded. That first summer my emotional state was expressed in bouts of sleep walking. For several years starting when I was ten, my parents also sent us to winter camp over Christmas break.

It was not until years later that I realized the significance of the word "camp."

I have struggled to understand their choice to send us away, especially starting at such a young age, given my parents' history with separation. But I never felt like I could ask without making them feel sorely criticized. Each summer they took exotic trips, just the two of them. Perhaps they wanted to travel the world unencumbered by children. Perhaps my father wanted a break from some of the tension at home between him and his equally strong-headed son. Perhaps my mother had some misguided notion this would help fortify us against future separation and loss akin to what she had endured.

She encouraged me to walk barefoot over grass for the pleasure of it. A few times, she just as casually encouraged me to take off my sandals and walk barefoot over gravel and stones "to toughen my feet." Perhaps this too was to prepare me for what might come.

• • •

In my early thirties, after my parents died, after the birth of my daughter, I began to hunger for information about their experience in the war. My cousin Danuta insisted it was too painful to talk about. And she admonished me not to ask questions of her mother, Marysia, then in her seventies, as "It would kill her."

It took me more than thirty years to get up the courage to ask Danuta again. I requested information about our mothers' parents as well as anything she might be willing to share about my parents' experience during the war. She would not, or could not, once again claiming these memories were too painful for her. In my disappointment I wrote a follow-up email, explaining that she was my only source for knowing my grandparents and that anything she could tell me would mean so much.

I waited hopefully for her response. In its stead I received the following email from her husband, in all caps, which made the words scream off the page.

FRAN I DON'T UNDERSTAND YOUR SELFISHNESS. THANKS TO YOUR INSISTENT QUESTIONS DANUTA IS NOW TAKING PILLS AND HAS NIGHTMARES WHICH HAVE SHATTERED HER COMPLETELY. THIS IS A LAST WARNING. IF YOU WRITE TO DANUTA ONE MORE QUESTION WHICH MAKES HER CRAZY I WILL BLOCK YOUR EMAIL SO THAT YOU WILL HAVE NO MORE CONTACT.

GEORGE

Reading this email, I had trouble catching my breath. In rapid succession I was flooded with shame, rage, and sorrow. I never asked again.

Jewess

After the war, some survivors embraced their Judaism more passionately, while others shunned it. My parents reflected both sides of this continuum. My father became profoundly Zionistic. My mother, on the other hand, in the aftermath of her experience with the war, wanted to have nothing to do with the religion that had cost her so dearly. My father wanted to move to Israel. My mother wouldn't hear of it.

My parents wanted children desperately but had difficulty getting pregnant. Children were the future. Children represented life. Birth and rebirth. They wanted to have children who would live happy, peaceful lives, free of tragedy. Children to make up in some way for what they had lost. Victory over Hitler's mission. The doctor told my mother she couldn't get pregnant because she was too nervous, and she should adopt. Determined as ever, she proved him wrong.

When my brother was born, my mother announced that she would not have him circumcised. My father insisted. But, she pleaded, during the war such evidence led to death. My father refused to back down.

A few years later, my mother chose to enroll Jules in a preschool run by nuns that had an excellent reputation. Filling out the registration form, under religion my mother wrote "Catholic." When she came home and admitted this to my father, he demanded she go back and correct it.

"I can't," my mother pleaded.

"You must, Irka!" commanded my father, just short of yelling.

"But what will I tell them . . . that I forgot?"

So, my mother went back, not a little sheepishly, and reported to the nuns that Jules was in fact Jewish.

And they told her they knew.

At a second-generation Yom HaShoah service, I recounted this story. As I stood on the synagogue's bimah, I was assailed by the sense that I had betrayed my parents. I was talking to a whole congregation about a Holocaust-related experience of theirs. This went against their strong desire for that unmentionable part of their lives to remain unmentioned.

• • •

When my daughter Cara Rachel was sixteen, she was president of her temple youth group. When she turned seventeen, she was elected president of the Michigan Region Reform Jewish Youth Movement. I was filled with pride. Cara has striking features—luscious dark wavy hair and brown fawn eyes. She took to wearing a Star of David around her neck. When I first saw it, my instinctive thought was that I wished she wouldn't wear it. I was mystified by my visceral reaction of discomfort. These words came to my mind: *Does she have to advertise it?*

Then I understood. My mother desperately attempted to prevent my brother's circumcision in order to hide evidence of his being Jewish, out of fear for his very survival. And now her granddaughter was choosing to proudly proclaim her Jewishness around her neck for all the world to see.

• • •

I wanted my daughter to experience having extended family, something I had precious little of growing up. A somber reminder of Hitler's mission. I envied my friends' Sunday visits to relatives, the photos of multiple generations that graced their walls and their family reunions. In graduate school, six women and I formed a "family by choice" to commemorate holidays and life events while living far from blood relatives. Thirty years later we are three generations strong and comprise thirty-eight members and one on the way. Stunningly this intentional family gave me the gift of kin. My daughter grew up with multiple "cousins" and "aunts and uncles," something I only dreamed of.

Lateness and Death

When I was young, I begged for a puppy. My mother refused. Her reason was simple: dogs die. Goldfish were permissible. When she found one floating belly up, she ran to the corner Woolworth's store to replace it before Jules and I woke up. We were not fooled, but the need to not acknowledge death was clear. Some thirty years later, when Cara's goldfish died, there were tears. We had a proper funeral, placed Goldie in an envelope, and said some words about how she had been a good goldfish. We buried her in the backyard. But when I was a child, my mother summarily flushed our goldfish down the toilet. We were permitted a budgie when we got a little older. On its death, we cried hard. In response, my mother said angrily, "I told you we shouldn't get a pet!"

My parents responded to anyone's falling seriously ill with disbelief and shock, as if this had no natural place in the life cycle. I was ten when my great-uncle Vucho Muti died and my mother barreled her way into my camp on a mission to alleviate my father's resulting depression. But my parents never told me that he had died. I believe they could not bring themselves to. I learned of his death because his wife and daughter came to our house without him, dressed in black.

In spite of my mother's need to be socially correct, she could not bear to attend funerals. Her solution was to sign the guest book in the funeral home, so her presence would be made known, and then flee. When my best friend Penny's grandfather died, her mother spoke of how he had lived a good and full life. This manner of handling a death was totally foreign to me.

. . .

Penny was the tallest girl in our seventh-grade class. I was the shortest. She was as big-boned as I was slight. She had fashion sense. I had none. We were mistaken more than once for mother and daughter, which pleased her no end and embarrassed me to death. However, in Penny's presence I laughed it off like "Isn't that hysterical?" Because I was that cool.

Our ritual after school was to go to Woolworth's and see and be seen by as many kids we knew as possible, sit in our favorite booth with the orange vinyl seating, and eat French fries with vinegar because that's the way you eat French fries if you live in Quebec. One day I accompanied Penny back to her house so I could admire the clothes her aunt had bought her in yet another shopping extravaganza. I was doing the obligatory oohing and aahing when her mother came down and announced in a nervous voice that my mother had called and I was to go home straight away. I knew I was in trouble.

My mother was in our kitchen, beside herself with why was I so late. She was shaking and carrying on as if I had done something criminal. I eventually gathered that she had gotten hold of my personal phone book and had systematically called all my friends and acquaintances in a desperate attempt to find me. Mortified, I hollered, "It makes me look like such a baby! How could you do such a stupid, stupid thing?" My mother's expression went blank. My father grabbed me by the shoulders and pulled me into the hallway. He looked at me gravely and delivered the stinging message, "Mummy's experience during the war was that if someone was five minutes late you never saw them again."

I had committed the gravest sin, the violation of my code to never add to my parents' suffering. But I was only twelve. Couldn't I just be mad that my mother had embarrassed me? Couldn't I just stamp my feet at the unfairness of it all? No. That was a luxury I didn't have.

When would I have suffered enough for people to protect me, to avoid hurting me at all costs, to make it their goal to not disappoint me and make me happy?

It was not until I suffered my own emotional crisis, and experienced a depression so debilitating that I had to leave graduate school and return to my parents' home, that I realized the answer to that question: Never. It will never be my turn.

For years I carried on a heated debate with myself: what did I owe my parents and what did they owe me? For the longest time, I struggled to figure out whose needs were greater, whose rights more legitimate. I wrestled with whether I should side with my parents' needs or my own. The heat of that debate eventually transformed into sorrow. As I left the self-centered world of adolescence, I could begin to put myself in my parents' heavy shoes. As I look back on that scene in our kitchen—of an emotionally wrought mother and her enraged daughter—I feel waves of sorrow for them both.

• • •

When I was in my twenties, I was expecting a visit from my father. He was hours late, which was unlike him. With annoyance I called my parents' home. When my mother answered her voice sounded shaky. To my bewilderment she would not put my father on the phone. I demanded to speak to him. She refused. I am not one to raise my voice, but after several rounds of this, I yelled "I want to speak to Dad this minute!" After a long hesitation she handed him the phone. His speech was garbled. Incomprehensible. That is how I learned my father had had a stroke.

His physical therapist said she had never worked with anyone who showed as much determination and perseverance to get better as my father did. In time, he fully recovered except for a slight telltale limp.

Five years later, at the age of fifty-eight, my mother developed breast cancer. In the 1980s this was no longer considered a death sentence. Yet she was convinced she would die. I reasoned with her that her cancer was not aggressive and, in all likelihood, she would survive, but then she became convinced that she would die on the operating table. I worried that given my mother's Holocaust history she might associate a mastectomy with mutilation. At the time lumpectomies were beginning to be heralded as a viable alternative to mastectomies. When I suggested researching a lumpectomy as a possible option, my mother's conservative doctor said her daughter should stop her "harmful meddling."

My mother survived. The cancer had not metastasized to her lymph nodes. She was told her situation going forward did not require much concern. But the horror of the experience never left her.

· · ·

Back when I was in eighth grade, one crisp autumn day, my mother and I were walking down Macdonald Avenue outside our apartment building, headed toward the neighborhood shopping area. She reached out and took my hand. I was appalled. The thought of being caught in public holding hands with my mother! I emphatically dropped her hand and shot her an exasperated look. She turned to me and sighed, "Ah, what I wouldn't give to be able to hold my mother's hand right now."

In that instant, I was overwhelmed with sorrow, rage, and guilt. Years later my therapist said of this story, "She brought out the big guns." He was taking my side. Had he been my mother's therapist, he would have taken hers.

Emotional Crisis and Beyond

The summer before graduate school I experienced my first unimaginable, unmanageable depression. The pursuit of higher education was consistent with everyone's expectation of me. An incapacitating depression was not. Both my parents and I engaged in outward denial about the seriousness of my condition. I should never have left my home in Montreal to move to school in Ann Arbor when I was so limited. But, perplexed and pained by my condition, my parents pushed me out. They didn't know what else to do. I didn't know either.

In Ann Arbor, I did not go to classes. I barely talked. I barely was. A psychologist surmised that I was reliving the Holocaust. Unhelpful. My mother called Bill Morse, the chairman of my department, crying hysterically. I was mortified. He later told me she loved me as an extension of herself. I didn't know what he meant at the time, but I knew he must be right.

My boyfriend of seven years, the boyfriend who followed me to Ann Arbor, the boyfriend who wanted us to marry one day, reached his limit and walked away.

I returned home to my parents and received better professional help—increased insight into my complicated relationship with my parents and the many-layered meaning of separation and loss for me. The same mother who could not tolerate my needing glasses or having the flu insisted I was undergoing age-typical mood swings and should stop my medication. I knew better.

A year later my doctoral program allowed me to return. How could they take me back? I had a series of incompletes on my first-year transcript; I was a failure as an academic and a human being. "I am fascinated by resilience," said Bill Morse. "After everything you went through, you wanted to come back." He gave me the gift of respect when I was cowering in shame.

Years later I received my PhD—a certificate of my knowledge and ability, as well as my mental capacities and mental health. I am grateful that before my parents died, they saw me graduate. Their pride was palpable. As I collected my diploma, my head was full of my mother's oft-repeated words, "Education is the one thing they can't take away from you." Nothing could have pleased them more—other than a grandchild. I never gave them a grandchild, which breaks my heart. But I did give them a son-in-law whom they adored. My mother said of Mark, "Now that's someone to go through life with," and she was once again right.

Lalka

Our morning begins with openmouthed delight at finding ourselves in each other's company. Ruthie announces at a fevered pitch, with flailing arms and legs, "I am Moana!" She is a precious if not credible two-year-old impersonator of her favorite princess hero. Moana and her grandmother glide together across the floor, in stocking feet, in our rendition of *Disney On Ice*.

Next, a Magic Carpet Ride on a silver blanket. Then a train ride, which looks much the same as Magic Carpet Ride, except this time I puff "Choo Choo" as I pull her around the room. The No Waking Bubby Up game consists solely of whispering to herself, "Don't! Don't! Don't!" as she stealthily tiptoes towards her goal and then triumphantly pounces on me, the pretending-to-sleep Bubby. I look into her eyes, those beautiful pools that are so dark I can't distinguish her pupils, and ask, "Are you a cow?" She vigorously shakes her head, "Nooooo," giggling as if my humor is unsurpassable. "Are you a hippo?" "Nooooo!" "Then you must be a giraffe!" I bask in her laughter and her loving gaze—rewards of my comedic effort.

She protests being put down for a nap, so enraptured by her world she doesn't want to stop engaging with it. This child is alive and magnificent despite Hitler's heinous plan. I call her Lalka—the name gifted to her by her great-grandfather through me. Lalka. I love the sound of it.

Early on in the COVID pandemic I feared I would miss out on Ruthie's fourth year. All the transitions and stages never to be recaptured. The last visit was full of "I'm ready for Bubby!" when she woke up from her naps. I lamented that she won't always crave my company above others as she does now, and that my turn was being shortened. I felt I was missing out on a significant portion of what has been termed the "magical" years. I experienced the loss as a dull ache. Part of me felt like I might never see Cara, her husband, and Ruthie again. Holocaust lens. Losing parents in a fatal car crash lens.

As the year went on, Ruthie and I learned how to connect through technology. Talking through puppets, and singing nursery rhymes, acting out *Little Red Riding Hood* and *Annie*, hiding from monsters in our blanket cave, never tiring of giggling over our "pippick" joke (Yiddish for belly button), and making up tales about princesses for countless hours, all on FaceTime, have served to strengthen our bond. My fears of impending loss and deprivation were not realized. My parents walked around with those fears because of the history they had lived through—a history that cast a shadow on my life. This evidence of my fears being unfounded showed me once again that it was their history, not my history, and that its lingering shadows need not define my future.

• • •

I believe in my thirties I would have found a way to ask about the Holocaust—certainly after my daughter was born. There are so many questions to which I ache for answers. Tell me about your experience during the war. What were your parents like? Tell me about yourself as a child. Tell me about myself as a child. How can I help you make the last chapter of your life what you want it to be? How can I care for you when it is my turn to do the caring? Tell me how to manage the pain of missing you, of your being taken abruptly, violently. Tell me what you want me to know. Tell me what I crave to know. Tell me. Tell me.

• • •

Joy Wolfe Ensor is a dear friend and fellow author in this anthology. Several years ago I had the honor of visiting her father as he lay dying, no longer speaking, barely responsive. I found myself chanting the famous Polish lullaby "*Ah, Ah, Kotki Dva*" to him. I tripped over the Polish, his native tongue, and badly bastardized the poem, yet the melody and cadence were true. He stirred, and I felt my father there with us. A gift from one survivor to another in the presence of their second-generation daughters.

• • •

The Generations After group is synonymous with the words "Never Forget," a call to conscience to the world. Never forget those six million European Jews; never forget what hatred can transform us into; never forget what must never be repeated. The group imparts a mandate to remember, as the children of survivors share their own recollections—service after service, year after year.

My parents sought to silence insufferable memories in an effort to protect their children and themselves. An impossible, self-defeating mission. Before I wrote this, I wondered to what extent I could grapple with the Holocaust in the absence of my parents, in the absence of having heard their stories, in the absence of their permission to know. I long for my parents to hear their own unspoken stories being told with pride, with love, and with purpose. I wish they could be in the congregation at a Generations After service, to hear me recount them. I also long for my parents to know the impact of it all on me and that I am okay—more than okay. It will have to be enough to sense them sitting on my shoulder.

In my parents' story, in my background story, there was so much good alongside the darkness. People who came through the Holocaust were exceptional almost by definition. They survived against all the odds. My parents were bent, but not broken. They were dignified, heroic, remarkable. Growing up in my family was replete with moments of warmth, joy, and beauty. When it comes to resilience, to perseverance, to accomplishment, to loving, I am my parents' daughter. I believe it never would have been in their script for me to join the Generations After project—they would have tried to forbid it—but here I am.

15

Not Made of Glass

Ruth Wade, daughter of Sidney "Sevek" Finkel

*Sevek (far right) leaving for Windermere, England from Prague,
Czechoslovakia, August 1945*

My father, Sidney "Sevek" Finkel, was eight years old when the Nazis invaded Poland. For four years, Sevek, his father Laib, and his twenty-five-year-old brother Izzy managed to stay together, enduring first the ghetto, and then slave labor and concentration camps. But when he boarded the cattle car to Buchenwald, Sevek was on his own. He had already seen bombers set the people and animals of his town on fire, watched his mother and sister board the cattle train to the Treblinka killing center, grieved for his other murdered sister and infant nephew, suffered several near-death experiences, and witnessed unspeakable acts of brutality inflicted by Nazis on a countless number of Jews. In order to survive he numbed himself, stopped caring, and gave up on love.

In 2006, at age seventy-five, my dad published a memoir, *Sevek and the Holocaust: The Boy Who Refused to Die*. In the following excerpt, Sevek sees his father again, in Buchenwald, days before Laib is transferred to another concentration camp, Dora-Mittelbau, which functioned as an underground ammunition plant. Laib would die there, of exhaustion, overwork, and starvation.

I have an indelible memory of my last meeting with my father. He came across me as I was standing with my friends in the compound. My father cried with joy when he saw me. He hugged me as tears ran down his cheeks. He had lost a lot of weight and he looked very weak and emaciated. He took a piece of bread from the knapsack from his shoulder and he handed it to me. The gesture of the bread showed his great love for me, since these were the only provisions he had for his transport out of Buchenwald. I took the bread, but I felt agitated and uncomfortable. Here standing before me was the one person in the world that I loved more than any other, and yet I was incapable of feeling affection. I bore no resemblance to the son that he knew. Sevek, the fun-loving, affectionate, boyish kid was dead. I now was more like an animal, with instincts only for survival. Likely, he was being sent to his death—I am unsure under what conditions we met—and yet I was silent. I turned my back on my own father without giving him the slightest bit of encouragement or acknowledgment.

Who was I? What kind of an animal had I become in the camps? This encounter was so powerful that it stayed with me for the rest of my life. Guilt plagued me and caused me to believe that I had betrayed my father. I left my father standing alone and walked back to my block to be with the young people. "Old people had no right to live; they were taking resources from the young," I thought to myself. My God, I was beginning to think just like the Nazis.[1]

I didn't know this story growing up, but the way my dad chose to survive even after the war ended affected our relationship in a profound way. I longed for his love and approval. His trauma-induced inability to provide tenderness and caring left me feeling frustrated and angry.

• • •

I don't remember living with my father. He moved out when I was two and remarried when I was four. He lived on the South Side of Chicago and I lived on the North Side, a world away. I saw him on occasional weekends and on school holidays, along with my brother Leon, who was two years older than me. As we waited for our father to pick us up, eyes fixated on the window, we competed to see who could spot him first. This helped me to get through the interminable wait. From what I recall, my dad was always late, and sometimes he didn't show up at all. When I was little it was a huge disappointment, but I was usually placated by his big hugs and our adventures at the zoo or trips to the toy store. When I got older, seeing him became agonizing. His first comment to me was always about my looks—I had put on a little weight, or I had lost a little weight. In my early teens, he gave me a book about hair and makeup. Was this a message? Was I supposed to win his love by improving my appearance? His two stepdaughters from his wife Jean's first marriage were of Swedish descent—blond, tall, thin—and he loved to boast about how beautiful they were. I took his bragging personally; clearly, I wasn't pretty enough. And when we went to his house, I got little attention—I was immediately sent off to play with the girls. When I confronted him about his focus on my looks, he would go off on a rant about how women had it so much better in the past. Modern, educated career women couldn't be happy, he said. Was he purposely pushing my buttons or did he really believe this? Either way, it was infuriating and offensive. When I plucked up the courage to talk to him about not spending time with me, he would deny it or make an excuse. Any confrontation on my part was met with a retort that left me feeling like I was crazy, like any deficit in the relationship was my fault.

As painful as this was, I always wanted to please him.

When I was sixteen, my dad went to England for some kind of reunion. I now know that it was a gathering of The Boys—the group of orphan survivors who flew from Czechoslovakia to English boarding schools after the war. He came home and demanded that I write a letter and become pen pals with the daughter of one of his friends. "What's her name?" I asked. He didn't know. Filled with exasperation and embarrassment, but wanting to make him happy, I addressed a letter to "The Sixteen-Year-Old Girl Who Lives Here." I carried on a pen pal friendship with the girl (her name was Marilyn) for many years, but I don't remember ever talking about our fathers and our relationships with them, let alone what they had been through.

In college and during my mid-twenties, I decided that I had two choices when it came to my dad. Acknowledge him and feel my self-esteem plummet or ignore him. Avoiding the relationship wasn't difficult. I didn't see him or talk to him very often anyway. But inevitably he would pop back into my life, I would end up feeling hurt, and the cycle would begin again.

Just after my twenty-sixth birthday, my dad told me he was an alcoholic and that he was in AA. He apologized for all he had put me through. He took ownership of his neglect and blame. I wasn't crazy after all! We began an adult relationship, but it was still rocky. Holidays at his house were anxious and depressing. There was little warmth, and everything seemed forced. We were all supposed to act like a big happy family, but my dad's other family was very cliquish and often went out of their way to not be in a room with me or my brother. When we spoke at the dinner table or my dad asked us a question, I felt their eyes rolling, mocking us. I endured this for several more years because it meant a lot to my dad, but I finally told him I couldn't come to his house for holidays anymore. We were going to have to create a different kind of relationship, one between just him and me.

• • •

I once attended a youth group talk with an Auschwitz survivor named Etta Jaffe, and we watched a graphic documentary about the Holocaust. I never associated these events with my dad. Maybe because he never spoke about his experiences during the war, maybe because I couldn't believe that anything this horrible could have happened to him, or maybe because my brother and I followed an unspoken rule not to ask. Reflecting back on that time, I find myself confused about what I did and did not know about my dad's past. Recently I've begun to wonder if my memory has been playing tricks on me. I did know some things . . . what *did* I know?

I always knew that my dad was born in Poland and that something bad had happened to him when he was young. This made me feel guilty. How could I have bad feelings about him when he had been through something unspeakable?

I knew that my Hebrew name was supposed to be Faiga, after my dad's mother. But the rabbi told my mother, "That's not a Hebrew name, it's a Polish name." I was relieved they had given me the Hebrew name of Ruchama instead. It was hard enough being named Ruth when everyone else my age was Susan or Debbie. I at least wanted a more "normal" Hebrew name. I never gave my grandmother Faiga another thought. More recently I've learned that I was named after my dad's Aunt Rachel. Why didn't they use her name as my Hebrew name? And why didn't he ever tell me about her?

As a child I knew that my brother Leon was named after my dad's father Laib. But we never asked one question about who he was and why he wasn't here. We never knew, until decades later, that he was my dad's hero and that what happened to him led to my dad's emotional downfall.

When I was twenty-five years old, my dad's older brother Izzy recorded his audio testimonial. I listened to the tapes and learned about the ghetto, the concentration camps, and their experiences with slave labor for the first time, but the quality of the audio was poor and Uncle Izzy's Polish-English accent was hard to understand. I remember being fascinated but then, strangely, I forgot about it. And my dad still wasn't talking.

Although Uncle Izzy and Aunt Lola had heavy accents, I never realized that my dad had an accent until a friend asked about it in college.

Was I in denial about my dad's past?

• • •

I've come to understand that my dad never intended to hurt me—his wounds were deep, and he was not capable of healing until he shed his survival mode and began telling his story. Thirty-three years old and pregnant, I wanted to know more about my grandparents, Laib and Faiga. I think I was finally ready to hear my dad's story and I became persistent in getting him to open up. He must have decided that it was time, too. I was the first person he told. He chose me. This was the act of love I had craved for so long.

I always think about the experience of my dad sharing his story in the context of *his* healing journey—his reclaiming his memories and becoming a storyteller and an educator. Now I am asking myself how *I* felt hearing his story for the first time. He was sitting in an overstuffed club chair by the window while I sat on the sofa across from him, listening in stunned silence.

He described two sisters I'd never heard of, Ronia and Frania. Frania was five years older than him, pretty and spirited. Boys liked her, and even though Sevek was just a little kid he felt very protective of her. Ronia, twenty years older than him, was married and spoke many languages, including Hebrew. She wanted to immigrate to Palestine with the Zionist youth movement, but her father wouldn't allow it, couldn't bear her being so far away. Ronia became pregnant when they were living in the ghetto. When it came time for her to give birth, Laib was able to smuggle her out to a Catholic hospital using false papers. After her identity was discovered, the infant boy was thrown out of the hospital window. Ronia was taken to the Jewish cemetery and shot.

From his club chair, my dad shared stories about more relatives I'd never heard of, about watching bomber planes swoop down so close he could see the pilot in the cockpit, and about his final meeting with his father. How long did he talk and what happened after? Did we hug? Did he get in his car and drive home? I don't remember.

I don't recall getting emotional, but looking back, that doesn't surprise me—I am Sevek's daughter. I've inherited his ability to numb my feelings when confronted with pain. Perhaps I was in shock. This was far from the *Hogan's Heroes* fantasies I'd entertained, where my dad was held captive by German buffoons and had escaped through the underground. I didn't know how to process this information.

A few months later, my dad, his wife, my husband, brother, nephew and I traveled to Washington, D.C., and visited the newly opened United States Holocaust Memorial Museum. I spent a long time in the Hall of Remembrance, thinking about what it would have been like to have an Aunt Ronia and an Aunt Frania. I sat quietly, contemplating the loss of a family I hadn't even known I had.

• • •

My dad was from Piotrków Trybunalski, a town of about forty thousand including fifteen thousand Jews. Sevek was a happy, spoiled, adventurous kid with four older siblings. The following passage from his book gave me a glimpse into his life before, which sounds so ordinary, down to the sibling rivalry between Sevek and his sister Lola.

On Fridays the house smelled delicious with the aroma of baking and cooking. When we finally all sat down at the dining room table, my mother would cover her eyes and say a blessing over the challah. Her voice sounded so soothing and beautiful to me. Dad would be relaxed and calm and acting very caring. Everything was so nice and I would be feeling very happy. And then Lola would start in on me. She would have to open her mouth and say something like, "I saw Sevek at the market this afternoon and he had no shoes on, and he went around begging for food. It was so disgusting." And then I would get angry and would be ready to go over where she sat and smack her one. But Frania, my youngest sister, would hold on to my hand and tell me to let it go. Father would come to my defense as always and tell the mean Lola to be quiet. I would get my revenge by sticking out my tongue at her. After dinner Dad would always say that he wanted me and Izzy to go to the synagogue with him. I liked going to the synagogue with Father. I would sit next to him and he would put his arms around me and cover us both with a prayer shawl that he wore. When he prayed, his eyes would close, and he would hug me and kiss my head. I felt so loved by him.

It makes my heart happy knowing that my dad was loved. But I wonder if he ever contemplated what kind of parent he wanted to be. Did he imagine being a father like his father, wrapping his child in a prayer shawl and giving away his precious bread? No, I don't think he ever did. I don't think he was capable of loving me the way his father loved him. I blame the Nazis; they took away my dad's ability to love fiercely. They stole the parent I should have had.

I'm grateful that I have the capacity to love my child with a ferocious intensity.

• • •

Only six percent of Piotrków Trybunalski's Jewish population survived the Holocaust. My grandmother Faiga and aunt Frania were amongst the Jews of the town murdered in the killing center of Treblinka. Frania was actually not selected to go to Treblinka. She and Lola were among the few chosen to stay behind to work as slave laborers in the ghetto. But Frania could not bear to be separated from her mother. Lola squeezed her sister's hand tightly, but Frania broke free and ran off to find Faiga. This is the only story from the Holocaust that my Aunt Lola ever told. Her inability to save her sister haunted her forever.

Every victim's death is a tragedy and each survivor's story is a startling combination of random luck and humanity. Sometimes people showed their humanity with seemingly small gestures: a look the other way, a piece of bread. Other times humanity involved bigger and riskier choices. I feel a need to tell these stories because they're examples of how our choices make a difference. And while many of my relatives were not on the receiving end of that lifesaving sliver of luck or humanity, my dad and uncle were. Here are just a few of the stories that fill me with awe.

When Izzy was called up for military duty at the front, he was injured and left for dead. German soldiers found him, and when Izzy spoke to them in fluent German, they mistook him for a Pole of German descent. They took him to a military hospital, where he was given medical attention for eleven months even though the staff learned that he was Jewish. He had heard of other Jewish soldiers being treated and then shot once they were released, but he travelled back home safely.

When the Nazis liquidated the ghetto, they announced that two thousand Jews could avoid deportation if they had work permits. Izzy was able to attain work permits from some former friends. He called them former friends because they only provided the permits in exchange for money. Luckily, he could pay, and my uncle and grandfather were able to remain in the ghetto. Sevek, however, was not yet thirteen, he was destined for the train to the Treblinka killing center with his mother. But Izzy and Laib saved Sevek—they hid him behind them during the Selection, and when a Nazi officer noticed him, Izzy bribed the Nazi to look the other way.

In the Bugaj slave labor camp, an SS officer held a gun to my father's temple and told him, "This bullet is going to enter your head." But he didn't pull the trigger. Young Sevek received a thrashing instead. My dad became famous in the camp for saying, "Go ahead, my ass is not made of glass" while enduring a sadistic beating.

In Buchenwald, political prisoners who assisted the Nazis in running the concentration camp created an underground movement to save as many children as possible by giving them lighter work assignments, providing a few extra pieces of bread, and housing them in disease-ridden barracks. The Nazis feared getting sick, so they tended to stay away from this area of the camp. Thus the children had a higher chance of survival.

Following a death march out of Buchenwald and a three-week cattle car train ride with no food or water, Sevek's train reached Theresienstadt concentration camp, where the Jews were then liberated. Sevek was so weak at this point that he succumbed to typhus. While miraculously recovering, he heard someone calling his name. Izzy had found him.

The Jews of Great Britain received permission and raised sufficient funds to transport seven hundred orphaned children to the safety of England after the war. On August 14, 1945, my dad flew in the first transport of three hundred children to Lake Windermere. Here he began his journey back to humanity.

In 2020, my cousin Anita, Izzy's daughter, attained documentation kept by the World Jewish Relief Agency, the organization that supported my dad throughout his stay in England. Reading through the pages, I learned the details of my father's difficult postwar adjustment. He had to learn the basic rules of civilized behavior. Sevek had not eaten a meal at a dining room table in years; didn't know how to use proper utensils; and hoarded or stole food whenever possible, not trusting there would be another meal. He didn't know the fundamentals of reading, writing, or math—school had ended for him at the age of eight. On top of that he had to learn English. With great effort and assistance, my dad made enormous progress, but he failed one qualifying exam, which led to ending his formal education. His self-esteem damaged, Sevek went to work while his friends continued their academic pursuits.

It saddens me to think about his suffering, how hard his life was even after liberation from the Nazis. But I have also come to appreciate my dad's resilience and courage. In 1951, at the age of nineteen, he persisted in acquiring his visa to immigrate to the United States. He worked hard, became a successful salesman and manager, completed his GED in his fifties, and triumphantly received an honorary doctorate from St. Xavier University in 2012 for his Holocaust education work. In his keynote commencement address to the university's winter graduating class, he talked about returning to Buchenwald earlier that year, and the anger he felt towards the Nazis. He said, "At first I thought 'How could they do this to me?' But then I said, 'to hell with them, I'm alive and doing well.'" The audience's applause was resounding.

• • •

My dad was truly surprised when he turned out to be a gifted speaker. As he shared his story more and more, he made incredible connections with teachers and students all over the country. He lovingly wrote me this letter in 1997, sharing the experience of his visit to a school in Cabot, Arkansas, where he was adopted by teacher Mary Bryant. Mary embraced my dad in a way that he had never experienced. She made him and his story the center of her middle school curriculum. More than that, her love and care lifted his spirits, making him believe that he had something of great worth to offer.

I got out of the car and walked with Mary, into a crowd of one hundred twenty children. All the kids were very excited and immediately surrounded me. The kids had raised eight hundred dollars by washing cars, walking for ten cents a mile, and doing a bake sale to bring me to their school. All the young people then proceeded to individually hug me, one by one. They sang Hebrew songs and danced Israeli dances; they had learned all this just to make me feel welcome.

I saw a sign on the south side of the building proclaiming in large letters, "The Future Home of the Sidney Finkel Survivor Garden." What was happening here was far beyond anything that I could have imagined. Mary could read my mind and said, "Yes, Sidney, it is true, this is your garden forever. The kids and people from the community have worked for weeks getting ready. We have big plans for this garden." They were going to put in a bench, and a stone with my name on it, and more plants. This was all joy and happiness. I couldn't help but think that my Higher Power had something to do with this. How else can you explain such an outpouring of love?

For a moment it washed away all my humiliation at being persecuted for being a Jew. Here were Christian people that were welcoming me with open arms.

I entered the school and walked on red paper that lined the corridor, in honor of me. There were signs on the walls saying, "Welcome Sidney." The principal pointed to paper links that were hanging on the walls and explained that the boys and girls had worked for months linking the chains, which stood symbolically for the six million Jews that had perished in the

Holocaust. They had actually been successful in making one hundred fifty thousand of them!

Mary had built the kids up so much that they considered me already a hero. I just hoped that I could meet their heightened expectation of me. I spoke with a lot of energy, gesturing with my hands and raising and lowering my voice. Lowering my voice to no more than a whisper when I told them of the tragic death of my family. These kids, all of them eighth graders, were paying attention. They were following my words closely, and there was a minimum of movement. I had reached them. My story was completely out of the realm of their experiences, but they could follow the adventures of Sevek. They could relate to being discriminated against and picked upon themselves. Many of these kids, Mary told me, came from broken families. At the age of twelve, some were doing drugs and were in trouble with the law. These kids crowded around me, hugging me and writing their names on the back of my school tee shirt that I wore. I had to sign my name on their books and have my picture taken with them.

When I started telling my story, I was amazed by the reaction. The students asked many of the same questions that I have been asking myself for years. Teachers and friends called my talks powerful and moving but myself, I didn't think of these talks as being anything special. I was simply telling my story.[2]

• • •

My father's story of survival enabled us to create a strong bond. With his appreciation and love, I have found myself immersed in helping him communicate his message of tolerance and resilience. We created a second edition of his book with information received from the Buchenwald archives, published it as an e-book, updated his website and video, and started a Facebook author page. I used to get annoyed with my dad. I'd travel to see him in Tucson, and after a giant bear hug, squeezing the breath out of me, he would sit outside, smoke his cigar, look at his Kindle, and ignore me. But since I started writing this narrative and reflecting more deeply on his life, I've let it all go, accepting him for who he is and just enjoying our times together. All of my exasperation has melted away. Our last time together, I referred to us as "Holocaust Buddies," and he nodded and agreed.

As my dad entered his mid-eighties and cut down on his speaking schedule and travel, I grew concerned about his legacy, and I began wondering, could I effectively tell his story? Some might say it's not my story to tell. Thankfully, I wasn't there, I didn't live it. But I am still compelled to speak. If I don't, when my dad is gone, who will bear witness? Who will provide the personal connection necessary to keep his story alive, and hopefully, in this small way, keep history from repeating itself?

I took on the challenge, meeting with the director of education at the Florida Holocaust Museum and developing a presentation. My hope was to give students a sense of the connection between me and my dad, as well as telling them the story of Sevek—once a kid just like them— who managed to survive through a dark period of time that lacked so much humanity.

My first audience was a class of fifth graders. My dad was so excited; he couldn't wait to hear about it. "I love fifth graders—they're the best!" he said. He was right about how great they were. When I saw the mesmerized looks on the kids' faces, I understood firsthand the awe my dad felt telling his powerful story and why he told it over and over again for so many years.

In the letter he sent to me, he wrote, "I didn't think of these talks as being anything special. I was simply telling my story." Expressing himself with humility is no longer my dad's style. He loves attention, even going so far as to have a "Holocaust Survivor" baseball cap made for himself and his survivor friends. He wears it out all of the time and people come up to him to shake his hand and even buy his meals. When he goes to the doctor, the whole office ends up hearing about (and buying) his book. But there are still times when he is taken aback by the response he gets. He may have thought he was simply telling his story, but we've both come to realize that it's so much more. Through his example, we offer young people a path to resilience and hope as they go through their own difficult times. In 2017, I accompanied my dad to a school talk in Indiana. Afterward, a boy of Sevek's age when he went to Buchenwald hugged my dad and told him that he had a brain tumor. But he wasn't going to give up, he said; he was going to survive, just like Sevek.

My father says that when he tells his story to an audience it makes him feel closer to his family. I get that. When I tell the story of Sevek, I feel closer to my dad. In 2020, he sent me my own baseball cap, embroidered with "My Dad is a Holocaust Survivor."

I plan to offer Sevek's story of hope to many people for many years to come. And I believe that someday the third generation will keep his story alive.

• • •

I love the story of how my parents met. My mom, who grew up in Chicago, met my dad at a wedding. They were at two different weddings in the same hotel; the wedding my dad was attending had a cash bar and the wedding my mom was attending had an open bar. So, my dad crashed the wedding with the open bar to get free drinks and asked my mom to dance so that he would appear to be a guest. They were married for seven years.

My dad was happy to have married a Jewish woman from a large boisterous family. Even though he didn't feel a connection with God himself, his heritage was important to him and he wanted to raise a Jewish family. He was pleased that my brother and I belonged to a synagogue and were bar/bat mitzvah. We went to Jewish summer camp, were involved in youth group, and sang in Debbie Friedman's "Sing Unto God" choir. My father told me that he wanted to believe in God, but during the Holocaust he saw that the most religious Jews were the first to be persecuted, and this had a lasting effect on him. He also thought the ultra-Orthodox were too passive, believing that whatever happened was "God's will." When he went to AA, he struggled with the idea of a higher power. Over time he came to believe that his higher power was his community: the friends who supported him, believed in him, and made him feel safe and smart and loved. I feel a similar way about being a second-generation survivor. Often when I meet 2Gs, I feel an instant rapport and am welcomed with open arms.

My Holocaust inheritance and love of Jewish heritage contributed to the way I raised my son Ike. He grew up identifying as a Jew, proud of his grandfather, aware of Sevek's story from a young age. It always seemed to be part of his fabric. I invited Ike to write a piece for a Yom HaShoah service in 2017, when he was twenty-four years old. Reading his narrative for the first time was emotional for me—no numbness. I was overwhelmed with joy realizing that Ike had inherited my father's optimism and resilience. Unlike the relationship between my dad and me, the connection between Ike and his grandfather has always been filled with a light, easy love.

I don't remember the first time I learned that my grandfather was a Holocaust survivor. My mother recounts that I was in her womb when he first began to talk about his story. In that sense, I suppose I've always carried his story with me. It's never been a burden. Of course it comes with a natural helping of Jewish guilt. How can I skip services to watch a football game if my grandpa has kept his faith through all the persecution he suffered? But mostly his story serves as a reminder of the power of love.

When I was eleven or twelve, I went with my grandpa when he spoke to a group of young students somewhere near his home in Arizona. While many of the details are lost on me today—the name of the school, the city we were in, the teacher who had invited us—I will always remember that day in the fluorescent-lit, gray-tiled elementary school auditorium. I had heard my grandpa's story many times, and read it many more, but on that day something specific stood out. As I observed teachers brushing back tears and watched the wonderment and curiosity on the students' faces, I could feel an overwhelming sense of love for my grandpa throughout the room. I could feel my grandfather reciprocate that same love as he paced across the stage sharing his story and warmly answering students' questions. It struck me that there was so much love in the room, brought out by a story of such anguish and heartbreak. I was amazed by the contrast between the immense pain my grandpa spoke about and the love I felt in that auditorium.

Later in life, my cousin Bari and I got the opportunity to travel to Winnipeg, Canada with our grandfather to introduce him as he accepted a storytelling award. The reception where he spoke was held at a wonderful family center with glass walls, overlooking a gorgeous park. The crowd was made up of distinguished academics and storytellers rather than fifth graders, and we were half a continent away, but I felt that same love surrounding my grandpa. After the nerves of public speaking faded, I saw the same scene that had taken place years ago in that auditorium in Arizona. I felt the love for my grandpa through the generous applause, and in the kind words the audience had for my cousin and me. I could feel his love in his smile and back-breaking hug. Again, I was blown away that my grandfather, who had experienced such horror, was able to bring so much love into the room.

As a part of the generations after, I think of my grandpa's story as my own. Seemingly since birth, I've known about the pain and cruelty he experienced as a young boy. But I've also time and time again experienced the love he has to give, and the love the world now has for him. I've seen that even from the darkest places love can grow and flourish. And that is the part of his story—my story—that I will always carry with me.

• • •

Forgiveness is often a theme for survivors and their children. I don't understand how one forgives the Nazis for their purposeful choice to systemically exterminate six million individuals because they were Jewish. But my dad says he had to forgive them in order to move on with his life. Closer to the heart, though, was my dad's need to forgive himself for turning away from his father when they met for the last time in Buchenwald.

In 2012, when my dad was invited to the sixty-sixth anniversary commemoration of the liberation of Buchenwald, he brought Jean, Leon, and me to the spot where he likely met his father for the last time. We stood in a circle, arms around one another, and Sevek forgave himself, speaking aloud to his father:

Ruth and Sidney, Tucson, Arizona, 2021

On this space of ground here I'm thinking of the day we met in Buchenwald. I was embarrassed and disappointed that I didn't act as the loving son that I should have, and I'm sorry. But I know that you can feel that I am here with your grand-children, Leon and Ruth. And I can see you smiling and can see how happy you are that I survived. You live in my spirit and I loved you and I'm sorry you didn't make it. I just want to tell you that I know that you're here with us and I feel your presence. And we are here on this spot to tell you that we all love you very much.

I am not a Holocaust survivor. But I am the daughter of a Holo-caust survivor. I didn't live the Holocaust, but I have lived the conse-quences. The abandonment, the anger, the blaming. And ultimately, the unbelievable awe of survival. I love my dad and I'm grateful that I am capable of loving him. Forgiveness starts with ourselves.

16

One Day the World
Will Be the World Again

Joy Wolfe Ensor, daughter of Henia Karmel and Leon Wolfe

Ilona and Henia Karmel, Stockholm, Sweden, 1946

There was barely enough room to hold all the memorial candles that my parents lit every Yizkor. The tiny galley kitchen in our New York City apartment was short of counter space, and the bookshelves were not flameproof, so the candles were arrayed on a rolling Salton hot table, tucked in the hallway outside my bedroom.

There was a candle for each of my grandmothers; another two for my grandfathers; and "one more for everyone else," including nine of my father's ten brothers and sisters and almost all of their offspring—the "sweet children of the family." The candles flickered through the night, casting shadows that danced on the walls and ceiling just outside my bedroom door.

Those flickers and shadows terrified me as a child. I dreaded having to cross their path to go from my room to the bathroom. I would hold off as long as I could, and then, covering my eyes and crouching low, skitter past the candles as quickly as I could, lest the ghosts in the flickers grab me.

It never occurred to me to ask my parents to roll the hot table to a different location. I never told them that I was frightened. I knew from my father's burning eyes and my mother's overflowing ones that the candles signified something terrible; both my parents seemed to retreat into a dark and distant place until the last of the candles flickered out. I couldn't grasp the enormity of their losses, but I imagined that somehow the dead lingered in those shadows.

What's a mother to do with the ghosts in the nursery? How does she bind up her own pain enough to pass the family legacy on to the next generation? When the time comes for her to explain to her children that they were named for murdered loved ones, how does she tell *that* story?

• • •

In 1943, in the midst of the horror and degradation of the Skarżysko slave labor camp, my twenty-two-year-old mother wrote a defiant line: "My name is Number 906. And guess what? I still write verse."[1] Henia Karmel and her sister Ilona had already endured the terror of the Nazi invasion. Their family had fled Kraków for the East, but after their father was captured and deported to his death, they decided they were better off returning to the relative safety and community of the Kraków ghetto.

From there, my mother, aunt, and grandmother were enslaved in Płaszów, Skarżysko, and Buchenwald. Along with the other prisoners, they were starved and beaten. They fell ill with typhoid and typhus. They watched as loved ones were taken off to their deaths. Their survival depended on contributing to the German war effort. Working under horrific conditions, they stuffed munitions with poisonous picric acid that infiltrated their lungs and yellowed their skin.

And yet, through all of this, Henia and Ilona wrote poetry, on sheets of paper smuggled into the barracks from the slave labor factory. In the progressive Jewish academy they'd attended until the outbreak of World War II, the sisters had studied Polish, learning Adam Mickiewicz's classical romantic verses and Julian Tuwim's experimental poetic forms. They loved Poland and her literature, even though, my mother lamented, Poland never loved them back.

MY LANGUAGE

> I can't look for a new homeland
> Because Poland
> Has captivated me with its poetry.
> I scratch on a steel plate
> My soul in blood, my language.[2]

In the summer of 1944, my mother, aunt, and grandmother were among the six thousand women of Skarżysko who were transported to the HASAG slave labor plant at Buchenwald. In April of 1945, as the war drew to a close, the Buchenwald inmates were gathered for a death march to elude the approaching American Army. Determined to preserve the poems, my mother sewed the manuscript into the hem of her prison uniform. I imagine her huddled in her bunk in the darkness, green eyes flashing, the needle moving swiftly through the thin fabric of her dress, forming tight stitches with a skill that I always envied, but could never match.

• • •

Lying in the twin bed in my tiny bedroom in New York City, down the hall from my parents, I was sometimes awakened by the guttural German and Polish cries of my father's nightmares, and sometimes by the sound of my mother, hop-hop-hopping on one foot from her bed to her bathroom.

As a child I thought it was normal that in the evenings, daddies took off their shoes and socks, their shirts and trousers, and mommies took off their skirts and blouses, their brassieres and girdles, and their wooden leg.

The leg was a triumph of the sculptor's art, the wood stained to match my mother's skin tone. It had two different screw-on feet to accommodate flats and high heels. The interior of the socket was sanded smooth beneath a heavy coat of varnish designed to protect the stump from abrasion and open sores.

My fascination with the leg's aesthetic was offset by the more sobering experience of watching my mother put it on. This involved a laborious maneuver—first lubricating the stump with Mennen's medicated talcum powder, which rose in a perfumed cloud that lodged in my nose and settled on the bed covers, before suctioning it into the socket. The process involved a nakedness that my older brother John was not permitted to witness; that intimacy was the province of a daughter. It was such a complicated and time-consuming ordeal that if my mother woke up in the middle of the night to pee, she would skip it—thus the hop-hop-hopping sound that punctuated my sleep.

My mother explained that she and my aunt had each lost a leg in "the accident in the war." As a young child I imagined that their legs had been blown off by a cannonball, leaving clean stumps behind. But later I gathered that some kind of motor vehicle had run them over.

I was a young adult when I first saw the letter that my mother and aunt had written from their hospital room following liberation. They'd had the foresight to make a handwritten copy of it. Once in this country, my mother translated the letter from German and saved it with her other papers. The addressee, Yitzhak Sternbuch, was a Swiss businessman who, with his wife Recha Rottenberg, smuggled Jewish refugees to safety.

Leipzig, 15 September 1945

Dear Mr. Sternbuch:

I hope you still remember us. We are relatives of Rela Rottenberg, and you also were in touch with our father. He and the rest of the family were gassed on November 17, 1942. Uncle Menashe Karmel, who also corresponded with you, was executed together with his mother and son in the Kraków camp in March of 1943.

A year ago, the two of us were brought to Germany, to the Buchenwald concentration camp. On April 13, 1945, as the Americans were approaching, the SS guards "evacuated" the camp. We spent the next two weeks without food or shelter. We slept in the woods and went crazy from hunger.

On the twelfth day of our wandering, when all escape roads seemed to be closed, the guards let us rest in a ditch. Suddenly a German tank appeared. Since we all wore prison garb, the tank drove deliberately into the ditch, and as we were sitting in the first row, we became the victims.

Taken to a hospital in Döbeln (Saxonia), our Mama, who was with us all throughout, died the next day.

The two of us were operated on, and each of us lost a leg. The remaining ones were badly fractured but worth saving.

For the last two weeks we are the wards of St. Elisabeth Hospital, brought here through the intervention of the local Jewish community.

Our situation is very pitiful. I am 24 and my sister 20 years old.

We paid a high price for being Jews.

You, Mr. Sternbuch, acted in the past as a liaison with our uncle, Gerson Rosenbojm, in New York. Would you by any chance still have his address? Please communicate to him our tragic fate and he will do his utmost to help us. He could be reached through the Jewish Community Council, or the "Joint." He himself escaped in 1940 from Belgium and made it to New York. Get in touch also with our uncle, Yehuda Karmel,

Palestine, Kibbutz Beth-Zerah, and our cousin, Joseph Karmel, London (exact address unknown).

For the time being, our hands are tied. Please help us as soon as possible. We are lonely and helpless. Our best thanks.

Henia Wolf, née Karmel
Ilona Karmel

P.S. We expect your prompt reply.

• • •

I was a sickly little girl and a notoriously fussy eater. My mother, frantic for my well-being, used every imaginable tactic to get food into me. She waved forkfuls of food before my mouth and chanted, "Here comes the airplane—open the airport!" She provoked me with nicknames like "String Bean" and "Soup Green." She performed dramatic recitations of the cautionary Polish children's tale "Hanna Nyatka," about a little girl so stubbornly skinny that when her mother treated her to a balloon from the vendor in the park, it lofted her high into a tree, leaving her stuck and frightened until the firemen came to rescue her.

Over seemingly endless bowls of green pea soup and plates of brisket, potatoes and spinach, my mother cajoled me to eat: "If you finish your soup down to the bottom, I will tell you the story of how my Aunt Dora became a pediatrician." "Eat your vegetables, and I will tell you the story of how I played in the park with my grandmother in Warsaw."

Those stories whetted my appetite. They followed a fairytale arc: an idyllic childhood, a time of suffering under a fearsome ogre, and finally the happy ending in which the ogre is vanquished and the heroes survive. My parents were the center of my universe, and the stories, told by the heroine herself, suffused me with a sense of nourishment and protection even greater than my mother's best culinary offerings.

The family lore went back to the 1400s, when the Karmels fled the Spanish Inquisition and settled in Kraków. Over the centuries, the family grew in size and stature, producing rabbis and scholars, tradesmen and merchants. Once upon a time, my mother said, when Kraków was the capital of the kingdom, the royal family paraded past a throng of adoring subjects. The royal prince spied a beautiful young woman and immediately fell in love. She was a Karmel, and the prince abandoned his throne to marry her. This story so charmed me as a child that I begged my mother to tell it over and over again.

• • •

Though more reticent than my mother, my father Löbel "Leszek" Wolf (later changed to Leon Wolfe) would occasionally surprise me with anecdotes about his life before the war. He was the youngest of eleven children in a Hasidic family. His father was a manufacturer, a philanthropist, and a Religious Party representative in Kraków's Jewish City Council. His older brothers, noting the opportunities newly opened to Jews in the era between the World Wars, encouraged him to pursue the secular education that had been inaccessible to them. They helped him enroll in the Hebrew gymnasium that Henia and Ilona also attended. Later, with his brothers' support, my father became the first in his family to attend university. At age twenty-three, when he was about to enter his last year of law school, the Nazis entered Kraków, deported most of the professors to Dachau, and forbade all instruction.

I collected my father's nuggets as they dropped. He adored his mother Sara. He revered his father Joachim. He was particularly close to his next-older brother and sister, Eli and Eva. During his childhood, he enjoyed weekend visits to his grandmother in the city of Wadowice and especially looked forward to playing soccer with her neighbor, a boy nicknamed Lolek who would grow up to become Pope John Paul II.

My father shared little about his suffering during the war while I was growing up, but I heard the cries from his nightmares. "He had a bad dream about the war," my mother would explain. Over time, she described his losses: his parents, Eli and Eva and seven more brothers and sisters, his countless nieces and nephews.

We could never have enough Salton hot tables to hold the yahrzeit candles for all of them.

ANNIVERSARIES

In my house no mourning candles will ever glisten.
Too many would have to burn—millions.

Then days of anniversaries would follow
Too many to honor the lost ones, it would take forever.

In my house no mourning candles will ever glisten.
I tell you, there's not even enough time to light them!

My whole life is already a prolonged day of mourning
Each minute is spent in grief

What would I do with little teardrop candles
When my heart is like a furnace

That burned up my happiness with the others?[3]

• • •

302

Having a princess ancestor was romantic, but what I wanted most of all was a grandmother. I turned to American television and depictions in children's books to create an imaginary one for myself: a pleasingly plump, soft-faced, white-haired lady who baked cookies, knitted sweaters, and rocked me on her lap. She never had need to utter a harsh word, never mind ward off a harsh blow.

My mother couldn't give me a grandmother like that, but she told me stories about the grandmother that I would have had, if only. Symcha Rosenbaum had grown up in Warsaw, and brought her big-city glamour and sophistication to Kraków when she entered into an arranged marriage with my grandfather Hirsch Karmel. She had a soft face and delicate hands. She loved yellow flowers, and even in the Kraków ghetto managed to find some to brighten their squalid quarters. Hardened by the terrors and losses of the war, she remained fiercely protective of Henia and Ilona. Toward the end, when her strength was ebbing, she tried to trick them into taking her meager allotment of bread, claiming it was extra rations that someone had smuggled to her from the factory.

Symcha held her daughters to account if even their language, never mind their behavior, became coarse. "Your grandmother always told us," my mother said, "'One day the world will be the world again. You have to remember how to behave.'"

"Symcha," translated into English, is Joy. This is the grandmother for whom I am named.

I never entirely gave up my fantasy of having a soft, round, white-haired grandmother in my life. I sometimes joke that I fell for my husband because his mother looked so much the part that I imagined her being my future children's grandmother. As for the grandmother I never knew, I use her moral compass as my guide: "One day the world will be the world again. You have to remember how to behave." It's the least I can do to carry on her good name.

• • •

When I was old enough, I began to ask my mother questions. What happened to Aunt Dora the pediatrician? What happened to the sweet children of the family? What happened to all the other characters in those vivid childhood tales? My mother had been waiting for this moment. "They died in the war," she would say. "Why?" I asked. Long pause. "It's what God wanted," my mother replied with the slightest shrug and a deep quivering sigh.

The answer didn't persuade me then; it does not persuade me now.

Nor, apparently, did it persuade my mother. Years later, ruing the interruption of her education when she was eighteen, she enrolled at a small Catholic college in our Bronx neighborhood. The nuns loved her from the start. And they loved her still when she ended an autobiographical essay by recalling this conversation and concluding, "God was invented by a mother who could no longer answer her child's questions."

• • •

My parents had been married for less than two years when the Kraków ghetto was liquidated and the Jews were deported to the nearby Płaszów camp and then dispersed to camps across the Reich. They promised each other that, should they both survive the war, they would return to Kraków and find each other. My father, after being liberated from a subcamp of Gross-Rosen, kept his word. At a newly established reunification center, he met my mother's cousin, who had been in the Buchenwald death march and had passed by the ditch after the "accident." In her last act before losing consciousness, my mother had ripped the manuscript of poems out of her dress and handed it to this cousin (whose name is unfortunately lost to me), beseeching her to find my father and give it to him.

The cousin had the manuscript in hand when she encountered my father. She told him that Henia, Ilona, and their mother had all been killed. By this time my father was numbed by news of death, but he had the presence of mind to ask her whether the women were actually dead when she last saw them. They were close to death, the cousin said, and could not possibly have survived. My father decided that he had nothing left to lose by searching for the women until he confirmed their fate. His civil service job that gave him access to Jeeps, vodka, and cigarettes, combined with the "Aryan" name he'd adopted during the war and maintained in postwar Poland where antisemitic pogroms persisted, afforded him safe passage across the country.

Word of the sisters' deaths had spread among the remnants of the Kraków Jewish community. Their poems had been part of an underground cultural life in the camps, and the survivors prevailed on my father to give them permission to hold a memorial program. My father, exhausted and heartbroken from his fruitless search, grudgingly acceded. He attended the service, standing at the back of a large cinema in Kraków, listening to the first postwar public reading of the sisters' poems.

The next week, word reached my father that the sisters were alive in the hospital in Leipzig. Using vodka and cigarettes to bribe the border guards, he crossed into East Germany and brought Henia and Ilona home.

My mother was already taking her first steps on a wooden leg but needed medical attention that was unavailable in the "Wild West" chaos of postwar Poland. Ilona's injuries were more severe. My father was able to obtain medical visas through the International Red Cross that, in March 1946, granted them all entry to Sweden.

Ilona received treatment in Stockholm's Karolinska Institute. During her two years of hospitalization, she took up smoking at her doctors' behest so that she wouldn't gain excess weight while bedridden. On her

Henia and Leszek reunited, Rychbach, Poland, 1945

own initiative, she took up the education that had been halted when she was thirteen, devouring stacks of books and learning English by correspondence course.

My mother gave birth to my brother in October 1946. He was named Johann Zwi (later Anglicized to John Howard) for his two lost grandfathers. During his earliest weeks, my mother wrote him a series of letters in a small red leather-bound journal. I first saw the journal when my brother read from it at her funeral. She had tucked an English translation of the letters inside it. They opened with this promise: "I will tell you about . . . all those you weren't given the opportunity to know and to love, all those who will live through you and those who will follow you, because I will create a legend to secure their immortality."

• • •

In the late 1940s, my parents, brother, and aunt were able to immigrate to the United States. Yitzhak Sternbuch, whom my mother and aunt had implored in their letter from their hospital room, had presumably located my great-uncle Gerson Rosenbojm, and he served as the family's sponsor. Gerson paid "key money" to the landlord of a building in Washington Heights (a neighborhood in northern Manhattan so dominated by German Jewish refugees that it was nicknamed "the Fourth Reich"), in order to bribe him to rent to Polish Jews. He helped my father find a job while my mother stayed at home with my brother, and he sent Ilona to the Hebrew Immigrant Aid Society (HIAS) for employment assistance.

The social worker at HIAS offered to place Ilona in a factory and laughed at her when she said that she wanted to attend college. Undeterred, Ilona enrolled in Hunter College in New York City and soon transferred to Radcliffe College, where she was accepted into Archibald MacLeish's creative writing program. Her short story, "Fru Holm," won a *Mademoiselle Magazine* award, and the magazine editor, Cyrilly Abels, included it in a *Best Stories* anthology. Ilona's senior thesis, an autobiographical novel entitled *Stephania*, was published by Houghton Mifflin in 1953.

In 1947, even before my mother and aunt had arrived in the United States, a New York-based fraternal organization of Jewish survivors had privately published their wartime poems. But the poems receded into obscurity as the sisters abandoned both Polish (which my mother always called "the language of my oppression") and poetry, establishing their English-speaking lives—and prose-writing careers—in America.

• • •

My mother, who had been stunningly beautiful in her youth, still cut a glamorous figure through much of my childhood. In Washington

Heights, being a Karmel from Kraków carried cachet, and to my young eyes my mother carried herself with poise and confidence. She enjoyed flirting with the men in our social circle, standing a little too close, her voice rising in a coquettish lilt. My father would glance away while I, sensing his embarrassment, hovered protectively nearby. My mother also loved her women friends. She could talk on the phone with them endlessly. When she entertained guests and the evening came to an end, she and her friends would linger in our apartment foyer for another hour or more, unwilling to part, hugging and kissing and saying good-bye, and then talking some more.

In her youth, my mother told me, she had been athletic and care-free, roaming the city with her friends, skiing in the Tatra Mountains in the winter, and enjoying long hikes and swims in the Zionist sum-mer camp intended to prepare her and other young people for kibbutz life. The mother I grew up with was burdened by the loss of her leg and, when we moved to the more upscale Riverdale section of the Bronx, by the loss of the "Karmel from Kraków" status that had buoyed her in the immigrant neighborhood. Here, she was an accented and lame outsider, her pockets empty of the American social currency of wealth, influence, and physical vitality.

Still vivacious in social gatherings, my mother struggled privately with anxiety and depression. She was ashamed of her physical muti-lation and did all she could to hide the fact of her wooden leg, which to her dying day she never referred to as anything other than "that damn thing."

"That damn thing." After losing everything, my mother chose new life. She doted on my brother and me. I can still see my mother skip-ping down Riverside Drive, in her own way, trying to keep up with me—hopping on her right foot and swinging the heavy wooden left leg around in an awkward arc. I found her determination and ingenuity amazing, and this assessment only grew stronger as I became older. At age four I looked daggers at a bus driver who dared give my mother an impatient glare when she was slow climbing the steep bus steps. I knew why those stairs were difficult for her; why didn't he? I identified with my mother more than I realized: to this day, when I bend over, I unconsciously extend my own left leg stiffly behind me, my body echoing its memory of my mother's movements.

"That damn thing." From a young age I learned to attend closely to my mother's well-being, to avoid causing her any more suffering. Growing up in a survivor community whose most valuable asset was their children, my first job was to be a "happy little Yankee." I could bring my parents pride and status by being clever, assimilated, and articulate in the English language, and by entertaining their guests with piano performances that were a stretch for my little fingers to play.

My mother was always loving and protective, but if I aired routine childhood complaints—that the other girls had fancier clothes or more freedoms—she fixed her gaze on me and said, "May this be the worst thing that ever happens to you." I took the message to heart. My hardships were nothing—nothing!—compared to what she and my father had endured. How could I be so self-indulgent as to claim struggles of my own when I had (as my mother often reminded me) two good legs, and two parents who loved me?

"That damn thing." Refusing to call attention to her disability by using a cane, my mother walked with her arm draped through mine for balance. Whether on outings to the markets on Broadway in Washington Heights, or to synagogue in Riverdale, or on more exciting adventures to downtown department stores and museums, I loved the intimacy and sophistication of what my mother described as a European way of walking. But the heavy pressure of her arm on mine also conveyed the weight of responsibility.

Our family doctor made frequent house calls, and I came to understand that what my mother called "rain pains" were not just charmingly accurate weather forecasts; they were part of the phantom limb pain she endured from her amputation. As I grew into awareness that many of the house calls were for what the doctor deemed her "nervous condition," I worried about my mother's moods, taking on the role of listener, feeling like a sponge absorbing her emotional overflow. I understood that bearing witness to my mother's anxiety was important, but I never felt capable of truly soothing her. Instead, I stood vigil with her every evening as she leaned out the window overlooking the #10 bus stop on Riverdale Avenue and 254th Street, waiting for my father's safe arrival home from work. Each time a bus stopped without discharging him, my mother's panic mounted. When, at last, she recognized his unmistakable gait from half a block away, she would hurry to wash her face and calm herself to mask the evidence of her distress.

In many ways, my mother was able to reclaim her spirit of beauty and strength. But the leg reminded us every day of all the losses that could never be restored. That damn thing.

• • •

I also witnessed my father's struggle to find a sense of professional place and identity in the new land. He had been accepted into a doctoral program in history at Columbia University, but had to decline admission because while they offered him a full scholarship, they did not provide a living stipend that would have helped support the family. Deeply disappointed, my father cobbled together part-time jobs for which he was overqualified. For most of my childhood, he worked in the mornings at a low-level job in the Jewish-dominated Diamond District on West 47th Street in Manhattan; in the afternoons, he worked as a teacher and then principal at a succession of yeshivas and Hebrew schools, a bitter concession to Orthodoxy after having rejected his Hasidic upbringing. My father often expressed his resentment that his livelihood depended on pleasing rabbis whom he considered less learned and forward-thinking than he was. The rabbis had made it clear that he was a charity hire. They thought he was lying when he referenced his university training ("Nu, come on, everybody knows there are no universities in Poland."). They patted themselves on the back for reassuring skittish parents that their children would be safe with a Holocaust survivor. Early on, one of those rabbis convinced my father to add an "e" to the end of his surname, Wolf, presumably to reduce the likelihood of the children's teasing him for having an "animal" name, and thus to reduce the risk of his erupting in fury in response.

My father returned home from work exhausted, not just from his long commutes but from the daily reminder that his dreams of being a lawyer or scholar had been crushed. Once, in his later years, as he was reflecting on his career, I commented, "You don't sound particularly proud of your jobs."

"Sweetheart," he replied, "pride in your work is a luxury. I had to put food on the table."

Home was my father's refuge from the humiliations of the workaday world. After dinner he changed out of his suit and, stretched out on the bed (most nights with me nestled by his side), tuned in to Walter Cronkite's reassurances—"that's the way it is"—and to television sitcoms in which anodyne family conflicts could be neatly resolved in a half hour. Imitating Robert Young in Father Knows Best, my father called me "Princess," and the nickname stuck. I emulated Patty Duke in her eponymous show, for a time calling my father "Poppo."

Reality intruded into our television set in April 1961, when the Eichmann trial began and aired every night for weeks. At age nine, I was too young to absorb the enormity of the witnesses' testimony, but there was no mistaking the stricken looks on my parents' faces. My best friend Beth and I debated what a fitting punishment would be for such a criminal. My idea was that Eichmann should be placed neck deep in a hole filled with strawberry jam and have swarms of bees set loose on him. But my fantasy never extended to his subsequent painful death because I couldn't get past my guilty (and unspoken) perception that this monster Eichmann—with his blue eyes, high forehead, square chin, thin lips, and thick horn-rimmed eyeglasses—in many ways resembled my father.

Eichmann's execution brought a small measure of justice to my parents, but it did not bring them peace. At least my father found pleasure in the sitcom *Hogan's Heroes*, which premiered in 1965. I don't think I can recall his ever laughing so uproariously as he did at the show's depiction of hapless and bumbling Nazis.

• • •

When I was in junior high school, my mother enrolled in a creative writing class taught by the writer and editor Martha Foley. As one of her first projects, she translated a short story, originally titled "Deportation Through the Eyes of a Child," that she had written in Polish shortly after the war. She retitled it "The Last Day," and submitted it to Ilona's former editor Cyrilly Abels, who was then working at *The Reporter* magazine. Cyrilly wrote an acceptance letter to my mother, adding in a postscript that she was about to leave the magazine to become an agent, and inviting my mother to be among her first clients.

My mother became a prolific short story writer. Three of her stories were accepted for publication, and two of them were reprinted in *Best American Short Stories*, which Foley edited at the time. One day Cyrilly declared that her new manuscript wasn't a short story but rather the first chapter of a novel.

I don't know if my mother had ever imagined this evolution from poet to short story writer to novelist, but she threw herself into this project with gusto. My father had always been my mother's greatest literary champion and personal assistant, driving her to and from class and typing her manuscripts for her. By the time my mother started working on her novel, I was in high school and had mastered typing. Beyond my regular chores, my most important household contribution was to be my mother's secretary. My mother wrote in barely decipherable longhand in wide-ruled spiral-bound notebooks, and dictated her words to me while I transcribed them, along the way making spelling and grammar corrections to her Polish-inflected English. The summer I turned sixteen, I wanted to attend summer camp, but my mother was at a critical point in developing her manuscript. She offered me the princely sum of $500 to stay home and work for her. Our compromise was that I took the typewriter to camp along with my mother's latest notebooks. During the other campers' free time, I sat on my bunk bed and typed; my parents drove up every week or two to deliver new notebooks.

I never experienced this as a burden, but rather as a front-row seat to my mother's creative process. I loved her characters, especially the heroine Halina, based on my mother during early wartime, who was an adolescent like me. In real life, I argued with my mother over her refusal to let me wear makeup, but while I typed, I was mollified by her description of Halina's eyelids (which she said had come to her when she looked in on me as I slept), so delicately shadowed with lacy veins that they needed no cosmetic enhancement.

I knew that the characters were barely disguised versions of our family members. Samuel Becker, for example, was based on my mother's uncle Jacob (Gerson's youngest brother), who now lived in the building right across Netherland Avenue from us. My mother told me that one morning, while musing about the next plot turn, she had decided to give Samuel Becker a stroke that left his mouth drooping badly on one side. She described the thrill of having such power over life and death, even in fiction. But soon afterward, Uncle Jacob had an actual stroke, with an identical disfigurement. My mother felt shaken and guilty, as if she had caused it by a literal stroke of her pen.

• • •

While my mother was working on her first novel, Ilona was completing her second; *An Estate of Memory* was published in 1969. The sisters were extremely close and also, to my eyes, completely different from one another. Ilona and her husband Hans Zucker were childless; Henia had two children. Ilona was the "country mouse," living in a house in a leafy suburb of Boston and buying her clothes in second-hand stores. Henia was the "city mouse," living in a rent-controlled apartment and fussing over her appearance, even though, she said, buying herself new clothes triggered nightmares about her mother standing starved and freezing in prison rags. Henia was "the beauty" (although Ilona had striking good looks) and Ilona was "the brains" (although Henia was highly intelligent). Henia kept an immaculate apartment and was an indifferent cook; Ilona's kitchen counters— much to my mother's horror—were a calamity of open cat food cans, overflowing ashtrays, and dirty pots and pans, but her cooking and baking were legendary.

The sisters squabbled—over books, over art, over whether the latest Pope was an antisemite—but I do not recall their ever arguing or competing over their writing. They exchanged drafts of their manuscripts and took each other's critiques to heart. Their shorthand was that Henia was the better poet and Ilona the better novelist, but their support for each other never wavered.

Cyrilly Abels submitted my mother's manuscript, *The Baders of Jacob Street*, to Tay Hohoff at Lippincott. Tay had edited *To Kill a Mockingbird*, and told Henia that *Baders*, like the original draft of

Mockingbird, was a diamond in the rough. She shepherded my mother through edits and, when I was a junior in college, to publication. Tay sent my mother—accompanied by a personal assistant—on an all-expenses-paid book tour around the country before bringing her home to give a talk and reading at our own neighborhood synagogue, my father and me beaming with pride from the front row.

• • •

During my college years, my mother was working on a story about her last spring in captivity. As the Passover holiday approached, it occurred to her that the Haggadah could have been written about the ways in which Jews were currently oppressed. My mother organized a secret Seder in her barrack, using slices of white sugar beet to stand in for matzo. Defying the prohibition on religious observances, she recited the Haggadah from memory, adapting the narrative from past-tense Egypt to present-tense Germany.

My mother had never before talked about that Seder in the camp, but now that she was writing about it, she was determined to reenact it. She started scouring the local produce markets for a sugar beet to place on our Seder plate, arguing with Ilona, who insisted that it wasn't a sugar beet they'd sliced to use in place of matzo, but rather kohlrabi.

At the time I was more bemused by my mother's excursions to the far corners of the Bronx in search of a random root vegetable than sensitive to her quest to honor a singular moment in her life in the camps. Her essay was published a few years later, and when I read it, I realized that I was the same age she had been when those events took place. The contrast between her experience in the camp and my own life of relative ease as a psychology graduate student could not have been more stark. No matter how hard I tried, I could not imagine myself in my mother's place. But my mother's writing opened a door for me, as it had for her. I realized that what I could do was to scour my local markets for a sugar beet to put on my own Seder table.

To this day, I read my mother's story at our Seders. A new generation of our intentional family has grown up hearing it. It brings me great joy when my daughters, and many of my honorary nieces and nephews, choose to read my mother's Seder story at their own Passover tables, in honor of her suffering and her courage.

• • •

My father encouraged me to apply to Sarah Lawrence College because, as he drove past it on the way home from his job at a nearby synagogue, he viewed it as the kind of finishing school for proper American young ladies that would represent his ultimate triumph as an immigrant. When he took me to the admitted students' tour and we learned from the barefooted, long-haired guide that the college had no requirements and no rules, I was delighted, but my father gasped, "It's complete anarchy!"

It was my mother who'd convinced me to apply only to colleges close to home. By this time she had passed the age that her own mother had been when she was killed in the war. My mother had no road map for this phase of her life, and—as I now realize—she was re-traumatized by the prospect of my separating from her. When I chose to live in the dorm at Sarah Lawrence, a scant ten miles from home, my mother wanted to move to Yonkers in order to live closer to my campus. I was a scholarship kid but my parents paid for me to have a phone in my dorm room so that my mother could call me every day. In those calls, she expressed her terror over her high blood pressure and my father's bleeding ulcers—ailments that I now understand were the physical expression of their chronic trauma. I shared my good grades and the PG-rated aspects of my social life, not in an attempt to be emotionally intimate with her, but as an offering of solace.

Even after my parents experienced greater professional success, my mother in publishing her writing, my father in attaining a prominent position (at last!) at the New York headquarters of the Jewish National Fund, their fear of catastrophic loss never abated. The freedoms that were open to me—traveling with friends, dating, engaging in political protest—terrified my parents. They expressed their fears readily in an attempt to hold me close and keep me safe. They did not hesitate to voice their vehement disapproval of my boyfriends. Woe betide any of those young men who came from our refugee community, because my parents would enlist their network of "spies" to vet the family and make sure that, during the war, they had "behaved properly" and had not stooped to saving themselves at others' expense by hoarding their food or, God forbid, collaborating with the Germans.

My mother continued to struggle with anxiety, and when her friends distanced themselves from her, she increasingly turned to me for companionship and comfort. Needing boundaries, I was often short with her. My mother felt this as rejection. I got angry during our tearful arguments, and then felt terrible shame and guilt for expressing it. I still viewed my parents as remarkable—they remained loving and proud and brave—but the weight of our relationship made it difficult for me to breathe.

When I applied to graduate schools, I chose to go to Michigan because it was the only program offering a fellowship package that didn't require me to add to my student loan debt. My parents understood that decision, but they were also baffled by it because, although they were familiar with both coasts, they had never been in the Midwest: "It's bad enough you thought about going to California, but to go all the way to *Michigan?*" Among my entering cohort, my parents were the first to visit: "We just want to make sure you're not living in a hovel." My mother continued to call on the phone almost daily. The geographical separation, and the opportunity to explore living in a region that was mine alone, helped me realize how much my parents' neediness and fear were stifling me.

Then, much to my own surprise, I fell in love with a non-Jewish man, my now-husband Doug Ensor. My parents experienced this as the ultimate betrayal of their wartime suffering. I was determined not to be forced to choose between pursuing my relationship with Doug and honoring and protecting my parents. This was a long and anguished process, with even more phone calls and frequent visits home. As I was in the midst of grappling with it, my college best friend wrote me a letter that opened with "Dear Joy, I think it's high time you told your mother to fuck off." It was obvious to me (if not to my friend) that I would never do that, but neither did I bow to my parents' pressure to leave the man I loved. Eventually they came not only to accept Doug but to love him deeply and—through being embraced by his family— to experience a new sense of belonging in the non-Jewish world.

• • •

After *Baders* was published in 1971, Tay Hohoff put my mother under contract for a second novel. In retrospect, it's not clear to me that my mother had another book in her. The writing didn't seem to bring her joy, and she labored for years to complete it. Tay passed away in 1974, and the new editor rejected the manuscript, billing my mother for the advance she had been paid. My mother endured dozens of rejections before *Marek and Lisa: A Love Story* was accepted by Dodd, Mead & Co. and published in 1984.

The rejections took a toll on my mother's health, which was already faltering. A publication party in Scarsdale, hosted by her childhood best friend Lilly, was just getting started when my mother suffered a heart attack. My brother and his family were turning on to Lilly's street when an ambulance screamed past them in the opposite direction. About an hour later, my phone in Ann Arbor rang with a collect call from my father. "It's about Mama," he said. I flew out on the next plane to New York.

• • •

"That damn thing." When the hospital called in the middle of the night to say that my mother had died, my father and I drove over to sit by her for the last time, to deal with the hospital bureaucracy, and to collect her few personal belongings that had been placed in a brown wax paper bag. As we were leaving at dawn to face the dolorous task of making funeral arrangements, we heard running footsteps behind us and a nurse calling, "Waiiiiit!" She had my mother's wooden leg slung over her shoulder: foot down, thigh and stump socket up. "Don't you want this?" No, we said. She hated that damn thing, we said. "No, really, wouldn't she want to be buried with it?" No, we said. Not in our tradition, we said. "Well, what should I do with it?" Send it to a needy hospital in Europe. Recycle the parts. Anything, just don't ask us to take it.

My mother died much too young, at age sixty-three. We grieved her deeply but, recalling the unfathomable losses during the war, we were grateful to be able to have a proper burial and shiva, and to mourn in the embrace of our community. At the funeral, my father recited Psalm 31 ("A Woman of Valor") in Hebrew, barely containing his tears; my husband Doug read it in English. The reading that captured my mother best was from the letter she had written to her newborn son thirty-six years earlier. Through her stories, through her writing, she had succeeded in giving us the opportunity to know and to love those we had lost. She had created a legend, at least for us, to secure their immortality.

• • •

By the time my mother died, Ilona had been on the MIT faculty for five years, teaching creative writing in the Program in Writing and Humanistic Studies. She was a striking figure on campus, carrying a heavy book-laden backpack on her tiny frame, her two walking sticks clacking down the hallways and up the all-too-many staircases. She was devoted to her students, especially the first-generation Americans. She rewarded them with her sumptuous homemade cakes and, when they fell in love with the craft she taught them, shooed them away from writing careers, telling them their immigrant parents hadn't sacrificed everything to get them to MIT only to have them throw it all away. In 1995, MIT named the Ilona Karmel Writing Prizes in her honor.

To the end of her life, Ilona remembered my grandmother's lesson about how to behave. On one occasion during her final illness, I took her to Mt. Auburn Hospital in Cambridge for a chemotherapy infusion. It was early in the morning, and the elevator filled up with medical staff at the start of a shift. A tall, white-coated doctor squeezed in, a huge steaming cup of Starbucks coffee in each hand. A woman in the back of the elevator murmured, "Mmm, that coffee smells so good—I wish I had some." The doctor, oozing charm, replied, "If I had any to spare, I would give you some." Ilona, desperately ill, bent over her crutches, and bald and ashen from chemo, observed, "It's what you do when you *don't* have anything to spare that's the mark of your character."

When Ilona died in 2000, her close friend and colleague Fanny Howe organized a memorial program, including readings and talks about her novels and short fiction. Fanny wanted to honor the early poetry as well. She arranged for two Polish speakers to prepare literal translations of a few of Ilona's poems, which she then adapted into

English poetic form. These translations sparked a seven-year labor of love during which Fanny worked on a larger collection of Ilona and Henia's wartime poems.

We were all thrilled, no one more so than my father. He had always wanted the poems translated so that they could be accessible to my brother and me, and to the English-speaking world at large. He followed every detail of the book's progress and spoke regularly with Fanny to provide her with historical background.

Fanny's adaptations were published in 2007 as *A Wall of Two: Poems of Resistance and Suffering from Kraków to Buchenwald and Beyond*. My father had died just weeks before.

• • •

Whenever my mother or aunt needed a new prosthesis, the German government paid the expenses, but they required documetation that the sisters were still amputees. Finally, Ilona wrote to the Germans: "Dear Sirs, My leg has not yet grown back, but I remain hopeful."

Years after the sisters died, the people of Kraków started to experience their own phantom limb pain from the loss of Jewish life there. In 2015, I received an unexpected voicemail from a Kraków physician named Aleksander Skotnicki. Aleksander was active in the "Jewish revival" in that city; he had also founded a center for dialogue to address our shared tragic history. He tracked me down on the Internet, seeking my permission for a Kraków publishing house to re-issue the Karmel sisters' wartime poems. Shortly thereafter, I received another message from the City Codes project that was part of Kraków's designation as a UNESCO City of Literature. They wanted to honor the sisters with a plaque on a "literary bench," including a QR code linking to their work.

The twin projects moved forward. When the poems were re-published, Aleksander engaged two young actresses to perform them in such venues as the Juliusz Słowacki Opera House. These were the first public readings since the long-ago memorial service in the nearby cinema. I could never have imagined such a turn of events in a city that had been the location of so much pain and loss, and I knew I had to witness it for myself. The next year, I traveled to Kraków with my cousin Marianne Karmel to see the bench and to meet its benefactors and supporters.

From the descriptions in Henia and Ilona's books and my parents' stories, Marianne and I were able to retrace their steps, street by cob-blestoned street. Marveling at the still-intact buildings in which the once-huge Karmel clan had lived, we were at first overwhelmed by the extent to which they had been hollowed out of their Jewish inhabi-tants, but we were also buoyed by the warmth and genuine respect of our many new friends.

I was, and remain, enchanted by Kraków. It's an exquisite city, and it lived up to my mother's most magical fairytale descriptions. It gives me hope that, in a way, Kraków now loves her back.

• • •

Our daughter Sarah was only two when my mother Henia died; Hannah, born two years later, was named for her. The girls were very close to my father and to Ilona, who shared their stories with greater ease now, from the vantage point of the lives they'd reclaimed. Our home was filled with family photos and with bookshelves devoted to the sisters' writings, and I did my best to convey the family lore to my girls in the gently unfolding manner that my mother used with me.

Sarah and Hannah are storytellers in their own right; they teach English at universities and are published writers. Hannah carries on her namesake Henia's poetic legacy, writing with a depth and emotional honesty that leaves me breathless:

METABOLISM

Pressing on my thumbnail to check capillary
response I am a dumb mess with information
and fear well I "come by it honestly" my mom
would say I now agree in ways she wouldn't like
and ditto for how I disagree I'm not in
a "3G" group for third generation survivors
of the Shoah I am perfectly glad with how
hard that work is for me and in my body
when I go to the local Holocaust museum I need
days of nothing after I need to be alone this
is how I want it I do not want more
or less of any of it I have a slow
metabolism take what my DO considers
placebo levels of all my pills and when I say
here are the four things I want to talk about
she says let's talk first about your anxiety[4]

• • •

Now Hannah and her wife have a daughter of their own. Her name is Ilona. The namesakes of the Karmel sisters dwell together under one roof: a reunion of souls that moves me beyond measure.

Since losing my mother, I have had many occasions to light memorial candles, as is our lot as we grow older. Today I no longer fear the flickering lights and dancing shadows; rather, I find them beautiful and comforting. They still hold ghosts, but of people I knew and cherished, who loved and cherished me back. When I light the candles with my family members, we share stories and remembrances. And if I walk by the candles in the night, I greet my beloveds. I tell them how blessed I am to be here to honor their memory, and to know that their good names are carried on through the generations after.

ENDNOTES

INTRODUCTION

1. Remarks at Legacy of Holocaust Survivors conference at Yad Vashem, 2002.

1. SCREAMS IN THE NIGHT

1. Lola Taubman, *My Story* (self-pub., 2012).

2. THE ATTIC FULL OF PHOTOGRAPHS

1. Excerpt of "The Last Holocaust Survivors," by Jonathan Ellis, Jan. 31, 2016, https://mashable.com/2016/01/31/holocaust-survivors/.

11. CHESED

1. Originally published in *The Village Voice,* 1978.

12. IF ONLY

1. A detailed analysis of the origins and history of Hungarian antisemitism can be found in my husband's book: Tamas I. Gombosi, *Phoenix,* 2018 (3rd edition), available from Amazon.

15. NOT MADE OF GLASS

1. Sidney Finkel, *Sevek and the Holocaust: The Boy Who Refused to Die* (self-pub., 2006).
2. Letter from Sidney Finkel to daughter Ruth Wade, 1997.

16. ONE DAY THE WORLD WILL BE THE WORLD AGAIN

1. Henia Karmel, "Snapshots," in Henia Karmel and Ilona Karmel,

A Wall of Two: Songs of Resistance and Suffering from Kraków to Buchenwald and Beyond, trans. Arie Galles (Berkeley, Calif.: University of California Press, 2007).

2. Henia Karmel, "My Language," in Karmel and Karmel, *A Wall of Two.*

3. Ilona Karmel, "Anniversaries," in Karmel and Karmel, *A Wall of Two.*

4. Hannah Ensor, "Metabolism," in *Love Dream with Television* (Blacksburg, Virginia: Noemi Press, 2018).

CONTRIBUTORS

Back row, left to right: Ruth Taubman, Avishay Hayut, Sassa Åkervall, Julie Goldstein Ellis, Rita Benn, Phil Barr. Middle row, left to right: Nancy Szabo, Ruth Wade, Ava Adler, Joy Wolfe Ensor, Fran Lewy Berg, Eszter Gombosi. Front row, left to right: Simone Yehuda, Irene Hasenberg Butter, Natalie Iglewicz, Cilla Tomas.

Ava Dee Adler, MSW grew up outside of Detroit and moved to Ann Arbor to attend the University of Michigan, earning both Bachelor's and Master of Social Work degrees. Her career included work with children in foster care, addiction, and medical social work. Ava and her husband, chef Burt Steinberg, raised their nephews, Matthew Powondra and Zachary Adler, and now have grandchildren Sasha, Levi, Ezra, Maya, and Nora. Ava has a passion for social justice and loves dance, theater, movies, and books.

Sassa Åkervall was born in Sweden to a Holocaust-survivor mother. Her professional background began in the media. Sassa worked in television, as a freelance writer, and is a published author of children's books. After moving with her husband and two small children to Ann Arbor in 2004, her career changed. Currently, she is running their family company which she started at the kitchen table a decade ago. The company manufactures and produces dental protection, invented by her physician husband.

Phil Barr, MPH met his wife Julie in the Detroit Zionist Movement. They moved first to San Francisco, where Phil became enamored with technology, then spent seven years living on a kibbutz in Israel before settling in Ann Arbor. Their children Maya and David are both married, and have given Phil and Julie three beautiful granddaughters, Evie, Margo, and Sylvia. Phil is a mechanic, tinkerer, programmer, sailor, and avid gardener, and works primarily in Healthcare Consulting. Julie, though retired from public education, remains forever the teacher and voice for social justice.

Rita Benn, PhD is a clinical psychologist and adjunct faculty at the University of Michigan. Her academic career focused on developing statewide early intervention policies and educational programs in Integrative Medicine. More recently, she established several local non-profits to advance the practice of mindfulness and teaches mindfulness meditation to educators, healthcare professionals and families coping with cancer. Dr. Benn and her husband Steve, both originally from Montreal, have three children and three grandchildren. In her spare time, Rita enjoys painting, writing poetry, and practicing yoga.

Fran Lewy Berg, PhD grew up in Montreal and moved to Ann Arbor for graduate study at the University of Michigan. She is a clinical psychologist. Her husband Mark is retired from a multifaceted career in development and research. Their daughter Cara is a Doctor of Nursing Practice, and they have a granddaughter, Ruth. Fran is currently writing her memoir, *Impact: The Story of a Daughter of Survivors*, from which the chapter in this book was adapted. She loves photography, kayaking, and hiking.

Irene Hasenberg Butter is a well-known peace activist, Holocaust survivor, and Professor Emerita of Public Health at the University of Michigan. Irene is a co-founder of Zeitouna, a dialogue group consisting of Jewish and Palestinian women working for a just peace, and a co-founder of the Raoul Wallenberg Lecture Series at the University of Michigan. She is the subject of two movies, *Never a Bystander* and *Refusing to Be Enemies, the Zeitouna Story*, and the author of *From Holocaust to Hope: Shores Beyond Shores, A Bergen-Belsen Survivor's True Story*. She received a PhD in Economics from Duke University.

Julie Goldstein Ellis, a graduate of the University of Michigan, has spent her life in Ann Arbor devoted to her family, volunteerism, elder care, and managing a consulting company. Her husband Charles is an emeritus professor at the University of Michigan Medical School. Their son Jonathan is an editor at *The New York Times* and their daughter-in-law Aly is a social media director in New York. Julie and her sister, Susan Goldstein, are dedicated to following in their survivor parents' footsteps to keep their extended family of many generations of cousins connected.

Joy Wolfe Ensor, PhD is a psychologist whose clinical, teaching, and leadership activities over forty-plus years have centered on the social determinants of health and the multi-generational legacy of trauma. She grew up in New York City and has lived in Ann Arbor since 1973. This writing project has deepened her attachment to Kraków, her ancestral home. Joy and her husband Doug, a fellow psychologist, have two daughters and one granddaughter. Joy has studied classical piano since age six and still tackles pieces that are a stretch for her little fingers to play.

Myra Sue Fox was a poet, musician, special education teacher, and fierce advocate for social justice. Her parents were Polish Jews who survived concentration camps. The presence of the survivor community as her extended family informed Myra of its rich Yiddish culture. Myra built a strong community around herself reflecting her congregation, her artistic passions, and her commitment to the children she served. When Myra succumbed to cancer in 2018, she was surrounded by her congregational family who sang to her and cared for her. Generations After continues to be inspired by her memory. Myra is survived by her son Joe.

Eszter Gombosi was born, raised, and educated in Hungary where her parents returned after their liberation from concentration camps. In 1979, her husband accepted a postdoctoral position at the University of Michigan in Ann Arbor, where he is currently a Distinguished University Professor of Space Science. Eszter spent her career as a mathematician at the University of Michigan, designing and implementing data management projects in the medical setting. She has two children and six grandchildren and is now retired.

Avishay Hayut was born in Tel Aviv, Israel. After completing his army service, he became a physical therapist and immigrated to New Jersey to further his education. In 1996, he met and married Regina Lambert-Hayut, a cantor who brought him to Ann Arbor for her job at Temple Beth Emeth. They have two college-age sons, Yoav and Alon, who study music. Avishay loves music, playing the guitar, participating in choir, and accompanying Regina at Temple services.

Natalie L. Iglewicz was raised in suburban Detroit. Her loving parents, both Holocaust survivors, led by example in valuing hard work, respect for others, and kindness. Natalie received degrees from the

University of Michigan, Eastern Michigan, and Wayne State University. Recently retired, Natalie was an educator for thirty-eight years. Her students included adjudicated youth and those with learning differences. Natalie and her husband, Reed Newland, live with their two children and two dogs in Ann Arbor.

Nancy Szabo is a teacher, artist, and poet. She grew up in Rockville, Maryland, with her father, a refugee from Hungary, her mother, and brother. Nancy received her BA from Wesleyan University, MS in Public Health from Harvard, and MA in Teaching from Johns Hopkins. Nancy has called Ann Arbor home since 2004. Her husband is a law professor at the University of Michigan. They have two children, Ben and Isabel.

Ruth Taubman is a jewelry designer working in Ann Arbor, New York, and California. She has a BFA from the University of Michigan School of Art, where she has taught in its Jewelry and Metals program. She has two sons and two stepsons with her partner, Steven Russman. She facilitated the publication of her survivor mother's memoir *My Story*. Ruth's zeal for life, drive, and positive nature are expressions of the legacy she carries forward from her parents, Lola and Sam.

Cilla Tomas, MSW grew up in Bern, Switzerland, and was a social worker in a psychiatric hospital near Zurich before immigrating to the United States. She earned a graduate degree at the University of Michigan and worked for another fifteen years in the United States, after which she launched a second career as a financial advisor. With her husband Jim Hallock, Cilla has a son, a stepdaughter, and three grandchildren. Now retired, she enjoys political activism, travel, hiking, fiber arts, movies, and reading.

Ruth Wade is a retired training and development executive. She currently teaches mobility and strengthening fitness, and volunteers at the Florida Holocaust Museum as a speaker and docent. Ruth also assists her Holocaust survivor father, Sidney Finkel, with the management of his speaking engagements and book *Sevek and the Holocaust: The Boy Who Refused to Die*. She grew up in Chicago, spent more than twenty years living in Ann Arbor, Michigan, and now lives in Largo, Florida. Ruth's son Ike is a data scientist with a degree from the University of Michigan.

Simone Yehuda, PhD, a retired Professor of English, has written two books of poetry, *Thaw*, and *Lifting Water*. A third, *Pieces of Thunder*, will be published next year. A playwright, her play *Willing* was produced Off-Broadway. She's now a screenwriter developing three thrillers, *The New Eve, Jerusalem Road*, and *Love and Homicide*. She lives in Ann Arbor, Michigan, with her husband, historian Barry Shapiro. Her daughters, physician Valerie Press and psychologist Corinna Press, live in Chicago and San Francisco, respectively.

ACKNOWLEDGMENTS

When we first came together in 2004 to create a new kind of Yom HaShoah service, we could not have imagined the journey that would lead to the publication of this book. Over the years we have had the extraordinary good fortune to encounter many wonderful people who offered their time, wisdom, and expertise, guiding us every step of the way with patience and care.

Thank you to Temple Beth Emeth in Ann Arbor, Michigan, our spiritual home and incubator of this project. We are deeply grateful to all the clergy, staff, board members, and congregants who embraced our vision for a new approach to Holocaust remembrance and education. Special thanks to Martha Solent, Rabbi Emeritus Robert Levy, Cantor Emerita Annie Rose, and Rabbi Lisa Delson, who saw the importance of sharing our family stories more widely, and to Rabbi Josh Whinston, Cantor Regina Hayut, and Rabbi Daniel Alter for their continuing support of what has become a tradition in our congregation.

For believing in our book and giving us encouragement and feedback, we thank David Behrmann, Henry Greenspan, Henry Hochland, Barbara Kriigel, Sharon Leder, Annie Martin, Lori Sagerin, Rabbi Barry Schwartz, Keith Taylor, Milton Teichman, and Jaimie Wraight. We also appreciate the support received from other Second Generation communities, including USHMM's Chicago Daughters of Survivors and Florida Holocaust Museum's Generations After.

For offering us invaluable advice, expertise and many hours of their time, we thank Carol Anderson, Barbara Bergren, Mary Bisbee-Beek, Susan Goldstein, Erica Klein, Kristin McGuire, Reed Newland, and Barbara Stark-Nemon.

Special thanks to our talented and patient editor Polly Rosen-waike, who guided each of us to develop our distinctive writing voices and themes, and helped shape a compelling narrative arc.

Kudos and thanks to David Wilk and the publishing team at City Point Press for embracing our project, understanding the importance of our message, and bringing this book to fruition.

Words cannot express our gratitude to our Generations After community, past and present, for their creativity, passion and devotion; for the abundant food, laughter, tears and conversation; and for being fully present and supportive in times of joy and sorrow alike. An important member of our group, Irene Butter, inspires us in many ways, and was the first to encourage us to more deeply explore our second-generation voices. Through our work together in Generations After, our relationships and focus strengthened, and our project became so much greater than the sum of its parts.

Finally, we are forever grateful to our families—our spouses, siblings, and children—for their patience and loving support. Above all we thank our extraordinary parents and other survivor relatives for inspiring us to share their stories, to carry the memories of our family members lost in the Shoah, and to honor their legacies in our own lives.